UPDATING LOGICAL DATABASES

**Cambridge Tracts in Theoretical
Computer Science**

Managing Editor Professor C.J. van Rijsbergen, Department of Computing Science,
University of Glasgow

Titles in the series

1. G. Chaitin   *Algorithmic Information Theory*
2. L.C. Paulson   *Logic and Computation*
3. M. Spivey   *Understanding Z*
4. G. Revesz   *Lambda Calculus, Combinators and Logic Programming*
5. S. Vickers   *Topology via Logic*
6. A. Ramsay   *Formal Methods in Artificial Intelligence*
7. J-Y. Girard, Y. Lafont & P. Taylor   *Proofs and Types*
8. J. Clifford   *Formal Semantics & Pragmatics for Natural Language Processing*

UPDATING LOGICAL DATABASES

MARIANNE WINSLETT

Department of Computer Science, University of Illinois

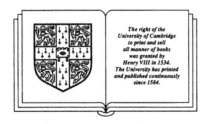

The right of the
University of Cambridge
to print and sell
all manner of books
was granted by
Henry VIII in 1534.
The University has printed
and published continuously
since 1584.

CAMBRIDGE UNIVERSITY PRESS

Cambridge
New York   New Rochelle
Melbourne   Sydney

PUBLISHED BY THE PRESS SYNDICATE OF THE UNIVERSITY OF CAMBRIDGE
The Pitt Building, Trumpington Street, Cambridge, United Kingdom

CAMBRIDGE UNIVERSITY PRESS
The Edinburgh Building, Cambridge CB2 2RU, UK
40 West 20th Street, New York NY 10011–4211, USA
477 Williamstown Road, Port Melbourne, VIC 3207, Australia
Ruiz de Alarcón 13, 28014 Madrid, Spain
Dock House, The Waterfront, Cape Town 8001, South Africa

http://www.cambridge.org

© Cambridge University Press 1990

First published 1990
First paperback edition 2005

A catalogue record for this book is available from the British Library

ISBN 0 521 37371 9 hardback
ISBN 0 521 61972 6 paperback

To David

CONTENTS

ACKNOWLEDGMENTS

This work has benefitted greatly from discussions with my mentors, colleagues, and students. I owe much to my dissertation committee: Gio Wiederhold, Moshe Vardi, and Christos Papadimitriou. My appreciation also goes to Tim Chou, Mukesh Dalal, Ken Forbus, Peter Gärdenfors, Matt Ginsberg, Haym Hirsh, Hirofumi Katsuno, Vladimir Lifschitz, Mike Mitchell, Karen Myers, Peter Rathmann, Ray Reiter, Ken Satoh, Alex Schäffer, Devika Subramanian, Allen Van Gelder, Jeff Ullman, and David Wilkins for their helpful insights, suggestions, advice, and comments. I also thank John Corbett for creating Figure 9.1.

Financial support for this endeavor came from an AT&T Bell Laboratories Doctoral Scholarship, an NSF Presidential Young Investigator Award, and from the Defense Advanced Research Projects Agency under contract N00039-84-C-0211 to Prof. Gio Wiederhold. I also owe much to the encouragement I received while working at Bell Laboratories, especially from Andy Salazar, Charles Roberts, and Bob Lucky.

Earlier versions of some of this material have appeared elsewhere; much of Chapters 1–7 and 9 was an outgrowth of my PhD thesis [Winslett 86c]. Chapters 2 and 3 are drawn in part from [Winslett 88a] and [Winslett 88b], respectively. Portions of Chapters 4 and 5 are derived from [Winslett 86b, 88b], and Chapter 8 is a refinement of [Winslett 88c].

CHAPTER ONE

INTRODUCTION

Nothing endures but change. —Heraclitus

Suppose that one wishes to construct, use, and maintain a body of information describing what is known about the state of the world. One would naturally wish to have a means of updating the information as more facts are gathered about the state of the world, and as the world undergoes change. But how can new facts be added to a body of knowledge when the new facts may contradict preexisting information? For example, given the new information that "b or c is true," how can one get rid of all outdated information about b and c, add the new information, and yet in the process not disturb any other information in the knowledge base? The simplest choice is to place the burden on the users, by requiring them to determine exactly what to add and remove from the knowledge base. But what is really needed is a way to specify the desired change intensionally, by stating a formula that the state of the world is now known to satisfy and letting the knowledge base update algorithms automatically accomplish that change.

In this book we examine application-independent means of updating data and knowledge bases, viewing them abstractly as finite sets of sentences in propositional and first-order logic. We anticipate that an appropriate treatment of updates can be designed for a particular application by coupling the relevant application-independent techniques with additional principles and heuristics that are specific to the application domain.

1.1. The Context

The problem of updating logical databases and knowledge bases has been studied in three research communities: databases, artificial intelligence (AI), and philosophy. We will briefly survey the origins of these efforts.

1.1.1. From the Database Community

In the late 1970s database researchers began to examine the problems posed by queries against databases containing incomplete information (e.g., [Biskup 81, Codd 79, Grahne 84, 89, Imielinski 83, 84, 85, Laurent 88, Lerat 86, Lipski 81, Liu 88, Reiter 84, 86 Vardi 86, Vassiliou 79, Yuan 88, 89, Zaniolo 84]). The type of incompleteness most often considered was that of *null values,* or attribute values that are known to lie in a certain domain but whose value is currently unknown; for example, one might know that Chien was an employee of some department, without knowing exactly which department—Emp(Chien, ?). Some researchers also considered the problems introduced by disjunctive information, such as Emp(Chien, CS) ∨ Emp(Chien, EE); and by "maybe" tuples, which are used to represent facts that might possibly hold, as when we think that Chien might possibly be an employee of CS.

The challenge of query processing in this environment is, first, to define what the correct answer is to such a query, and justify that definition; and second, to develop a means of producing the desired query answer efficiently. For example, if the user asks whether Chien is an employee of CS and we know only Emp(Chien, ?), how should we answer this query? Null values complicate query answering because nulls cannot be treated like ordinary data values by the query processor. For example, a null occurring in one tuple is not necessarily equal to a null occurring in another tuple: Emp(Chien, ?) and Emp(Nilsson, ?) do not together imply that Chien and Nilsson are in the same department.

Eventually database researchers realized that at least some portion of the power of a theorem prover was needed in order to answer queries correctly when the database contains incomplete information. Recent investigations have focussed on means of limiting the representational power of the database in order to decrease the computational complexity of answering queries.

A second type of incompleteness arises in database applications, caused not by missing information but rather by schema attributes that are not applicable for a particular tuple. For example, the "spouse's name" attribute for an unmarried employee might receive the special null value "inapplicable." "Inapplicable" nulls indicate a mismatch between the database schema and the real world that the schema is intended to represent. In theory, one can revamp the schema of the database to prevent the occurrence of "inapplicable" nulls, for example along the lines of the structural model [Wieder-hold 90]. In practice, however, the resulting schemas may be sprawling and untidy, so that from an engineering point of view it may be better to keep the imperfect schema and devise a means of handling "inapplicable" nulls directly. Researchers have produced widely differing proposals for handling "inapplicable" nulls (see, e.g., [Atzeni 87, Vassiliou 79, Zaniolo 84]). We will not consider "inapplicable" nulls in our study of updates.

As the problems of query answering in incomplete databases began to be understood, attention was also given to the problem of updating incomplete databases. As an example of the difficulties posed by even simple updates, suppose that we have the following two relations, containing one null value.

EMPLOYEE	DEPT	SALARY
Chien	?	30,000
Nilsson	CS	40,000

MANAGER	DEPT
Nilsson	CS

Suppose that the database user wishes to give all the computer scientists a raise. Here is an expression of that update in a generic database manipulation language:

```
RANGE OF t IS EmpDeptSal

MODIFY t.SALARY TO BE t.SALARY*1.1
WHERE t.DEPT = CS
```

What happens to Chien's salary? How can we express the fact that Chien's salary depends on an unknown value in another field of the tuple, and how can that relationship be determined automatically?

Matters are more complicated if instead the user wishes to give Chien's boss a raise:

```
RANGE OF t IS EmpDeptSal
RANGE OF t2 IS EmpDeptSal
```

```
RANGE OF s IS ManDept
MODIFY t.SALARY TO BE t.SALARY*1.1
WHERE t2.EMP = Chien AND t2.DEPT = s.DEPT
AND s.MANAGER = t.EMP
```

What happens to Nilsson's salary? How can we express the fact that his salary depends upon an unknown value in a different relation, and how can that fact be derived automatically?

Unfortunately, although it is syntactically simple to allow null values in relational tables and update requests, any reasonable semantics for these updates will lead to result relations that cannot be stored as simple tables. Even with tight restrictions on the appearance of nulls, one quickly leaves the realm of the relational model, as in the example above. For that reason, in applications where performance rather than flexibility is of primary concern (such as traditional data processing applications), we recommend that system support for automatic special handling of null values be modest, and that nulls not be permitted to appear in indexed attributes (e.g., keys and join attributes). The approaches outlined in this book are more suitable for applications where power and accuracy is of greater concern than performance.

For these reasons, we cast aside the traditional relational restriction of databases to tables and instead view databases as simple, restricted theories in first-order logic with equality. We use an extension of the logic framework set forth by Reiter for the null value and disjunctive information problems [Reiter 84]. Given a relational database, Reiter shows how to construct a *relational theory* whose model corresponds to the world represented by the database, and extends this framework to allow disjunctive information, null values, and "maybe" information to be expressed in the relational theory. The use of a logic framework has three advantages: it allows a clean formalization of incomplete information; it allows a definition of the meanings of query and update operators without recourse to intuition or common knowledge; and it frees us from implicit or explicit consideration of implementation issues, by not forcing incomplete information into a tabular format. Through framing the update question in this paradigm, we also gain insights into the more general problem of updating general logical theories, and lay groundwork for use in applications beyond ordinary databases, such as AI applications using a knowledge base built on top of base facts.

The techniques discussed in this book apply directly to the problem of updating databases with incomplete information. Such a capability is needed not only in the case where the user directly requests the incorporation of uncertainty into the database, but also when updates indirectly spawn incomplete information, as in updating through views [Bancilhon 81, Dayal 82, Keller 82, 85a] and in natural language updates [Davidson 84ab].

Updates through even the simplest views can produce incomplete information in the relations underlying the view. For example, suppose the user requests the insertion of the tuple (Chien, CS) into the Employee view, and suppose that the underlying relation from which the view was formed contains an additional attribute, e.g. Salary. Associated with each updatable view will be a view update translation policy, i.e., a method of translating updates expressed against views into updates on base relations. For the insertion of employee Chien, the view update interpretation policy will probably give Chien a null value for her salary. Similar problems arise in views formed by selection and/or joins of relations, and for updates that request deletion or modification of tuples. Given a view update policy, the techniques discussed in Chapters 3–5 can be used to implement those updates, and to process subsequent updates against the incomplete base relations.

Updates expressed in natural language also introduce incomplete information, as they are expressed against the user's mental "view" of the database, which may not be very closely related to the actual database schema. Once an interpretation policy has been established for natural language updates—no easy task!—again the techniques offered in this book can be used to carry out the updates.

1.1.2. From the AI community

In artificial intelligence one often wishes to construct a problem-solving agent that has a base set of knowledge and beliefs about the world. If the world is under flux, the agent must be able to incorporate new, possibly contradictory knowledge into this set of beliefs. Thus many subareas of AI must confront the problems of theory revision: discourse understanding, learning, diagnosis, reasoning about the effects of actions, planning, belief revision [Appelt 88, Baker 89, Borgida 85, Davidson 84ab, de Kleer 86, 87, Doyle 79, Drummond 86, Finger 87, Foo 89, Forbus 89, Ginsberg 88ab, Levesque 84, Lifschitz 87, Myers 88, Reiter 87, Shoham 88, Winslett 88c].

For example, in research on planning, the goal is to devise a sequence of actions that will transform the world from its current state to some desired goal state. In order to do this, one must be able to revise the knowledge base in accordance with the known effects of the actions to be performed.

Work on planning often assumes that the effects of an action can be completely specified by two sets of facts, the members of one to be added to the knowledge base, and of the other to be deleted from the knowledge base. This restriction makes it difficult or impossible to represent actions having far-ranging, complex, context-dependent effects. It also breaks down in the face of incomplete information, when the updatable portion of the knowledge base is no longer simple atomic statements. Yet even with the assumptions of complete information and of very simple actions, the planning problem is so difficult that a finer-grained examination of the modeling of individual actions has only recently been undertaken.

The latter area of work, that of reasoning about the effects of actions, seeks to formalize a means of drawing the same common-sense conclusions about the effects of an action as would a human, given the same initial information about the world state and the action to be performed. Abstractly, the problem is that of adding a formula ω, describing the known effects of the action, to a knowledge base that may contradict ω. The work on reasoning about the effects of actions draws on prior work in planning, non-monotonic reasoning, common-sense reasoning, belief revision, and temporal reasoning, and can also be seen as a driving force behind some of the recent developments in the study of updates and in the related application areas. Much of the emphasis in the study of actions is on knowledge representation (e.g., [Baker 89, Lifschitz 87, McCarthy 86, Shoham 88]) rather than on updates per se.

Levesque directly considered the problem of updating knowledge bases with his TELL operation [Levesque 84]; however, TELL could only eliminate models from the set of models for the knowledge base, not change the internal contents of those models. In other words, one could only TELL the knowledge base new information that was consistent with what was already known. This is an important and vital function, but an agent also needs to be able to make changes in the belief set that contradict current beliefs. For example, the agent should be able to change the belief that block A is on block B if, for example, the agent observes an arm removing A from B.

In each area of application, the generic approach to theory revision must be tempered by application-specific principles and heuristics to focus and guide revision. We do not believe that any general-purpose, domain-independent means of updating knowledge bases will "do the right thing" under all circumstances. In complex applications such as those listed above, we see the update techniques presented in this book as forming the lowest layer of the theory revision system, with application-specific mechanisms residing at a higher level to filter incoming information and translate it into appropriate low-level updates. At yet a higher level, the choice of knowledge representation for a complex application is also crucial, as all of our proposed update mechanisms depend on the choice of language used to describe the world. The ability of the update layer to offload the burden of higher layers will be commensurate with the suitability of the choice of language.

While the goal of a perfect application-independent approach to updates is perhaps more noble, we think it unrealistic. Drawing an analogy to the database world, it would be unrealistic to expect that one could automatically translate updates expressed against views to the desired updates on the base relations: syntactically identical view definitions may require radically different interpretation policies, and one must understand the semantics of the domain in order to select the correct interpretation policy. Until one can encode a complete understanding of a domain into a knowledge base, then, an application-dependent layer will be needed to help guide the update interpretation layer.

The work on belief revision in the AI community has focused on the problem of revising derived beliefs when an underlying set of base beliefs changes [de Kleer 86, Doyle 79]. This work has culminated in the development of a number of types of *reason maintenance systems*. A reason maintenance system is a program used in conjunction with an inference engine such as a theorem prover. Given a set S_1 of facts that are currently believed to be true, the inference engine can determine the set S_2 of facts that one is justified in inferring from S_1. The reason maintenance system can record the justification relationships between members of S_1 and S_2. Then, should one no longer believe a fact $\alpha \in S_1$, the reason maintenance system can quickly determine those members of S_2 that one is no longer justified in believing. The bookeeping powers of the reason maintenance system also help to determine quickly what new facts one is now justified in inferring when S_1 changes. Reason maintenance systems can be used with many different types of inference engines; they are not tied to any particular policy on *how* beliefs should be revised. Rather, the goal has been to devise efficient means of recalculating S_2 when S_1 changes. Thus a reason maintenance system can be a particularly useful component of the implementation of a particular theory revision strategy.

1.1.3. From the Philosophical Community

From the time of Aristotle, philosophers have debated the meaning of actions and the nature of beliefs and belief revision; more recently has come the study of the revision of scientific theories, and of logical theory revision [Alchourrón 85, Gärdenfors 88ab, Goodman 83, Harman 86, Hintikka 62, Oddie 78, Pollack 76]. Also shedding light on the update problem are philosophical studies of the meaning of counterfactual statements ([Lewis 73, Rescher 64], and [Ginsberg 85, Jackson 89] from the AI community), such as "if the computer hadn't crashed, I would have finished on time."

Most of the philosophical studies have a different flavor than the work described in this book. We are more oriented toward engineering concerns; we are not so interested in the philosophical adequacy of a system as in its potential utility as a tool, to be used in conjunction with other tools within the restricted domain of a particular application, to achieve the limited goals of that application. For us, counterexamples to our approaches indicate the nature of the help that must be supplied by other system tools, or show that the approach is not appropriate for the application at hand, rather than serving to discredit the approach itself. The work from the philosophical community has been of greatest value to us through showing, often in an anecdotal fashion, where the boundaries lie in the effectiveness of an approach.

1.2. Overview

Chapter 2 surveys and classifies proposals for update semantics, for the particularly simple case where the knowledge base is a finite set of propositional formulas. The goal of Chapter 2 is to give an idea of the range of possible choices and the means of determining what semantics is appropriate for a particular application.

Chapter 3 introduces a formalization of databases with incomplete information, called *relational theories*, and presents in detail two choices of semantics for updating relational theories. Chapter 4 presents algorithms for implementing those semantics, and Chapter 5 extends the semantics and algorithms to the case where variables appear in update requests.

When null values occur in a relational theory, updates can cause unacceptably large growth in the theory when many data tuples "unify" with one another. Chapter 6 presents a lazy evaluation scheme coupled with simple user-supplied cost limits, that can be used to avoid undesirable expense during execution of updates against databases that suffer from this unification problem. The goal of lazy evaluation is to delay execution of too-expensive updates as long as possible in the hopes that more information about the null values causing the expense will arrive in the interim. The techniques proposed have a strong flavor of database concurrency control.

Chapter 7 gives a means of enforcing simple integrity constraints, such as functional dependencies, for relational theories. Chapter 8 looks at means of handling more general types of knowledge under update, with reference to a particular application, the problem of reasoning about the effects of actions.

Clearly queries and updates will be more expensive in databases with incomplete information; how high might that extra cost be in a typical database scenario? Chapter 9 describes an implementation of the Update Algorithm of Chapter 5, and gives experimental results. The discussion focuses on the size of the stored database after a long series of updates that insert, reference, and remove incomplete information, and on the number of disk accesses required to answer a set of queries after that series of updates.

CHAPTER TWO

CLASSES OF UPDATE SEMANTICS

According to the empirical philosophy, however, all ideals are matters of relation. It would be absurd, for example, to ask for a definition of "the ideal horse," so long as dragging drays and running races, bearing children, and jogging about with tradesmen's packages all remain as indispensible differentiations of equine function. You may take what you call a general all-round animal as a compromise, but he will be inferior to any horse of a more specialized type, in some one particular direction.
—William James, *The Varieties of Religious Experience*

Given a knowledge base encoded as a set of first-order sentences T, one would naturally like to be able to update T as new information arrives. Unfortunately, there is no clear-cut application-independent choice of semantics for updating T, and a variety of candidate semantics have appeared in the database, AI, and philosophical literature [Abiteboul 85, Alchourrón 85, Appelt 88, Borgida 85, Dalal 88, de Kleer 87, Fagin 83, 86, Foo 89, Forbus 89, Gärdenfors 88ab, Ginsberg 86, 88ab, Goodman 83, Harman 86, Hegner 87, Jackson 89, Katsuno 89, Lewis 73, Liu 88, Oddie 78, Pollack 76, Reiter 87, Rescher 64, Satoh 88, Weber 86, Winslett 86abc, 88bc]. These works vary widely in motivation, terminology, and goals; the applications discussed in these papers range from logical theory revision, counterfactuals, and philosophy of language (all active areas of research among modern philosophers, as well as the likes of Aristotle, Hume, and Mill) to diagnosis, database updates, reasoning about the effects of actions in the physical world, and discourse understanding. These different applications make the proposals hard to compare, even though at a deep level they all address similar issues.

This chapter offers a survey and categorization of a number of these proposals, restricted to propositional logic. Our goal is to expose the differences between semantics that are relevant when one is deciding which semantics to use for a particular application.

Section 2.1 describes the two basic classes of semantics: those based on the formulas present in the database or knowledge base T (*formula-based*), and those based solely on the models of T (*model–based*). Section 2.2 introduces a second dimension of differentiation based on the permissiveness/restrictivity of semantics, that is, based on how few or many models they admit as the result of a given update.

Section 2.4 summarizes the factors that must be considered when choosing an update semantics for an application, and presents additional measures that differentiate various semantics. We recommend that semantics be evaluated on the basis of (1) the needs of the intended application, (2) computational tractability, (3) expressive power, (4) comprehensibility, and (5) extensibility.

We shall make three initial simplifying assumptions about the information being represented in the database or knowledge base. (Section 2.4.5 discusses the effect of dropping these restrictions.) In addition, we will use a number of notational conventions, as described below.

First, we adopt the open-world assumption. In other words, those propositions[1] not occurring in T may be either true or false.

Second, we only consider the update operation of unconditionally inserting a new formula into the database or knowledge base. "U" will always designate an update and "ω" will always designate the formula being inserted by U. U will be written *insert ω*. We will assume that ω is satisfiable, as otherwise the update is not very interesting.

Third, the information must be expressed as a finite set of propositional formulas, where all formulas represent *data*, as described in the next paragraph. "T" will be used to designate such a set of formulas. A model of T is the assignment of a truth value to every proposition in such a way that all formulas of T are satisfied. "M" will be used to designate a model of T. Throughout this book, we will use the term *theory* to designate a finite set T of formulas; the set of formulas will not be closed under logical implication. If T is first-order rather than propositional, we make the additional requirement that T contain only sentences, that is, have all its variables appear within the scope of quantifiers. $U(T)$ will designate a theory resulting from applying U to T.

While the distinction between knowledge and data is in general a subtle phenomenon, for our purposes a very simple pragmatic definition will suffice. *Data* is mutable information that may be changed as the result of an incom-

---

[1] We use the terms "proposition" and "propositional symbol" synonymously.

ing update. *Knowledge*, or data about data, is information that cannot be changed using an ordinary update. For example, in the traditional database world, the database schema, integrity constraints, view definitions, and the closed-world assumption are all knowledge, as they cannot be changed by ordinary updates. The tuples residing in relations are the data portion of a traditional relational database.

In an actual application, T will contain formulas representing knowledge as well as data. One must differentiate between these two types of formulas in T, because one will undoubtedly wish to apply different update semantics and procedures to the different types of formulas. For example, in general one is more reluctant to change knowledge than data. Chapters 3–7 will consider the case where T contains the types of knowledge found in an ordinary database management system: schema information, a closed world assumption, and simple integrity constraints. Chapter 8 examines the problem of updating theories containing arbitrary collections of knowledge.

2.1. Formula-Based and Model-Based Semantics

This section discusses the first division of the taxonomy, into formula-based and model-based semantics.

2.1.1. Model-Based Semantics

Under the model-based paradigm, the semantics of an update U is based not on the formulas present in T, but rather on the individual models of T. U is applied to each model individually, rather like an ordinary database update, in order to make ω true in each model. When U is applied to a model M, a set $U(M)$ of models is produced. The following principle formalizes this idea.

MB1.   *The formula ω must be true in every model in $U(M)$.*

The scope of the effect of an update is another consideration. For example, in inserting $a \vee b$, can the truth valuation of another proposition c change in M? Recall that for now T is assumed to contain only data; there are no rules in T to assert, for example, that c must be true if a and b are true. For this reason, it is reasonable to limit the effects of U to propositions occurring in ω:

MB2.   *Let U be the update insert ω. Then for any model M' in $U(M)$,*

M and M' agree on the truth valuations of all propositions not occurring in
ω.

For a particular update U and model M, MB1 and MB2 together determine the maximal set of models that could possibly comprise U(M). But
not every model that could be in $U(M)$ according to MB1 and MB2 need
appear there; one may wish to *prune* some candidate result models, so that
$U(M)$ contains fewer members. We will return to this point shortly.

If T has multiple models, then any one of those models could in fact
be the correct picture of the current state of the world. It is hard to see
why $U(T)$ should have any additional models beyond those obtained from
updating the individual models of T; since one of those models does in fact
correctly describe the current state of the world, and its updated counterpart
should correctly describe the new state of the world, why introduce any extra
models into $U(T)$? This principle can be codified as follows:

MB3.

$$\text{Models}(U(T)) = \bigcup_{M \in \text{Models}(T)} U(M).$$

So far, we have no criteria that prevent $U(M)$ from always being the
empty set[2]:

MB4. *If ω and T are satisfiable, then $U(T)$ is satisfiable.*

One can formulate a stronger version[3] of MB4, which we will discuss in
Section 2.2.1:

MB4'. *If ω is satisfiable, then $U(M)$ is nonempty.*

---

[2] In the case of first-order theories, MB4 must be weakened if updates of facts about
equality, such as Jones $\neq$ Smith, are not fully supported (as is the case with the semantics
we discuss in Chapter 3). The appropriate reformulation of MB4 in this case is to add
the qualification that some model of ω and some model of T have the same constant
interpretations. Also, note that if T contains knowledge as well as data, MB4 is no
longer reasonable; if ω is inconsistent with a known integrity constraint, for example,
one might reasonably leave $U(T)$ undefined.

[3] The same provisos hold as in the previous footnote. In first-order theories with restricted
facilities for updating facts about equality, one needs to add the qualification to MB4'
that some model of ω has the same constant interpretations as M.

We would also like to guarantee that $U(M)$ can be determined by knowing just U, M, and the other models of T:

MB5.   *Let M_1 be a model of T_1, and M_2 a model of T_2, such that $M_1 = M_2$. If T_1 and T_2 are logically equivalent, then $U(M_1) = U(M_2)$.*

One might wish to strengthen MB5, by requiring that $U(M)$ depend only on U and M. This heuristic can be formalized by omitting the requirement in MB5 that T_1 and T_2 be logically equivalent:

MB5'.   *Let M_1 be a model of T_1, and M_2 a model of T_2, such that $M_1 = M_2$. Then $U(M_1) = U(M_2)$.*

In database terms, MB5' may be rephrased as follows: The database with incomplete information represents a set of models, or complete-information databases, each different and each one possibly the real, unknown world. The correct result of an update is that obtained by storing a separate database for each model and running the update in parallel on each separate database. A necessary and sufficient guarantee of correctness for any more efficient and practical method of update processing is that it produce the same results for updates as the parallel computation method. Equivalently, we require that the diagram below be commutative: both paths from upper-left-hand corner to lower-right-hand corner must produce the same result.

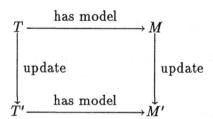

MB5' guarantees that $U(M)$ is the same whether we know for sure that M does describe the current state of the world (i.e., M is the only model of T), or only suspect that M might be the current state of the world. Intuitively, MB5' corresponds to the principle that knowing less about the state of the world will not cause us mistakenly to discard the correct picture of the world.

When the set of propositions is finite, MB5' entails MB4', as one can construct a theory having a model M as its sole model, and MB4 will guarantee that $U(M)$ is nonempty.

MB4' and MB5' seem so intuitively desirable that it may be difficult to see how they are inappropriate for some applications. The difficulty with MB4' and MB5' is that they do nothing to prevent growth in the number of models of T; i.e., they do not include any heuristics to try to eliminate ("prune") unlikely models of T. Since the time required to answer queries can grow exponentially with the amount of uncertainty in T (as measured by the number of disjunctions), one might wish to forgo MB4' and MB5' in favor of another heuristic that selected from T those models deemed most likely to represent the correct state of the world. Doing so opens the possibility that the actual state of the world will be seen as too unlikely and discarded from T; but for the sake of fast query answering, such a risk may be acceptable. In the terminology of Section 2.2, MB4' and MB5' prohibit the use of global measures when pruning $U(M)$. We will explore such heuristics in Section 2.2.

We will take the least common denominator of these heuristics as the definition of model-based semantics.

Definition. *A semantics is* model-based *iff it satisfies principles MB1, MB2, MB3, MB4, and MB5.*

Notice that a model-based semantics need not put any restrictions on the particular *formulas* in $U(T)$; rather, principles MB1 through MB5 just specify what the *models* of $U(T)$ should be.

The subsequent chapters of this book will focus on model-based semantics. At times the theories of interest to us will be more complex than those considered here, and we will find it convenient to relax principle MB2 when that time comes.

Example 2.1. Suppose $T = \{a \lor b\}$. Then, by MB1 and MB2, the model-based effect of *insert a* on the models of T is as follows[4]:

Model M_1:	$\{a,\ b\}$	$U(M_1) \subseteq$	$\{\{a,\ b\}\}$
Model M_2:	$\{a,\ \neg\ b\}$	$U(M_2) \subseteq$	$\{\{a,\ \neg\ b\}\}$
Model M_3:	$\{\neg\ a,\ b\}$	$U(M_3) \subseteq$	$\{\{a,\ b\}\}$.

---

[4] In the examples, truth valuations are only listed for propositions occurring in T and U; that is, the models shown are restricted to the propositions in T and U. Due to the open–world assumption, truth valuations of all other propositions can be either true or false; further, by MB2, their truth values are not affected by U.

The subset inclusion can be replaced by an equality for semantics satisfying MB4′.

Example 2.2.   Suppose $T = \{a \wedge b\}$. Then the model-based update *insert* $\neg a$ has the following effect on the models of T:

Model M_1: $\{a,\ b\}$ $U(M_1) \subseteq \{\{\neg\ a,\ b\}\}$

In Example 2.2, one might think that the result of U was completely determined by MB1, MB2, and MB4. However, a semantics might employ pruning heuristics based on propositions not occurring in T; recall that the models listed in the examples are actually partial models. If the only propositions are a and b, or if the semantics satisfies MB4′, then the subset inclusion in Example 2.2 can be replaced by an equality.

Example 2.3.   Let $T = \{\neg a, \neg b\}$, and let U be the update *insert* $a \vee b$. Then under a model-based semantics, the result of this update must be some subset of the following:

Model M_1: $\{a,\ b\}$
Model M_2: $\{\neg a,\ b\}$
Model M_3: $\{a,\ \neg b\}$.

How do MB1 through MB5 relate to the Gärdenfors Postulates, a well-known set of desiderata for update semantics (see, e.g., [Gärdenfors 88ab])? The Gärdenfors Postulates are phrased in terms of updates applied to the logical closure of a theory, rather than to the models of a theory; Katsuno and Mendelzon have rephrased the postulates in terms of operations on unclosed theories, which can easily be expressed as operations on models [Katsuno 89]. Let U_1 be the update *insert* ω_1, U_2 the update *insert* ω_2, and U the update *insert* $\omega_1 \wedge \omega_2$. Then, following Katsuno and Mendelzon, the Gärdenfors Postulates are:

(GP1) $U_1(T) \models \omega_1$.
(GP2) If ω is consistent with T,

$$\mathrm{Models}(U(T)) = \mathrm{Models}(T \cup \{\omega\}). \qquad (2.1)$$

(GP3) If ω_1 is satisfiable, then $U_1(T)$ is also.

(GP4) If ω_1 and ω_2 are logically equivalent, and T_1 and T_2 are logically equivalent, then $U_1(T_1)$ is logically equivalent to $U_2(T_2)$.

(GP5) $\text{Models}(U_1(T) \cup \{\omega_2\}) \subseteq \text{Models}(U(T))$.

(GP6) $\text{Models}(U(T)) \subseteq \text{Models}(U_1(T) \cup \{\omega_2\})$, if the latter is nonempty.

Stepping through the postulates, we find that GP1 is the same as our MB1, and GP3 is very close to MB4. Part of GP4 is captured in our MB5; we hesitate slightly to embrace the remainder of GP4 (the case of logically equivalent inserted formulas) on the grounds that syntactic differences between formulas may be an easy way of capturing different user intents, which can be used to guide pruning heuristics. Nonetheless, all the model-based semantics presented in this chapter, except the standard semantics, obey GP4, as shown in Section 2.4.3. Postulates GP5 and GP6 place restrictions on the scope of an update, by requiring that the measure used for "minimal change" meet certain criteria. In that sense GP5 and GP6 are analogous to our MB2; but MB2 is a simplistic restriction, satisfactory for our investigations in this chapter but inappropriate when T contains knowledge as well as data. GP5 is appropriate for all applications with which we are acquainted. Our difficulties with accepting GP2 and GP6 for some applications will be described in Section 2.2.1.

2.1.2. Formula-Based Semantics

In a formula-based semantics, one does not examine the models of T, but rather the formulas in T itself; formulas, not propositions, are the units of change. Informally, a formula-based semantics is one in which U is accomplished by adding ω to T, unless the resulting theory would be inconsistent. If $T \cup \{\omega\}$ is inconsistent, then the idea is to remove formulas (as few as possible) from T before adding ω, so that $T \cup \{\omega\}$ becomes consistent. There are two sticky points in this description: first, the meaning of the phrase "as few as possible"; second, the course of action if there is more than one candidate set of formulas to remove from T.

First let us consider the meaning of removing "as little as possible" from T. *Subset inclusion* is the most popular measure of minimality; in other words, don't remove a set S of formulas from T if removing a proper subset of S will suffice to make T and ω consistent.

Definition. *Given a theory T and an update* insert ω, *a subset S of the formulas of T is a* minimal set *iff*

1. $T - S \cup \{\omega\}$ *is consistent, and*

2. $T - S' \cup \{\omega\}$ *is inconsistent, for S' any proper subset of S.*

The following example shows how a simple update can have multiple minimal sets.

Example 2.4.   Let T be $\{a, b\}$ and let U be *insert* $\neg a \vee \neg b$. Then T will become consistent with ω if either a or b is removed; both $\{a\}$ and $\{b\}$ are minimal sets.

The principle of removing only a minimal set from T conflicts with the measures advocated by many authors in the case where there are multiple candidate minimal sets of formulas for removal, and for that reason many proposed formula-based semantics do not actually adhere to this principle, as will be described in Section 2.3.2. However, in the case where there is but a single minimal set, one can characterize the formula-based approach as follows.

FB1.   *The result of inserting ω into T is $T - S \cup \{\omega\}$ if S is a unique minimal set.*

No matter how many minimal sets there are, ω should hold after the update:

FB2. $U(T) \vdash \omega.$

We can also legislate preservation of consistency:

FB3.   *If ω is satisfiable, then so is $U(T)$.*

It is hard to characterize the behavior of formula-based semantics when there is more than one minimal set. The difficulty is that theory syntax is very important in formula-based approaches, yet in order to solve the multiple minimal set problem, formula-based semantics are willing to take liberties with theory syntax. For example, one cannot codify the principle "nothing extra is added" in a natural manner when there is more than one minimal set. We can, however, characterize the nature if not the syntax of the information that must remain in T after update:

FB4.   *If α is a formula of T that does not occur in any minimal set, then $U(T) \vdash \alpha$.*

Definition. *A semantics is* formula-based *iff it satisfies principles FB1 through FB4.*

Example 2.5. If T contains just the formula $a \lor b$, then under any formula-based semantics, inserting a produces the new theory $\{a \lor b, a\}$, as a is consistent with $a \lor b$.

Examples 2.1 and 2.5 show that it is possible for $\text{Models}(U(T))$ to be the same under both a model-based and a formula-based interpretation of U.

Formula-based semantics satisfy principles MB1 and MB4 but do not in general satisfy MB2 or, if suitably translated, MB3, MB4', or MB5, as the following examples illustrate. When choosing between a formula-based and a model-based semantics for an application, it is particularly helpful to consider these examples in the context of the application. In Examples 2.2 and 2.6, different models are produced depending on whether U is given a model-based or a formula-based interpretation.

Example 2.6. If $T = \{a \land b\}$, then the formula-based update *insert* $\neg a$ produces the new theory $\{\neg a\}$, as $\{a \land b\}$ is the unique minimal set.

Examples 2.6 and 2.7 show another peculiarity of formula-based semantics, their dependence upon the syntax of formulas of T. This pair of examples shows that it is unwise to consider the use of formula-based semantics in applications where inserted formulas have irregular, unpredictable syntax, as logically equivalent but syntactically different theories may behave differently under formula-based updates. In model-based updates, the syntax of the theory is irrelevant (MB5).

Example 2.7. If $T = \{a, b\}$, then the formula-based update *insert* $\neg a$ produces the new theory $\{\neg a, b\}$, as $\{a\}$ is the unique minimal set.

Formula-based and model-based semantics will coincide if T is initially empty and the only formulas ever inserted into T are propositions and negations of propositions. This case is very close to that of ordinary relational databases, in which one has complete information about the state of the world.

Formula-based semantics include those of [Fagin 83, 86, Ginsberg 86, 88ab]. Much of the philosophical literature on hypothetical reasoning also has a formula-based flavor (see, e.g., [Gärdenfors 88ab, Pollack 76]), in the sense that the formula is regarded as the unit of change; however, these approaches typically use the logical closure of T rather than just the formulas present in T, and use of the logical closure keeps these semantics in the model-based camp. In any case, not all philosophers accept a logic-based approach to hypothetical reasoning. Even those who do would not accept FB1, because they aim at a *philosophically adequate* account of the phenomena they investigate, and therefore rely on definitions of "minimal change" that are more sophisticated than mere set inclusion. For example, a more sophisticated measure of minimality might involve adding formulas other than ω to T. The reader is referred to [Gärdenfors 88b, Oddie 78, Pollack 76] for accounts of the philosophical subtleties of "minimal change."

2.2. Permissive and Restrictive Semantics

We now describe a means of classifying semantics beyond the formula-based/model-based distinction. This section shows how a partial order can be imposed upon the sets of formula-based and model-based semantics, based on how restrictive or permissive the semantics is. Section 2.2.1 explores the permissive/restrictive spectrum for model-based semantics, and Section 2.2.2 does the same for formula-based semantics.

2.2.1. Permissive and Restrictive Model-Based Semantics

Given theory $T = \{a, \neg b\}$ and the model-based update *insert $a \vee b$*, what should be the result of this update? Rather than any single obvious choice, we are confronted with a spectrum of reasonable candidate semantics. At one extreme lies the permissive viewpoint that *every* way of making ω true in a model of T should be in the result of the update [Abiteboul 85, Winslett 88b]. In other words, under this point of view the new theory should have three models:

Model M_1: $\{a, \neg b\}$
Model M_2: $\{\neg a, b\}$
Model M_3: $\{a, b\}$

From this "permissive" pole the spectrum stretches to the other extreme, where lie the minimal-change semantics. The idea behind a minimal-change semantics is that not *every* way of changing a model to satisfy ω should be included in $U(M)$; rather, M should be changed as little as is necessary to make ω true there. For the current example, one interpretation of "minimal change" is not to change T at all, since ω is already true in all models of T.

The philosophical justification for these more restrictive "forward pruning" semantics is an Occam's razor argument: one should make only those changes in a set of models that are strictly necessary, as the smallest possible set of changes is in some sense the simplest explanation of the need for the update. This argument is more compelling in the case where T contains large amounts of knowledge as well as data; under these circumstances the number of candidate result models for an update may be simply overwhelming, and heuristics, such as the minimal-change approach, are needed to prune the more unlikely candidates from consideration. For example, given the sighting of a pigeon outside the window, one can construct arbitrarily fanciful explanations for the pigeon's presence (if, indeed, it is a pigeon at all, rather than a taxidermist's relic or a fleeting hallucination). Most of these explanations, however, do not bear consideration unless other observations cast doubt on the normal interpretation of the pigeon-sighting.

One may apply minimal-change criteria locally, on a model-by-model basis, or globally, considering multiple models simultaneously when determining the effect of an update on a particular model. Looking for a globally minimal change in models amounts to pruning the set of candidate models *backwards* in time, as well as forward. The rationale behind backward pruning is that the more a model agrees with the new information contained in an update, the more likely that model is to be the actual state of the world. This may seem counterintuitive at first: after all, updates are mainly intended for use in describing *changes* in the world, so a model where the formula to be inserted is already true would seem an unlikely model. In practice, however, this heuristic accords well with human intuitions about the desirable effects of updates in some applications.

For example, a popular backward pruning heuristic is to retain only those models of T where ω is true, when such models exist [Borgida 85, Dalal 88, Gärdenfors 88b, Satoh 88, Weber 86]. In other words, if ω and T are consistent,

$$\text{Models}(U(T)) = \text{Models}(T \cup \{\omega\}). \tag{2.1}$$

Formula 2.1 is certainly appropriate when ω is supplying additional information about the current unchanged state of the world, rather than recording a change in the state of the world; but when ω may represent a change in the state of the world, the utility of formula 2.1 is not so clear; it conflicts with MB4' and MB5'. Katsuno and Mendelzon express the problem nicely [Katsuno 89]:

> ... suppose a represents the fact that a book is on the floor and b means that a magazine is on the floor. Then, ψ [(the theory $\{(a \wedge \neg b) \vee (\neg a \wedge b)\})$)] states that either the book or the magazine is on the floor, but not both. Now, we order a robot to put the book on the floor. The result of this action should be represented by the revision of ψ with a. After the robot puts the book on the floor, we know a, but we do not know whether b is true or not. Hence, the new state of the world should be described not as $a \wedge \neg b$ [(as formula 2.1 would suggest)], but as a [(as in, e.g., the minimal-change semantics defined below)].

We mentioned earlier that the Gärdenfors Postulates GP2 (formula 2.1) and GP6 will not be appropriate for all applications, because they involve backward pruning. For example, consider GP6 when ω_1 is just $\top$, and ω_2 and T are consistent with one another. Then GP6 reduces to formula 2.1, which is not reasonable in all applications.

For model-based semantics, the spectrum of possibilities for restrictiveness leads to a natural partial ordering on semantics:

Definition.   *Given two semantics S_1 and S_2, S_1 is as permissive as (resp. as restrictive as) S_2 if for every update U and theory T, Models($U(M)$) under S_1 is a superset (resp. subset) of Models($U(M)$) under S_2, for all $M \in$ Models(T).*

Generally, the more restrictive a semantics, the more global the nature of the information it uses in determining $U(M)$, and the fewer models it produces as the result of an update. As described in Section 2.1, the more restrictive semantics have the advantage of keeping down the number of models of T, which may help to speed query answering. On the other hand, permissive semantics are sound in the sense of MB4' and MB5', and many restrictive semantics are not. In addition, giving a global aspect to update semantics complicates algorithms for minimal-change semantics, as will be seen in Chapter 4; a decision on the interpretation of an update cannot be made locally at an individual model, but rather must consider information present in other models.

We will now describe several model-based semantics with different degrees of restrictiveness. First, we have an extremely permissive semantics, whose first-order analogue will be presented in Chapter 3:

Definition. *The* standard semantics *is the model-based semantics where $U(M)$ is the maximum set of models such that MB1 and MB2 hold.*

More explicitly, under the standard semantics $U(T)$ is given by MB3, and $U(M)$ is the set of all models M' such that

(1) ω is true in M' and
(2) M' agrees with M on all propositions not occurring in ω.

Under the standard semantics, all three result models in Example 2.3 would be produced. Insertion of a tautology such as $p \lor \neg p$ can change the models of a theory under the standard semantics:

Example 2.8. Let T be $\{a, b\}$, and let U be *insert* $a \lor \neg a$ under the standard semantics. Then Models$(U(T))$ is

Model M_1: $\{a, b\}$
Model M_2: $\{\neg a, b\}$

Let us now consider a semantics that is more restrictive than the standard semantics. Under Hegner's semantics, ω is put into a normal form before insertion [Hegner 87]. The advantage of normalization is that one can identify and remove tautologies within ω, which may help to eliminate unintended result models. Under Hegner's semantics (restricted to the propositional case), one first puts ω into conjunctive normal form, and then simplifies ω as much as possible. In the process redundant and tautological conjuncts are removed, so that propositions that need not occur in ω do not occur there. Then one inserts the normalized version of ω using the standard semantics. As a side effect of normalization, if ω_1 and ω_2 are logically equivalent, then *insert* ω_1 and *insert* ω_2 will always produce the same result models (GP4).

Example 2.9. Under Hegner's semantics, *insert* $a \lor \neg a$ reduces to the insertion of the empty formula, which does not change the models of T.

We next present a yet more restrictive semantics, perhaps the most natural choice for a minimal-change semantics. We will call it *the* minimal-change semantics, and will present its first-order analogue in Chapter 3. The minimal-change semantics employs forward but not backward pruning; it satisfies MB4' and MB5'.

Definition.   *Let* diff(M, M') *be the set of all propositional symbols on which models M and M' differ (i.e., to which they assign different truth valuations).*

Definition.   *Let S be $U(M)$ under the standard semantics. Then under the* minimal-change *semantics, $U(M)$ contains every model M' such that*

(1)   *$M' \in S$; and*
(2)   *There is no model $M'' \in S$ such that* diff(M'', M) *is a proper subset of* diff(M', M).

Under the minimal-change semantics, only result models M_2 and M_3 are produced in Example 2.3. The minimal-change semantics agrees with Hegner's semantics on Example 2.9.

One can be yet more restrictive than the minimal-change semantics. Another possibility, still using only forward pruning of models, is to use local cardinality counting to strengthen the second criterion in the definition of the minimal-change semantics [Forbus 89]:

(2)   There is no other model $M'' \in S$, such that diff(M'', M) is of smaller cardinality than diff(M', M).

Example 2.10.   Let T be $\{\neg a, \neg b, \neg c\}$ and let U be *insert $a \vee (b \wedge c)$.* The set of all result models satisfying MB1 and MB2 is

M_1: $\{a, \neg b, \neg c\}$
M_2: $\{\neg a, b, c\}$
M_3: $\{a, b, \neg c\}$
M_4: $\{a, \neg b, c\}$
M_5: $\{a, b, c\}$

A minimal-change semantics with local cardinality counting produces only M_1; the minimal-change semantics produces both M_1 and M_2; Hegner's and the standard semantics produce models M_1 through M_5.

We next describe a semantics that uses global criteria to perform both forward and backward pruning of models [Satoh 88]. Satoh's semantics is more restrictive than the minimal-change semantics, and is incomparable to minimal-change with local cardinality counting. We will use an auxiliary definition that measures the degree of difference between two sets of models:

Definition. *For sets of models S_1 and S_2, we define*

$$\mathrm{diff}(S_1, S_2) = \bigcup_{\substack{M_1 \in S_1 \\ M_2 \in S_2}} \mathrm{diff}(M_1, M_2).$$

Also, we define $\mathrm{minDiff}(S_1, S_2)$ as the set of all $d \in \mathrm{diff}(S_1, S_2)$ such that no member of $\mathrm{diff}(S_1, S_2)$ is a proper subset of d.

Example 2.11. Consider the following set of models:

M_1: $\{\neg a, \ \neg b, \ \neg c\}$
M_2: $\{\neg a, \ b, \ c\}$
M_3: $\{a, \ \neg b, \ \neg c\}$
M_4: $\{a, \ b, \ c\}$

Then

$\mathrm{diff}(M_1, \ M_2) = \{b, \ c\}$
$\mathrm{diff}(M_1, \ M_3) = \{a\}$
$\mathrm{diff}(M_1, \ M_4) = \{a, \ b, \ c\}$.

Therefore $\mathrm{minDiff}(\{M_1\}, \{M_2, M_3, M_4\}) = \{\{a\}, \{b, c\}\}$.

Definition. *Let U be an update to be applied to a theory T, and let S be $\mathrm{Models}(U(T))$ under the standard semantics. Under Satoh's semantics, M is a member of $\mathrm{Models}(U(T))$ iff*

(1)   *$M \in S$; and*
(2)   *There is a model M' in $\mathrm{Models}(T)$ such that $\mathrm{diff}(M, \ M') \in \mathrm{minDiff}(S, \mathrm{Models}(T))$.*

Satoh's semantics in effect discards those models of T for which the changes needed to make ω true are not as small as they are in other models of T. In effect, only those models of T that are closest to ω are retained. One could of course use the minimal-change semantics in the definition of S in Satoh's semantics, as Satoh's semantics is more restrictive than either the standard or minimal-change semantics. Satoh's semantics does not satisfy MB4′ or MB5′.

Example 2.12. Let $\mathrm{Models}(T)$ be

M_6: $\{\neg a, \ \neg b, \ \neg c\}$
M_7: $\{\neg a, \ b, \ c\}$

If U is *insert* $a \vee (b \wedge c)$, then the standard semantics will produce all five result models of Example 2.10. Under the minimal-change semantics, $U(M_6) = \{M_1, M_2\}$, and $U(M_7) = \{M_2\}$, so the same result models as in Example 2.10 are produced:

M_1: $\{a, \ \neg b, \ \neg c\}$
M_2: $\{\neg a, \ b, \ c\}$

Under minimal-change with local cardinality counting, $U(M_6) = \{M_1\}$, and $U(M_7) = \{M_2\}$, so Models($U(T)$) $= \{M_1, M_2\}$. The differences between models M_1 and M_2, M_6 and M_7:

diff(M_1, M_6): $\{\{a\}\}$
diff(M_2, M_6): $\{\{b, \ c\}\}$
diff(M_1, M_7): $\{\{a, \ b, \ c\}\}$
diff(M_2, M_7): $\{\{ \ \}\}$

Therefore minDiff($\{M_6, M_7\}$, $\{M_1, M_2\}$) is $\{\{ \ \}\}$, and Models($U(T)$) $= \{M_2\}$ under Satoh's semantics. M_6 falls victim to backward pruning under Satoh's semantics, because M_6 is further away from ω than is M_7.

Note that the definition of minDiff used set inclusion as the measure of minimality. If desired, one could use a cardinality test instead, as is done in Dalal's semantics [Dalal 88]. The resulting semantics is more restrictive than Satoh's or minimal-change with local cardinality counting. By the inclusion of a global test for minimality, both Satoh's and Dalal's semantics satisfy the heuristic of formula 2.1. More generally, cardinality counting is a "mixin" that can be used in lieu of set inclusion in any pruning heuristic.

Example 2.13.   Let T be $\{\neg a, \neg b, \neg c\}$, and let U be *insert* $(a \wedge b) \vee (c \wedge d)$. Then T has models

M_8: $\{\neg a, \ \neg b, \ \neg c, \ \neg d\}$
M_9: $\{\neg a, \ \neg b, \ \neg c, \ d\}$.

Under the minimal-change semantics, $U(M_8) = U(M_9) = \{M_{10}, M_{11}\}$:

M_{10}: $\{a, \ b, \ \neg c, \ \neg d\}$
M_{11}: $\{\neg a, \ \neg b, \ c, \ d\}$

Under minimal-change with local cardinality counting,

$U(M_8) = \{M_{10}, M_{11}\}$
$U(M_9) = \{M_{11}\}.$
$\text{Models}(U(T)) = \{M_{10}, M_{11}\}.$

Under Satoh's semantics, minDiff($\{M_8, M_9\}, \{M_{10}, M_{11}\} = \{\{a, b\}, \{c\}\}$, so that Models($U(T)) = \{M_{10}, M_{11}\}$ still. However, under Dalal's semantics, we find that Models($U(T)) = \{M_{11}\}$, so that M_8 falls to backward pruning.

The semantics given here do not by any means exhaust the set of possibilities. For example, Weber proposes global consideration of the set of models, in the manner of Satoh, to determine minDiff(Models(ω), Models(T)); Weber then applies the standard semantics, except that M and the members of $U(M)$ must agree on all propositions not occurring in minDiff(Models(ω), Models(T)) [Weber 86]. Borgida proposes a semantics identical to the minimal-change semantics, except that if ω is consistent with T, the heuristic of formula 2.1 is employed [Borgida 85]. One could also place a priority ordering on propositions, so that differences on certain propositions carried more weight than others when computing a minimal change. As another example, particular applications may have domain-dependent heuristics (such as the principle of continuity of physical parameters in qualitative physics [Forbus 89]) that allow intelligent pruning of the set of models and candidate result models, through use of priorities and other means.

2.2.2. Permissive and Restrictive Formula-Based Semantics
Is it meaningful to order formula-based semantics on the basis of restrictivity? At first glance it might seem not, since principle FB1 implies that every formula-based semantics subscribes to a minimal-change philosophy. But reasonable minds may differ on exactly what constitutes a formula-based minimal change in those cases where FB1 does not apply: the case of the multiple minimal sets, which has been a Waterloo of sorts for formula-based semantics. There are three main approaches advocated in the literature: the set-of-theories approach, the cross-product approach, and the WIDTIO paradigm.

2.2.2.1. The Set-of-Theories Approach
A semantically acceptable solution to the minimal set problem, advocated by [Fagin 86], is for the result of an update with multiple minimal sets to be the *set* of all theories resulting from removing a minimal set from T and then adding ω. Fagin et al call such a collection a *flock*. For example, if $T = \{a, b\}$ and U is *insert* $\neg a \vee \neg b$, then under the set-of-theories approach

two result theories are produced: $T_1 = \{a, \neg a \vee \neg b\}$, and $T_2 = \{b, \neg a \vee \neg b\}$. Under the set-of-theories approach, the knowledge base is not a single theory T but a *set* of such theories $\{T_1, T_2, \ldots\}$. An incoming update U is applied to all the theories in the stored set separately, and the models of the knowledge base are the set union of the models of the theories in the knowledge base.

Interestingly, the set-of-theories approach has a strong tinge of MB3 in its handling of multiple theories: note that each theory in a flock is updated independently of all others, with the result that an analogue of MB3 applies to the theories in a flock. A less egalitarian approach would be more in keeping with the formula-based credo. For example, if ω is true in some model of a flock, one might prefer to throw away all theories in the flock that are inconsistent with ω, as a backward pruning heuristic. This treatment has some empirical basis in scientific theory revision. Given a set of competing theories and a new piece of information to be explained, one is likely to favor those theories that predict or at least are consistent with the new information, and discredit those that contradict it.

The disadvantage of the set-of-theories approach is that it is difficult to see how to construct an efficient implementation of the semantics.

2.2.2.2. The Cross-Product Approach

Another approach is to merge the candidate result theories given by the set-of-theories technique into a single theory T by, loosely speaking, taking the disjunction of all the formulas in the candidate theories [Fagin 83]. More precisely, consider the cross product of the formulas in the n candidate theories. For each n-tuple of formulas $[f_1, f_2, \ldots, f_n]$ in the cross product, T contains the formula $f_1 \vee f_2 \vee \cdots \vee f_n$. For example, if $T = \{a, b\}$ and U is *insert* $\neg a \vee \neg b$, then under the cross-product approach $U(T) = \{a \vee b, a \vee \neg a \vee \neg b, \neg a \vee \neg b \vee b, \neg a \vee \neg b \vee \neg a \vee \neg b\}$. The models of the resulting theory are the union of the models of the candidate result theories.

The disadvantages of the cross-product approach are, first, that it is difficult to see how to construct an efficient implementation of the approach; and second, that it is hard to understand the effect of a series of updates. The formula-based approaches are all very dependent on the syntax of T, and the cross-product approach makes extensive alterations in that syntax, making it hard to predict the effect of updates.

2.2.2.3. The WIDTIO Approach

Another choice is to remove from T all formulas of all minimal sets—When

In Doubt, Throw It Out (WIDTIO). For example, if $T = \{a, b\}$ and U is *insert* $\neg a \vee \neg b$, then under the WIDTIO approach $U(T) = \{\neg a \vee \neg b\}$.

The major disadvantage of the WIDTIO approach is that it tends to remove information from T gratuitously. On the other hand, the WIDTIO approach is easy to implement [Ginsberg 86, Reiter 87], a major advantage. The typical manner of executing *insert* ω involves three steps:

- Find all minimal proofs (defined below) of $\neg\omega$ from T.
- Remove from T every formula that is used in a minimal proof.
- Add ω to T.

There are several hidden assumptions in this algorithm. In the first step, a theorem prover is used to ferret out all the possible ways that ω is inconsistent with T, by proving $\neg\omega$ from T in all possible ways. This assumes that a theorem prover sufficiently powerful to do so is on hand, and that computational resources are not limited. Further, the theorem prover must be sufficiently clever to find the "minimal" proofs: those proofs such that no proper subset of the formulas of T used as the basis for the proof would be sufficient to prove $\neg\omega$. If no minimal proofs are found, then presumably ω is consistent with T and can be added to it. If a minimal proof of $\neg\omega$ is found, then intuitively it represents one way that ω and T are inconsistent; and the removal from T of any one of the formulas used in the proof would eliminate that particular inconsistency. To eliminate *all* inconsistencies, it would suffice to remove from T one formula from every minimal proof of $\neg\omega$. In other words, a minimal set can be constructed by picking one formula from each minimal proof[4]. Which formula to pick? That is the multiple minimal set problem again, which the WIDTIO method avoids by computing only the union of all minimal sets. A lower complexity class results as in theory the set of all minimal proofs need not be computed.

Ginsberg reports satisfactory performance for this approach in a pilot implementation [Ginsberg 86]. In their work on planning, Ginsberg and Smith argue that this approach is at least as efficient as the contending approaches for representing the effect of actions on the state of the world (e.g., situation calculus) [Ginsberg 88a]. However, their analysis depends on strong assumptions about the shape and distribution of proof trees, which

---

[4] Well, almost. The result may not be a minimal set due to the occurrence of the same formula in multiple minimal proofs. Choosing a minimal set from a collection of minimal proofs is itself an *NP*-complete problem (vertex cover), and the number of minimal proofs may be exponential in t.

have not been verified experimentally; and since no effort has gone into optimizing other approaches, it is too early to draw conclusions.

2.2.2.4. Restrictiveness

It would seem natural to use the formulas of T as the basis for measuring restrictivity of formula-based semantics. In the case of multiple minimal sets, however, this approach breaks down because the set-of-theories and cross-product approaches tinker with the structure of T, and the resulting theories are incomparable. For that reason, we use models of T to determine restrictiveness.

Definition.   *Formula-based semantics S_1 is as permissive as S_2 if for every sequence of updates $U_1 \cdots U_n$ and theory T ($\{T\}$, for set-of-theories semantics), the models of $U_n(\cdots(U_1(T)))$ under S_1 are a superset of the models of $U_n(\cdots(U_1(T)))$ under S_2.*

WIDTIO semantics are more permissive than set-of-theories and cross-product semantics. The latter two are incomparable with respect to restrictivity, as the following example shows.

Example 2.14.   Starting with the theory $\{a, b\}$, successively perform the updates (1) *insert* $\neg a \vee \neg b$, (2) *insert* $a \wedge b$, (3) *insert* $\neg a$, and (4) *insert* $\neg b$ under the cross-product and set-of-theories semantics. Just after update (3), the cross-product models are a proper subset of the set-of-theories flock's models, while after update (4), the reverse holds.

Example 2.14 shows that the models of a theory can diverge after a series of updates, depending on whether the cross-product or set-of-theories semantics is used. However, after a *single* update, Models($U(T_1)$) is the same under the cross-product and set-of-theories semantics [Fagin 86].

2.3. Embellishments

The methods suggested above can be modified in many ways, by incorporating additional pruning heuristics. For example, in both formula-based and model-based semantics, one can "layer" the formulas or propositions according to a priori notions of the immutability of the information represented by them [Fagin 83, Ginsberg 86, Pollack 76, Winslett 88c], and prefer changes at lower levels to changes at higher ones. This heuristic is particularly popular for applications in which causality needs to be (sketchily) taken into account. In formula-based semantics one can use application-dependent heuristics [Drummond 86] and cardinality tests for minimality, just as in model-based semantics. One could also use Satoh's backward pruning with the set-of-theories approach, to prune out flock members that are unlikely to represent the actual world.

A particularly interesting example of formula layering is introduced in a model-based semantics[5] proposed in [Gärdenfors 88b]. The idea here is to apply WIDTIO update semantics not to T, but rather to Cn T, the set of all logical consequences of T. The WIDTIO approach makes sense here because if there is a finite set of candidate result theories for an update, then the union of the models of those theories is exactly the set of models of the intersection of those theories. However, one must introduce formula layering in order to make this work; otherwise, after inserting a formula ω into T, if ω does not already follow from T then the models of $U(T)$ will be simply the models of ω [Fagin 83]. This rather unintuitive fact holds because, in some sense, Cn T contains too much information, so much that nearly every formula of T will find itself in a minimal set. To counter this problem, Gärdenfors and Makinson have proposed a method of prioritizing the formulas of Cn T into layers, called *epistemic entrenchment* [Gärdenfors 88ab]. Under epistemic entrenchment, the insertion of a formula ω into Cn T will not lead to a trivial theory when ω and T are inconsistent. Further, the prioritization of formulas can be derived automatically from a priority ordering on just the atomic formulas occurring in T. Intuitively, epistemic entrenchment prefers shorter, simpler formulas over longer ones, when deciding which formulas of Cn T to retain under update.

2.4. Evaluating Semantics for a Particular Application

This section summarizes the factors to consider when choosing an update semantics for a particular application, and presents additional technical measures that differentiate semantics. The analysis is organized around a five-point framework for evaluation of semantics:

---

[5] Strictly speaking, this semantics is not model-based because it does not satisfy MB2 (the requirement that an update only change the truth valuations of propositions occurring in ω). We look mildly on this violation, however, because, as mentioned earlier, we will abandon MB2 when considering theories containing knowledge as well as data. When knowledge is present, the truth valuation of one proposition can affect the truth valuation of another proposition, and so the effect of an update can reasonably extend beyond the propositions of ω, to all propositions logically related to those in ω.

- The needs of the intended application.
- Computational tractability.
- Expressive power.
- Comprehensibility.
- Extensibility.

The following subsections examine each of these criteria in turn.

2.4.1. The Needs of the Intended Application

It is impossible to judge the appropriateness of a semantics for theory revision without an application in mind, because without an application, one has no intuitions about what revisions are appropriate in a given case. As different semantics produce different results given the same update, it is vital to keep applications in mind as a means of ensuring that a proposed semantics actually gives intuitively desirable results in some realistic scenario. Examples 2.1 through 2.14 are the most helpful examples to consider when looking for an update semantics for a particular application.

For example, the Occam's razor principle is appropriate in a diagnosis application. In diagnosis one wishes to make as few changes as possible in a description of the correct functioning of a device in order to make the description conform to the actual observed behavior of the device. When the observed behavior is provided as the new information in an update, the updated theory should not include *every* possible combination of conditions that would lead to the observed behavior, but rather only the minimal combinations of such conditions. The diagnosis of the problem consists of the minimal changes in the theory (if formula-based) or models (if model-based) needed to "explain" the behavior of the device.

For example, in diagnosing faults in circuits, T is a description of the correct functioning of the circuit, plus information on what inputs were applied to the circuit. (In this application, T will contain knowledge as well as data, but this does not affect our point here.) T will then entail a formula ϕ that gives the circuit outputs that will be obtained if the circuit is functioning correctly. Let ω be a formula giving the circuit outputs that were in fact obtained. Updating T by inserting ω will give a new theory of the device's behavior that is consistent with the observed behavior of the circuit [Reiter 87]. If in fact T entails ω, then the circuit is behaving as expected, and Models(T) should not be changed by the update. This means that the standard semantics is not appropriate for use in this application; instead one needs to use a minimal-change semantics. The diagnosis of the problems in the circuit will be the minimal changes in T or in Models(T) that make ω true. Further, one strongly prefers single-fault diagnoses over double-fault diagnoses, so that cardinality of sets of changes should also be used as a pruning heuristic. One can also use domain-dependent heuristics regarding which types of faults are more common, to prune out unlikely diagnoses.

In applying theory revision techniques to the AI problem of reasoning about the effects of actions (discussed in Chapter 8), again a minimal-change semantics gives more intuitively desirable results. In this application one needs a means of modeling causality; lacking semantic models of causality, one can use layering of formulas, predicates, or atoms as a syntactic tool to capture some of the effects of causality. Cardinality testing does not seem appropriate for this application, though some researchers report success with its use [Forbus 89].

2.4.2. Computational Tractability

A *computationally tractable* semantics is one for which an algorithm with a reasonable running time can be found to implement the semantics. Tables 2.1 and 2.2 present worst-case complexity results for different semantics, operating on a propositional theory T containing t occurrences of propositional symbols. The entries depend on a number of assumptions, discussed below.

First, we assume that the length of ω is bounded by a constant ≥ 3; this assumption will certainly be met by human-generated updates.

Second, we assume that the information in the update is incorporated completely into T. One could, of course, find more efficient algorithms by defining the knowledge base as an ordered sequence of update requests, but then the burden of determining the logical consequences of an update is thrust entirely upon the query-answering mechanism.

Third, the upper bound for WIDTIO in Table 2.1 is a bound for the problem of determining whether a particular formula is in any minimal set; a WIDTIO algorithm could be constructed by making t calls to such a procedure. (We suspect that the problem of determining whether a particular formula is in any minimal set is NP^{NP}-complete; in other words, it is complete for the class of problems that can be solved in non-deterministic polynomial time given an oracle for non-deterministic polynomial time problems.) For the cross-product and set-of-theories approaches, the lower bound in Table 2.1 follows from the fact that there may be that many minimal sets, and our assumption that a cross-product or set-of-theories algorithm must com-

Table 2.1. *Worst-Case Complexity Classes.*

Semantics	Lower Bound	Upper Bound
Model-Based		
Standard,		
Hegner's,		
Minimal-Change,		
M-C with Local CC	constant time	$O(\log t)$
Satoh's	NP-Hard	P^{NP}
Formula-Based		
Cross-Product	exponential in t	exponential in t
Set-of-Theories	exponential in t	exponential in t
WIDTIO	NP-Hard	NP^{NP}

pute all minimal sets. The lower bound for Satoh's semantics rests on the assumption that an implementation of Satoh's semantics must determine whether ω and T are consistent.

Finally, the cost of actually writing down the result theories is given in Table 2.2. For the cross-product and set-of-theories approaches we assume a completely naive storage organization, where the theories are written out as we would write them down on paper, using the usual boolean connectives. (We conjecture that these bounds hold even for clever storage schemes. In addition, any system that avoids redundant storage will introduce corresponding complexities into the query processors for the knowledge base.) Further, we assume that the number of disjunctions generated by the cross-product approach is kept down by generating only one permutation of the formulas making up each disjunct.

Chapter 4 gives algorithms for the standard and minimal-change model-based semantics that require time logarithmic in the size of the knowledge base and time linear (standard semantics) to exponential (minimal-change semantics) in the size of ω. Intuitively, the complexity increases because more cases must be considered in a restrictive semantics; the desired effect of the update must be spelled out for each possible context within a model.

According to Tables 2.1 and 2.2, formula-based semantics are intractable in the worst case; for example, there may be an exponential number of minimal sets or minimal proofs. Also, even should there be a reasonable

Table 2.2. *Worst-Case Increase in t When U is Performed.*

Semantics	Increase
Model-Based	
Standard,	
Hegner's,	
Minimal-Change,	
M-C with Local CC,	
Satoh's	$O(1)$
Formula-Based	
Cross-Product	exponential in t
Set-of-Theories	exponential in t
WIDTIO	$O(1)$

number of proofs and minimal sets, these semantics require use of a test to see whether ω is consistent with T, which is NP-complete for propositional theories, and undecidable for first-order theories.

Table 2.1 would seem to imply that model-based semantics are more tractable than formula-based semantics. We do not, however, expect this advantage to carry over to the case where T contains significant amounts of knowledge as well as data, as in the applications discussed in Chapter 8. In this case the most promising approach for model-based semantics is to use an assumption-based truth maintenance system [de Kleer 86] to keep track of the logical relationships between atomic formulas (e.g., as done in [Forbus 89]). This style of implementation attacks an undecidable problem in the first-order case, just as the formula-based approaches do, and in addition has large storage requirements.

In the remainder of this section, we present justifications for the entries in Tables 2.1 and 2.2.

We begin with the table entries for the WIDTIO semantics. WIDTIO need never increase the size of T by more than the length of ω, giving the upper bound of $O(1)$ in Table 2.2.

WIDTIO has an NP^{NP} upper bound in Table 2.1. A formula ϕ of T is in some minimal set iff there exists a subset T' of T such that $T' \cup \{\omega\}$ is satisfiable and $T' \cup \{\omega, \phi\}$ is unsatisfiable. There are up to 2^t possible choices of T', but one can nondeterministically guess a choice of T' and then quickly verify whether ϕ is in a minimal set for that choice of T' by two calls to an oracle for satisfiability. Therefore determination of the union of all minimal sets is in NP^{NP}.

The lower bound of NP-hard for WIDTIO in Table 2.1 follows from the fact that determining whether T and ω are consistent is an NP-complete problem.

We next consider the other formula-based semantics. Consider the theory containing the following formulas:

$$
\begin{array}{lll}
a_1 & b_1 & c_1 \leftrightarrow (\neg a_1 \vee \neg b_1) \\
\cdots & \cdots & \cdots \\
a_n & b_n & c_n \leftrightarrow [c_{n-1} \wedge (\neg a_n \vee \neg b_n)]
\end{array}
$$

The number of minimal sets for this theory and the update *insert* c_n is exponential in n. For example, there are 2^n minimal sets containing one each of a_i and b_i, for $1 \le i \le n$. This gives the exponential lower bounds for cross-product and set-of-theories semantics in Table 2.1.

The exponential upper bound in Table 2.1 for the cross-product and set-of-theories approaches was determined by considering the maximum possible number of minimal sets. There are at most 2^t subsets of T. Given a particular subset T' of T, whether T' and ω are consistent can be checked in $O(t2^t)$ time. If the subsets of T are generated and tested in decreasing order of size, whether a subset T' is a proper subset of another subset can be tested in $O(t2^t)$ time, assuming subsets are kept sorted on formula number. That means that all minimal sets can be found in $2^t[O(t2^t) + O(t2^t)] = O(t4^t)$ time.

The exponential lower bound for the cross-product approach in Table 2.2 follows from the same example used to establish the lower bound for cross-product and set-of-theories in Table 2.1. In this example, no minimal set is of size greater than n. Therefore, every disjunction of $n + 1$ or more formulas of T occurs in the cross-product theory $U(T)$. This means that the size of $U(T)$ is exponential in t.

The lower bound for the set-of-theories approach in Table 2.2 is established using the same example, for which there are exponentially many different result theories.

Now consider the exponential upper bound for the set-of-theories approach in Table 2.2. If a result theory T' in $U(T)$ has i formulas of the n

occurring in T, then there are at most $\binom{n}{i}$ choices for T'. In addition, if all $\binom{n}{i}$ of these are result theories, then they must be of average size $1 + it/n$ each. This gives a maximum length for $U(T)$ of

$$\sum_{i=0}^{n} \binom{n}{i}(1 + it/n) = O(t2^n) = O(t2^t).$$

The exponential upper bound for the cross-product approach in Table 2.2 is based on the case where every disjunction of the n formulas of $T \cup \{\omega\}$ occurs in $U(T)$. In this case, there are $\sum_{i=1}^{n} \binom{n}{i}$ formulas in $U(T)$. A disjunction of i formulas of T will have average length $i(t + c)/n$, where c is the size of ω, giving a size for $U(T)$ of

$$\sum_{i=1}^{n} \binom{n}{i} i(t + c)/n = O(t2^t).$$

For model-based semantics other than Satoh's, one can fill out a table in constant time giving, for each possible combination of truth valuations of the propositions of ω in M, the acceptable truth valuations for those propositions in $U(M)$. The update techniques described in Chapter 4 can then be used to make the necessary changes in T in $O(\log t)$ time. This bound assumes that the storage of T is organized in a particular manner, described in Chapter 9, so that a proposition can be located and replaced throughout T in $O(\log t)$ time. This updating method will increase the size of T by an amount at most exponential in the size of ω, giving the upper bound in Table 2.2 for most model-based semantics.

For Satoh's semantics, the lower bound in Table 2.1 follows from our assumption that an implementation of Satoh's approach will require determination of whether T and ω are consistent. For the upper bound, we will sketch an implementation approach that shows that updates can be accomplished in time polynomial in t, given an oracle for satisfiability. This sketch makes heavy use of notation and concepts that will be introduced in Chapter 4.

Let k be the number of propositions occurring in ω. Begin by determining the result theory T' for the minimal-change semantics. This can be accomplished in $O(\log t)$ time using the algorithm presented in Chapter 4.

Then for each of the 2^k subsets S of the propositions occurring in ω, we call an oracle for satisfiability to determine whether T' is consistent with the following formula:

$$\bigwedge_{f \in S} (f \not\equiv f_U) \wedge \bigwedge_{\substack{f \text{ occurs in } \omega \\ f \notin S}} (f \equiv f_U).$$

If the oracle reports that the two are consistent, then that means that S is the difference between some model of T and some model of T'. After 2^k calls to the oracle, we have determined exactly which choices of S are in diff(Models(T), Models(T')); call this set DiffSet. The next step is to determine which elements of DiffSet are minimal under set inclusion; this can also be done in time exponential in the size of ω. Let MinDiffSet be that subset of DiffSet. Then the final step of the algorithm is to add to T' the formula $f \leftrightarrow f_U$, for every proposition f of ω not occurring in MinDiffSet; and to add the formula

$$\neg\Big(\bigvee_{\substack{d \in \text{MinDiffSet} \\ f \in d}} \bigwedge_{\substack{g \text{ occurs in } \omega \\ g \notin d}} (g \leftrightarrow g_U)\Big) \quad \rightarrow \quad (f \leftrightarrow f_U),$$

for every proposition f that occurs in MinDiffSet. These two guarantee that a proposition's truth value does not change unless it is part of a globally minimal change in a model that will make ω true.

The worst-case size increase caused by Satoh's semantics is given by the increase in size for the minimal-change semantics plus the cost of the preceding formula; these will both be exponential in k in the worst case, but independent of t, giving the $O(1)$ bound in Table 2.2.

2.4.3. Comprehensibility

The user must be able to look at an update and understand what it will do: the update must be *comprehensible*. Comprehensibility can be addressed by informal arguments and by more formal means. One formal tool for measuring comprehensibility or trickiness is update equivalence: Do two updates that look similar produce the same effect when applied to a theory? If two updates look different, do they produce different effects? Update equivalence theorems can be used to evaluate how well a given semantics meets intuition: if a pair of updates should be the same according to intuition, but an equivalence theorem says that they are different (or vice versa), then the discrepancy can be registered as a mark against that semantics.

One might also ponder the question of when two *theories* are equivalent in the sense that they will have the same set of models after any series of updates. Note that by MB5, under any model-based semantics, theories T_1 and T_2 are equivalent iff they are logically equivalent. This is not true in the formula-based world [Fagin 86], as illustrated by Examples 2.6 and 2.7. In general, formula-based semantics are extremely sensitive to the syntax of the formulas in T. Conjunction must be used with care in the formula-based approach; tying two formulas together with conjunction means that they live or die as one in the knowledge base.

Theorem 2.1. *Under any WIDTIO semantics, consistent theories T_1 and T_2 are equivalent iff every subset of T_1 is logically equivalent to a subset of T_2, and vice versa.*

Proof of Theorem 2.1. (Sufficiency) Suppose that every subset of T_1 is logically equivalent to a subset of T_2, and vice versa. Given an update U, we will show that every subset of $U(T_1)$ is logically equivalent to a subset of $U(T_2)$, and vice versa, and the sufficiency of the subset equivalence condition will follow.

Suppose that the subset equivalence condition is not satisfied by $U(T_1)$ and $U(T_2)$. Then there must be a formula s_1 of, say, $U(T_1)$ such that s_1 is not logically equivalent to any subset of $U(T_2)$; otherwise the subset equivalence condition would be satisfied. Formula s_1 is logically equivalent to a subset S_2 of T_2. But some formula ϕ of S_2 must be in a minimal set for T_2, because ϕ is not in $U(T_2)$. Because ϕ is part of a minimal set for U and T_2, there must be a subset T_2' of T such that $T_2' \cup \{\omega\}$ is consistent and $T_2' \cup \{\omega, \phi\}$ is inconsistent. Find a subset T_1' of T_1 that is logically equivalent to T_2'. Then $T_1' \cup \{\omega\}$ is consistent, but since $s_1 \rightarrow \phi$, $T_1' \cup \{\omega, s_1\}$ is inconsistent. Therefore s_1 must be a member of some minimal set, a contradiction.

(Necessity) Let T_1 be a theory containing a subset that is not logically equivalent to any subset of T_2. We will show that T_1 and T_2 cannot be equivalent.

If T_1 is the empty set, or is not logically equivalent to T_2, or contains only one formula, then the theorem follows immediately. Otherwise, there must be a non-tautological formula ϕ_1 of T_1 such that ϕ_1 is not logically equivalent to any subset of T_2, as otherwise the subset equivalence condition would be satisfied. T_1 must also contain another non-tautological formula, ϕ_2. For now let us assume that these are all the non-tautological formulas of T_1:

$$T_1 = \{\phi_1, \phi_2, \tau_1, \tau_2, \dots, \dots\},$$

where each τ_i, if present in T_1, is a tautology. Further, ϕ_1 cannot logically entail ϕ_2, as otherwise the theorem follows. Consider now the update U_1: *insert* $\neg\phi_2$.

The formula $\neg\phi_2$ must be satisfiable, as ϕ_2 is not a tautology. The result theories are

$U_1(T_1) = \{\phi_1, \neg\phi_2, \tau_1, \tau_2, \ldots\},$
$U_1(T_2) = \{T_2', \neg\phi_2, \tau_1', \tau_2', \ldots\},$

where T_2' is a subset of the non-tautological formulas of T_2, T_2' is not logically equivalent to ϕ_1, and each τ_i', if present in T_2, is a tautology. If $U_1(T_1)$ and $U_1(T_2)$ are not logically equivalent, then the theorem follows. Assuming that they are logically equivalent, we have

$$(T_2' \wedge \neg\phi_1) \rightarrow \phi_2$$
$$(\phi_1 \wedge \neg T_2') \rightarrow \phi_2,$$

where T_2' is taken here to be the conjunction of all the formulas of T_2', and $\neg T_2'$ is satisfiable; or else T_2' is the empty set, in which case we have

$$\neg\phi_2 \rightarrow \phi_1.$$

Consider now the update U_2: *insert* ϕ_2. This update produces

$U_2(U_1(T_1)) = \{\phi_1, \phi_2, \tau_1, \tau_2, \ldots\},$
$U_2(U_1(T_2)) = \{T_2', \phi_2, \tau_1', \tau_2', \ldots\},$

from which as before we can conclude that

$$(T_2' \wedge \neg\phi_1) \rightarrow \neg\phi_2$$
$$(\phi_1 \wedge \neg T_2') \rightarrow \neg\phi_2,$$

unless T_2' is the empty set, in which case we have

$$\phi_2 \rightarrow \phi_1.$$

Therefore we have

$$(T_2' \wedge \neg\phi_1) \rightarrow (\phi_2 \wedge \neg\phi_2)$$
$$(\phi_1 \wedge \neg T_2') \rightarrow (\phi_2 \wedge \neg\phi_2),$$

which means that T_2' and ϕ_1 must be logically equivalent, a contradiction of our assumption; or else T_2' is the empty set, and we have

$$(\phi_2 \vee \neg\phi_2) \rightarrow \phi_1,$$

which means that ϕ_1 is a tautology, again a contradiction of our assumption. We conclude that the theorem holds when T_1 contains two formulas.

If T_1 contains $n > 2$ non-tautological formulas, say $\phi_1, \ldots, \phi_n$, let us reduce T_1 to a two-formula theory by update U_3: *insert* $\neg(\phi_2 \wedge \cdots \wedge \phi_n)$. If this inserted formula is not consistent with ϕ_1, then ϕ_1 logically entails $(\phi_2 \wedge \cdots \wedge \phi_n)$, an impossibility, as mentioned above. Therefore inserting this formula produces

$U_3(T_1) = \{\neg(\phi_2 \wedge \cdots \wedge \phi_n), \phi_1, \tau_1, \tau_2, \ldots\},$
$U_4(T_2) = \{\neg(\phi_2 \wedge \cdots \wedge \phi_n), T_2', \tau_1', \tau_2', \ldots\},$

where again T_2' is a subset of T_2 that is not logically equivalent to ϕ_1. In addition, ϕ_1 is not logically equivalent to $U_4(T_2)$, since if it were then it must be the case that ϕ_1 entails $\neg(\phi_2 \wedge \cdots \wedge \phi_n)$, which is untrue. Therefore the problem reduces to the case where T_1 contains just two non-tautological formulas.

Theorem 2.1 has an analogue for the cross-product semantics and for singleton sets under the set-of-theories approach [Fagin 86].

Now let us formalize the definition of update equivalence. We are interested in determining whether two updates are guaranteed to produce the same effect, regardless of what formulas are present in T:

Definition. *Update U_1 under semantics S_1 is equivalent to U_2 under S_2 iff for any theory T, $U_1(T)$ is equivalent to $U_2(T)$.*

It is easy to show that all model-based semantics that do not employ backward pruning are equivalent for insertions of conjunctive formulas. Recall that a model-based semantics does not employ backward pruning iff it satisfies MB4', i.e., for all updates U and models M, if $U(M)$ is empty then ω is unsatisfiable.

Theorem 2.2. *Let U be the update insert ω, where ω is a conjunction of propositions and negations of propositions. Then for any two model-based semantics S_1 and S_2 that satisfy MB4', U performed under S_1 is equivalent to U under S_2.*

Proof of Theorem 2.2. Let M be a model of a theory T. By principle MB1, all the conjuncts of ω must be true in every member of $U(M)$. By principles

MB2 and MB4′, there is exactly one model in $U(M)$, if ω is satisfiable, and none otherwise. Therefore by MB3, Models($U(T)$) is the same for any choice of model-based semantics satisfying MB4′. We conclude that U under S_1 is equivalent to U under S_2.

The cross-product, set-of-theories, and WIDTIO semantics only diverge when an update has more than one minimal set. Therefore, if T is initially the empty theory, then after any series of insertions of conjunctive formulas, the result theory will be the same whether the cross-product, set-of-theories, or WIDTIO approaches are used. It is the introduction of disjunctive information—incomplete information—that causes the formula-based approaches to diverge.

As Theorem 2.3 shows, update equivalence conditions are also simple for pairs of updates under the same formula-based semantics, or under model-based semantics with a minimal-change flavor.

Theorem 2.3.   *Let S be the set-of-theories, cross-product, WIDTIO, minimal-change, minimal-change with local cardinality counting, Satoh's semantics, or Dalal's semantics. Then updates U_1: insert ω_1 and U_2: insert ω_2, under S are equivalent iff ω_1 and ω_2 are logically equivalent.*

Theorem 2.3 lists specific model-based semantics, rather than being applied to all model-based semantics that are at least as restrictive as the minimal-change semantics. For Theorem 2.3 to hold for all minimal-change semantics, we would have to add a constraint like GP4.

Proof of Theorem 2.3.   First assume that ω_1 and ω_2 are logically equivalent. Let S be one of the model-based semantics listed in the theorem statement. For a particular choice of M, the minimal changes in M that make ω_1 true and survive pruning must be the same as those for ω_2. Therefore $U_1(M) = U_2(M)$, and by MB3, Models($U_1(T)$) = Models($U_2(T)$).

For a cross-product, set-of-theories, or WIDTIO semantics, the minimal sets for ω_1 and ω_2 must be identical if ω_1 and ω_2 are logically equivalent, and therefore $U_1(T) = U_2(T)$.

Now suppose that ω_1 and ω_2 are not logically equivalent. If T is the empty theory, then Models($U_1(T)$) will be the models of ω_1, and similarly for U_2, under all the semantics we are considering. But then Models($U_1(T)$) $\neq$ Models($U_2(T)$), and the theorem follows.

Moving to informal measures of comprehensibility, one argument for set-of-theories and WIDTIO semantics is that the formulas in these types of theories are always user-sensible; every formula in such a theory occurred in some user update request. The cross-product and model-based semantics do not share this advantage. However, if the user only has access to the information in the knowledge base via a fixed query language, as is the case in ordinary relational databases, then the user will never see the formulas in the knowledge base, and hence their exact form does not matter.

2.4.4. Expressiveness

An update language must have adequate *expressive power*. One must be able to express every type of update, every transition between sets of models, needed for the application. For example, some permissive semantics can be used to move from any set of models to any other set, and hence have satisfactory expressive power. Further, the application's commonly used transitions between sets of models should not be overly difficult to express; for example, permissive semantics are not suited for diagnostic applications. On the other hand, sufficiently restrictive semantics require additional operators to allow movement to a state of lesser knowledge, as does any semantics where logically equivalent inserted formulas lead to equivalent updates. For example, if the user wants to say that there is no longer any information about the truth or falsity of a particular proposition a, this can be done by inserting $a \vee \neg a$ under the standard semantics. Under a restrictive semantics, however, such an insertion would be equivalent to inserting "true," and would therefore have no effect on the models of the theory. In general, if an update is needed to express a loss of knowledge—i.e., one formerly believed that some proposition was true but now one is unsure—a minimal-change semantics does not offer a mechanism to accomplish the change, since every model of the old theory already satisfies the formula being inserted. A new "masking" operator is required for this type of update, as Theorem 2.4 shows.

Theorem 2.4.   *Let T_1 and T_2 be consistent theories such that Models(T_1) is a proper subset of Models(T_2). Then for no update U does Models($U(T_1)$) = Models(T_2), under a formula-based or under a model-based semantics at least as restrictive as the minimal-change semantics.*

Proof of Theorem 2.4.   First consider the minimal-change model-based semantics. Suppose that U: *insert* ω is such an update, and let M be a model of T_1 and therefore also of T_2 and of $U(T_1)$. Then by MB1, ω must be true in M, and so Models($U(T_1)$) = Models(T_1) under the minimal-change semantics. Therefore such an update U cannot exist for any semantics as restrictive as the minimal-change semantics.

Now consider a formula-based semantics. Suppose there exists such an update U: *insert* ω. Then ω must not be consistent with T_1, as otherwise U would just restrict the models of T_1 further. But if ω is inconsistent with T_1, then

$$\text{Models}(T_1) \not\subset \text{Models}(U(T_1)),$$

and since $\text{Models}(T_1) \subset \text{Models}(T_2)$, it cannot be the case that $\text{Models}(U(T_1)) = \text{Models}(T_2)$.

The WIDTIO semantics suffers on the expressivity score due to its penchant for formula deletion. Under WIDTIO, one runs the risk of depopulating the knowledge base by removing every formula that is even slightly controversial. Every removal of a formula lets in more models, with excessively weak theories a definite possibility in the long term. It remains to be seen whether WIDTIO is reasonable for real applications; perhaps the addition of application-dependent heuristics to eliminate unlikely minimal sets would give satisfactory performance.

Formula-based semantics and model-based semantics satisfying formula 2.1 are peculiar in their lack of distinction between *change-recording* updates and *knowledge-adding* updates [Keller 85b]. A knowledge-adding update gives new information about the current state of the world by eliminating some models which were previously considered to be possible. A change-recording update records an actual change in the state of the world; either time has passed, or the user was in error about the previous state of the world. With formula-based semantics, an insertion is given a knowledge-adding interpretation if possible (principle FB1), and otherwise is considered change-recording. This makes it impossible for the user to express certain types of information in a formula-based context. For example, suppose that the user discovers that p is now true, without knowing whether p was true already (knowledge-adding) or has just become true (change-recording). In other words, any of the models of T *might have been an accurate description of the world a few moments ago*, both models where p was true and models where p was false. If the user requests *insert* p, then the models where p was false will be eliminated: U will be interpreted as knowledge-adding, as long as p is true in some model of T. If one of those models was in fact the correct description of the world, that correct description is now lost.

2.4.5. Extensibility
How well do different types of semantics extend to new classes of theories and updates? Our analysis still holds for the relative merits of different seman-

tics under many natural extensions: adopting the closed-world assumption, allowing simple database-like first-order theories, permitting variables to occur in updates, allowing null values in updates, allowing selection clauses in model-based updates. (Selection clauses do not make sense for most formula-based semantics.) When nulls are permitted in updates, restrictive model-based semantics may become difficult to understand, because the minimal change needed to make ω true will depend on what value the null assumes in each model.

Another direction of extension is to make T first-order and allow knowledge and derived information to be part of T. Formula-based semantics and their implementations extend easily to this scenario, though the problem becomes undecidable when quantifiers appear. An extension of the minimal-change semantics to the case of knowledge and derived information is presented in Chapter 8. Essentially, if T contains formulas designated as knowledge rather than data, $U(M)$ is defined to be the set of "closest" models to M in which all of the knowledge formulas of T are true, and the formula being inserted is also true. Permitting arbitrary knowledge to appear in T forces an entirely different implementation approach for model-based semantics than that presented in Chapter 4; model-based implementations of updates for knowledge bases are a current research topic.

If different types of knowledge are permitted in theories, then all the proposals tendered for formula-based semantics so far are delete-happy. Often if new information conflicts with old knowledge, one wants not to delete the old axiom but rather to modify it or take some other course of action. For example, if a closed-world assumption limits the set of true propositions, then the user should be able to assert that a new proposition p is true, by modifying rather than eliminating the closed-world assumption.

CHAPTER THREE

MODEL-BASED SEMANTICS FOR UPDATES

... when an entire body of beliefs runs up against recalcitrant experiences, "revision can strike any-where," as Quine has put it. —Hilary Putnam, *Representation and Reality*

Incomplete information occurs when, due to insufficient knowledge about the state of the world, there is more than one candidate database to represent the current state of the world. In the database world, one can imagine the user keeping a set of relational databases (even an infinite set, if one imagines vigorously), knowing that one of these databases corresponds to the actual state of the world, but needing more information to know which database is the correct one.[6] If the user wants to apply an ordinary relational update to this set of candidate databases, then the natural definition of the semantics of the update is to apply the update to each candidate database individually.

Though this imaginary scenario paints a clear picture of the semantics of ordinary updates when incomplete information is present, it is unsuitable for direct implementation in most applications, due to the prohibitive expense of storing multiple databases. A more compact representation of the candidate databases is required for the sake of efficiency. Our solution is to represent sets of databases as the models of simple *relational theories* in first-order logic, using an extension of Reiter's relational theories [Reiter 84]. Our relational theories are sufficiently powerful to represent in one the-

---

[6] Heuristic guidelines may be available that give likelihood estimates for the different possible states of the world [Nilsson 86, Pearl 88, Zadeh 79]. How to incorporate these into an update algorithm is an interesting open question.

ory any realistic[7] set of relational databases all having the same schema and integrity constraints. Section 3.1 gives a formal description of the language and Section 3.2 of the structure of relational theories.

Another problem with the simple approach outlined above is that ordinary relational updates are not sufficiently powerful to express all desirable transformations on a set of candidate databases. For example, with ordinary updates there is no way to add new candidate databases to the set, or eliminate old candidates that are now known to be incorrect. Section 3.3 proposes a syntax and Sections 3.5 and 3.6 two semantics suitable for updates to relational theories; both of these semantics are first-order versions of semantics introduced in Chapter 2. Section 3.4 examines update equivalence under one of these semantics. Finally, Section 3.7 discusses the treatment of facts about equality.

3.1. Preliminaries

Relational theories are a method of representing multiple candidate databases in a single first-order theory. The language L implicitly underlying a relational theory is ordinary first-order logic with equality, with a few special features:

- L contains three disjoint types of constants:
    o   Constants representing the elements in the domains of database attributes, called *data constants*.
    o   An infinite set of constants $\epsilon_1, \epsilon_2, \epsilon_3, \ldots$, used to represent null values. We will call these constants *nulls*, and will often use ϵ to designate an arbitrary null.
    o   For use in the construction of an update algorithm, an infinite set of constants $U_1, U_2, \ldots$, to serve as update identifiers. We will often use U to designate an arbitrary update identifier.
- The predicates of L fall into four disjoint groups:
    o   The equality predicate.
    o   A finite set of *data predicates* of arity 1 or more, representing the relations of the database.
    o   For each data predicate R, one *history predicate* of arity

---

[7]   Not every set of relational databases can be represented as the models of a first-order theory. However, it is highly unlikely that any application of this work will ever run up against that particular limitation of logic.

one greater than the arity of R. Also, a single unary history predicate H. The history predicates are present for technical reasons; they are useful in the construction of an algorithm for performing updates.

o   The 0-ary "predicates" T and F, which always are interpreted as "true" and "false," respectively.

L does not contain any functions other than constants, as other functions do not arise in relational databases.

We now present some standard terminology used in the remainder of this work.

Atomic formulas, or *atoms*, are well-formed logic formulas that do not contain any logical connectives or quantifiers ($\land, \lor, \neg, \forall, \exists$, etc.), such as Manages(x, Smith). *Ground* atomic formulas are atomic formulas not containing variables, such as Manages(Smith, Chien). Ground atoms over data predicates, such as Manages(Smith, Chien), are a subclass of atomic formula that will be particularly relevant to us; we designate them by a special term, the *data atoms*. A ground atom over the equality predicate, such as Smith $= \epsilon_1$, will be called an *equality atom*. Similarly, an atom over a history predicate will be called a *history atom*. Formulas not containing nulls, such as Smith $\neq$ Chien, are called *null–free*.

Often we will be interested in the effect of replacing variables and/or nulls in a formula by particular nulls and data constants. A *substitution* $\frac{x_1 \cdots x_n}{y_1 \cdots y_n}$ specifies the simultaneous replacement of distinct variables or nulls $x_1, \ldots, x_n$ by variables or constants $y_1, \ldots, y_n$, respectively. For example, given a formula α, $(\alpha)_c^x$ is the formula obtained by simultaneously replacing all occurrences of x by c. If σ is the substitution $\frac{x_1 \cdots x_n}{y_1 \cdots y_n}$, then we will write $(\alpha)_\sigma$ as shorthand for $(\alpha)_{y_1 \cdots y_n}^{x_1 \cdots x_n}$. Finally, σ can also be written as a formula, $x_1 = y_1 \land \cdots \land x_n = y_n$, called the *wff form* of σ. The wff form of the identity substitution (i.e., where no substitutions are specified) is the truth value T. In the discussions that follow, σ will be assumed to be in wff form whenever that follows logically from the context; for example, assume σ is in wff form in $\alpha \land \sigma$. If S is a set of formulas and σ a substitution, then $(S)_\sigma$ is the set of formulas obtained by applying σ to all the members of S.

On occasion we will speak of a more exotic type of syntactic replacement, that of one atomic formula for another. For example, $(\alpha)_{\text{Emp(Nilsson,CS)}}^{\text{Emp(Nilsson,}\epsilon)}$ calls for the simultaneous replacement of all occurrences of Emp(Nilsson, ϵ) in α by the atom Emp(Nilsson, CS). Atomic formula substitutions do not have a wff form.

We will say that two atoms f and g *unify* if there is a substitution σ under which f and g are syntactically identical. If f and g unify under both σ_1 and σ_2, then σ_1 is *as general as* σ_2 if there exists a substitution σ_3 such that $((f)_{\sigma_1})_{\sigma_3}$ is $(g)_{\sigma_2}$. We will choose a particular substitution, called the *most general substitution*, as the canonical unifier of the pair of atoms, through imposition of an arbitrary lexocographic ordering on unifiers:

Definition. *A substitution σ is the* most general substitution *under which atoms f and g unify iff*

(1)   *f and g unify under σ; and*
(2)   *Let σ' be any other substitution under which f and g unify. Then σ must be as general as σ' and*
    (a)   *either σ contains fewer individual substitutions than σ'; or*
    (b)   *σ and σ' contain the same number of individual substitutions, and σ precedes σ' in lexocographic ordering.*

Example 3.1. Let f be the atom $\mathrm{Emp}(x,y)$, and let g be $\mathrm{Emp}(z,y)$. Then f and g unify under many different substitutions:

$$\sigma_1: \quad \frac{x}{\epsilon_1} \ \frac{z}{\epsilon_1}$$
$$\sigma_2: \quad \frac{x}{y} \ \frac{z}{y}$$
$$\sigma_3: \quad \frac{x}{y} \ \frac{z}{w}$$
$$\sigma_4: \quad \frac{x}{z}$$
$$\sigma_5: \quad \frac{z}{x}$$

Of these substitutions, σ_4 and σ_5 contain the fewest individual substitutions, and one of those two will be the most general substitution. Also, σ_1 is not as general as σ_2, but σ_2 is as general as σ_1. Similarly, σ_2 is not as general as σ_3, but σ_3 is as general as σ_2. As a more complex example, $R(x,y,x)$ and $R(\epsilon_1,\epsilon_1,c)$ unify under substitution $\frac{x}{c} \ \frac{y}{c} \ \frac{\epsilon_1}{c}$, which is as general as any other unifier.

In the remainder of this book, except when specifically noted otherwise, in substitution $\frac{x_1\cdots x_n}{y_1\cdots y_n}$, y_1 through y_n must be constants.

3.2. Relational Theories

Relational theories are a means of encoding databases with incomplete information. Our definition of a relational theory is an extension of that of Reiter [Reiter 84].

A relational theory T consists of a *body* and a set of *completion axioms*. The body of T may be any finite set of ground formulas, such as ¬(Manages(Smith, Chien) ∧ Manages(Chien, ϵ_1)).

The completion axioms are an analogue of the *closed-world assumption*, modified to be suitable for relational theories. In ordinary relational databases, the convention is that all atoms not explicitly mentioned in the database are false; that is, the database contains only those atoms that are known to be true [Clark 78, Lifschitz 85, Reiter 80]. An analogue of this closed-world assumption is needed for relational theories, so that we need not list things known to be false explicitly in T. The appropriate closed-world assumption for relational theories is that the only atoms that may be true in a model of T are those that unify with atoms occurring in the body of T. This means that, for example, if Manages(Smith, Chien) does not unify with any atom of T, then Manages(Smith, Chien) is false in all models of T. If Manages(Smith, ϵ_1) occurs in T, however, then Manages(Smith, Chien) might possibly hold in some model of T, as the two atoms unify under substitution ϵ_1=Chien.

More formally, the closed-world assumption is codified in the completion axiom section of T, which contains one completion axiom for each n-ary data predicate R of T. If R does not occur in the body of T, then R should be uniformly false in all models of T, and the appropriate completion axiom is $\forall x_1 \cdots \forall x_n \neg R(x_1, \ldots, x_n)$. Otherwise, R does occur in the body of T, and in this case T contains the axiom

$$\forall x_1 \ldots \forall x_n \ (R(x_1, \ldots, x_n) \to \bigvee_{\sigma \in S} \sigma),$$

where S is the set of all substitutions σ such that some atom in the body of T unifies with $R(x_1, \ldots, x_n)$ under most general substitution σ.

Example 3.2.   If the body of T is
Manages(Lopez, Smith)
¬(Manages(Smith, Chien) ∧ Manages(Chien, ϵ_1)),
then the completion axiom for T is
$\forall x \forall y$(Manages(x,y) →
    [(x=Lopez ∧ y=Smith) ∨ (x=Smith ∧ y=Chien) ∨ (x=Chien ∧ y=ϵ_1)].
T will have models in which ϵ_1 is equal to a data constant from the underlying

language, such as Lopez or Chien, and models in which ϵ_1 is not equal to any data constant, meaning that Chien manages a person whose name is not even in the underlying language.

The completion axioms need not actually be stored along with the body of T, because they can be derived mechanically from the body of T. For example, if the body of T contains just the formulas $R(c)$ and $R(\epsilon_1)$, then the appropriate completion axiom is $\forall x(R(x) \rightarrow (x{=}c \lor x{=}\epsilon_1))$. We say that an atom $P(c_1, \ldots, c_n)$ is *represented* in the completion axiom for P if $(x_1 = c_1) \land \ldots \land (x_n = c_n)$ is a disjunct in the completion axiom. For example, $R(\epsilon_1)$ is represented in the completion axiom $\forall x(R(x) \rightarrow (x{=}c \lor x{=}\epsilon_1))$, and $R(d)$ is not represented there.

There is another possible type of completion axiom, the *domain completion axiom* [Reiter 84], that we have not included in the definition of relational theories. The domain completion axiom takes the form

$$\forall x((x = c_1) \lor \cdots \lor (x = c_n)),$$

implying that there are a finite number of elements in the universe, and they are all known and named by constants of L. This completion axiom can be maintained during updates via the same techniques used for other completion axioms, as will be discussed in more detail in Chapter 7.

In a database context, one always assumes that different constants appearing in a database in fact designate different objects; this is called the *unique names assumption*. For example, Smith $\neq$ Chien is an implicit assumption made by anyone perusing a table about managers. On the other hand, it is not reasonable to assume that Smith $\neq \epsilon_1$, because ϵ_1 is a null and hence could very well designate the same person as "Smith." The correct version of the unique names assumption for relational theories is that all data constants and update identifier constants must satisfy the unique names assumption, but nulls need not.

The unique names assumption is just one of several features of models that we can standardize in a database context, as the full power of first-order logic is not needed. Standardizing these features will simplify presentation of our results, and close analogues of the results will still hold for relational theories using the usual first-order definition of "model." We will describe these standardizations, and then present our new definition of "model."

First, we will assume that the universe of a model contains only elements that are interpretations of the constants of L. Since L is countably infinite, in conjunction with the unique names assumption for update identifiers, this standardization will guarantee that all models have countably infinite universes.

Second, to enforce the unique names assumption and to simplify the mapping between constants of L and universe elements, we will require that the interpretation of a data constant or update identifier constant c in a model be the universe element c.

Third, we wish to adopt a standard convention for the interpretation of nulls that are not equal to any data constant. For a null ϵ_i, if the interpretation of ϵ_i is not identical to that of some data constant, then we require that the interpretation of ϵ_i be ϵ_j, where j is the smallest integer less than or equal to i such that $\epsilon_i = \epsilon_j$ is true in M. In other words, in those models where a null is not equal to any universe element named in L, we will use the nulls themselves as the universe elements, rather than allowing the universe to contain elements with arbitrary identifiers.

Definition.   *A standard model M of a theory T consists of:*

- *A subset U of the constants of L, called the* universe *of M.*
- *A mapping from the constants of L to the universe, called the* inter-
  pretation of the constants, such that
    - *Every universe element is the interpretation of some constant of L.*
    - *The interpretation of a data constant or update identifier c is the universe element c.*
    - *The interpretation of a null ϵ_i is either a data constant symbol or else ϵ_j, where j is the smallest integer such that $\epsilon_i = \epsilon_j$ is true in M.*
- *For each data or history predicate P, if P has arity n, then M contains an n-ary relation over U^n, called the* interpretation *of P. The 0-ary predicates T and F are interpreted as "true" and "false," respectively.*
- *All formulas of T must be satisfied by M, in the usual sense.*

In this work, all models under discussion are assumed to be standard models; so, for example, we will say that a formula α is satisfiable iff it is satisfied by some standard model.

Each standard model M includes a mapping from the nulls of L to elements in the universe of M. The effect of this mapping will often be of particular interest, and to allow easy reference to this information, we will define a special formula associated with M, its *null substitution*. The null substitution σ of M is a substitution of constants for all the nulls of L, such that σ includes the substitution $\frac{x}{y}$ iff the universe element y is the interpretation of the null x in M. If M is a model of T, then M is also a model of $(T)_\sigma$. Although σ is infinite, only a finite portion of it will be of interest to us at any given moment, because relational theories are finite and so only finitely many nulls can occur in them.

The predicate interpretations in a model of a relational theory look quite similar to an ordinary relational database. There is at least one important difference, however: a relational database instance only contains information about data predicates, not about the equality predicate or history predicates. For that reason we define the *alternative world* of a model M, written World(M), as the structure produced by restricting M to data predicates (i.e., removing the relations that are the interpretation of history predicates). Worlds(S), for S a set of models, is $\bigcup_{M \in S}$ World(M). Denoting the set of models of T as Models(T), we write Worlds(T) as shorthand for Worlds(Models(T)). Alternative worlds contain just the information that would be of interest to a database user, while models may be cluttered with history atoms of no external interest. Intuitively, an alternative world is a snapshot of the tuples of a complete-information relational database. The alternative worlds of a relational theory look like a set of ordinary relational databases all having the same schema.

The history predicates do not actually extend the expressive power of L; with a few minor restrictions, for every relational theory T there is a relational theory T' not containing history predicates, such that Worlds(T) = Worlds(T') [Winslett 86c].

3.3. A Syntax for Updates

As mentioned earlier, traditional relational update languages are not sufficiently powerful for use when incomplete information is present. The traditional languages also lack semantics that are sufficiently formal for a rigorous examination of the properties of these languages. This section presents a data manipulation language that remedies these two deficiencies. Appropriate subsets of traditional update languages, such as those of SQL and QUEL without aggregation, may be embedded in this language. In this chapter, only updates without variables will be considered; Chapter 5 extends this approach to updates with variables.

Our syntax for updates is extremely simple. Let ϕ and ω be ground formulas with no occurrences of history predicates. Then an *update* takes the form *insert ω where φ*. If the selection clause of an update is simply T, we will often write *insert ω* rather than *insert ω where* T.

The reader may wonder what has happened to the traditional relational data manipulation operations of *modify* and *delete*. Under the semantics presented in Sections 3.4 and 3.6, any *delete* or *modify* request can be phrased as an *insert* request, using negation. To simplify the presentation, *delete* and *modify* are omitted right from the start; details of the mapping will be presented at the end of Section 3.4.

Example 3.3.   Suppose the database schema has two relations, Mgr(Manager, Department) and Emp(Employee, Department). Then the following are updates, with their approximate intended semantics offered parenthetically:

- *insert* Emp(Chien,ϵ) $\wedge$ (ϵ=CS $\vee$ ϵ=EE) *where* ¬Mgr(Nilsson,English).
  In alternative worlds where Nilsson doesn't manage English, insert the fact that Chien is in one of CS and EE.
- *insert* ¬Emp(Chien,ϵ) *where* ¬Mgr(Nilsson,ϵ) $\wedge$ Emp(Chien,ϵ).
  For some department Nilsson does not manage, delete the fact that Chien is in that department.
- *insert* F *where* ¬Emp(Chien,English).
  Eliminate all alternative worlds where Chien isn't in English.
- *insert* ¬Emp(Chien,English) $\wedge$ Emp(Chien,ϵ) *where* Emp(Chien,English).
  In any alternative worlds where Chien is in English, reduce that belief to just believing that he is in some department.
- *insert* ¬Emp(Chien,ϵ).
  Insert the fact that Chien is not a member of every department.

We do not intend this language for use directly by database users; rather, a simpler, less powerful interface would be more appropriate. The interface should encourage the user to invoke updates that are inexpensive to perform (see Chapters 6 and 9).

3.4. The Standard Semantics

We will use a particular model-based semantics, hereafter called the *standard semantics*, extensively for illustrative purposes. The salient properties of the standard semantics are, first, that it agrees with traditional semantics in the case where the update request is to insert or delete a single atom, or to modify one atom to be another. Second, under the standard semantics an update *insert* ω *where* ϕ cannot change the truth valuations of any atoms except those that unify with atoms of ω. For example, the update *insert* Emp(Chien, CS) cannot change the department of any employee but Chien, and cannot change the truth valuation of formulas such as Mgr(Nilsson, CS).

Third, the new information in ω is to represent the *most exact and most recent state of knowledge obtainable* about the atoms that the update inserts; and the update is to *override all previous information* about those atoms. These two criteria have a syntactic component: one should not necessarily expect two updates with logically equivalent ωs to produce the same results. For example, the update *insert* ⊤ is different from *insert* Emp(Chien, CS) ∨ ¬Emp(Chien, CS); one update reports no change in the information available about Chien's department, and the other reports that whether Chien is in CS is now unknown[8]. More formally:

Definition. *Let U be an update and let M be a model of a relational theory T with null substitution σ. Then under the standard semantics, $U(M)$, the set of models produced by applying U to M, contains just M if ϕ is false in M. Otherwise, $U(M)$ contains every model M' with the same constant interpretations as M, such that*

(1)   *ω is true in M'; and*
(2)   *M' agrees with M on the truth valuations of all atoms α such that $(\alpha)_\sigma$ does not occur in $(\omega)_\sigma$.*

The test in (2) for atoms occurring in ω is an analogue of MB2; it makes use of σ, the null substitution for M, because σ tells us which of the possible unifications with atoms of ω actually take place in M. For example, in the update *insert* Emp(Chien, ϵ_1), the atom Emp(Chien, English) does unify with an atom of ω. In a model M where $\epsilon_1 = $ CS, however, this unification does not materialize, and so the truth valuation of Emp(Chien, English) should not change in M when this update is performed. In a model where $\epsilon_1 = $ English, the truth valuation of Emp(Chien, English) might change as a result of performing the update.

One advantage of this approach to nulls in updates is that σ associates

---

[8]   There is another obvious, and perhaps more useful, choice one could make in choosing a model-based semantics: that the models of T be changed as little as possible to make ω true. This *minimal-change* semantics will be discussed in Section 3.5. The algorithms associated with the minimal-change semantics are more complex, so that starting with the standard semantics offers pedagogical advantages.

any null ϵ that occurs in both U and T with the same element in M, so that the user can directly refer to entities such as "that department that we earlier noted that Chien is in, though we didn't know exactly which department it was." If U is *insert ω where ϕ*, then $(U)_\sigma$ will refer to the update *insert $(\omega)_\sigma$ where $(\phi)_\sigma$*.

Example 3.4. If the user requests *insert* Emp(Chien, CS) $\vee$ Emp(Chien, EE), then three models are created from each model M of T: one where Chien is in both CS and EE, one where Chien is in CS but not EE, and one where Chien is in EE but not CS—regardless of whether Chien was in CS or EE in M originally.

Example 3.5. Consider the update U: *insert* ¬Emp(Chien, CS) $\wedge$ Emp(Chien, ϵ) *where* Emp(Chien, CS). If Emp(Chien, CS) is false in M, then M is unchanged by the update: $U(M) = \{M\}$. Otherwise, if ϵ=CS is true in M, then $U(M)$ will be the empty set, as $(\omega)_\sigma$ is unsatisfiable, where σ is M's null substitution. And if Emp(Chien, CS) and $\epsilon\neq$CS are both true in M, then $U(M)$ will contain a single model, in which Chien is an employee of the department that is the interpretation of ϵ in M.

For simplicity, the semantics of U has been defined in terms of U's effect on the model M rather than in terms of U's effect on World(M). However, because the semantics is independent of the truth valuations of history atoms in M, U will have the same effect (i.e., produce the same alternative worlds) on *every* model whose alternative world is World(M).

The remarks at the beginning of this section on correctness of update processing may be summed up in the following definition:

Definition. *Given two relational theories T and T', T' accomplishes update U if*

$$\text{Worlds}(T') = \bigcup_{M \in Models(T)} \text{Worlds}(U(M)).$$

Example 3.6. If $\forall x$ ¬Emp(x, English) is true in M and we then insert Emp(ϵ_1, English) $\vee$ Emp(ϵ_2, English) into M, then $U(M)$ will contain one model M', in which the interpretation of Emp contains one or two tuples, depending upon whether $\epsilon_1 = \epsilon_2$ is true in M.

Under these definitions, the traditional relational operations of *delete* and *modify* can be phrased as *insert* requests as follows: to delete an atom t in all alternative worlds where ϕ is true, use the update *insert* $\neg t$ *where* ϕ. For example, *insert* $\neg$Emp(Chien, EE) will "delete" the atom Emp(Chien, EE) from the Emp relation in every model. To modify an atom t to be a different atom ω, use the update *insert* $\omega \wedge \neg t$ *where* $\phi \wedge t$. For example, to change Chien's department from EE to CS, use the update

insert Emp(Chien, CS) $\wedge \neg$Emp(Chien, EE) *where* Emp(Chien, EE).

The standard semantics will not be the best choice of update semantics for every application. In particular, the standard semantics allows many result models for updates; for some applications, it will be helpful to have heuristics to filter out the more unlikely result models. The minimal-change semantics, presented in Section 3.6, offers such a filter, in a domain-independent manner. In addition, the standard semantics' treatment of equality will not be appropriate for every application, as explained in Section 3.7.

3.5. Update Equivalence Under the Standard Semantics

To illustrate the properties of the standard semantics, we offer in this section three theorems on update equivalence. We begin with a simple sufficient criterion for equivalence:

Theorem 3.1.   *Let U_1 and U_2 be two updates under the standard semantics:*
U_1: *insert* ω_1 *where* ϕ,
U_2: *insert* ω_2 *where* ϕ.
If ω_1 and ω_2 are logically equivalent and the same atoms occur in ω_1 and ω_2, then U_1 is equivalent to U_2.

Proof of Theorem 3.1.   Assume that ω_1, and therefore ω_2, is satisfiable, as otherwise the theorem follows immediately. Consider the effects of U_1 and U_2 on a model M of T. U_1 must produce a model M' from M, since ω_1 is satisfiable. We wish to show that World(M') $\in$ Worlds($U_2(M)$). If ϕ is false in M, this follows immediately. Otherwise ω_2 must be true in M', because ω_1 and ω_2 are logically equivalent; and therefore rule 1 in the standard-semantics definition of *insert* is satisfied for U_2 by M'. Rule 2 in the definition of *insert* is also satisfied for U_2 by M', since U_1 and U_2 contain the same atoms.

To see that the criteria of Theorem 3.1 are sufficient but not necessary, consider the two equivalent updates *insert f where f ∧ g* and *insert g where f ∧ g*. These two updates fail the test of Theorem 3.1 because ω_1 and ω_2 contain atoms whose truth valuation is logically entailed by both ϕ and ω. To produce necessary and sufficient criteria, it will be advantageous to remove all such atoms from ω by *reducing* ω:

Definition.   *Let U be the update* insert ω where ϕ *under the standard semantics. The reduction of ω with respect to ϕ, written reduce(ω, ϕ), is formed from ω by making the following substitutions for every data atom g in ω:*

1.   *If ϕ and ω both logically entail g, replace g by* T *throughout ω.*
2. · *If ϕ and ω both logically entail ¬g, replace g by* F *throughout ω.*

This definition may seem a bit odd for the case where ϕ is unsatisfiable, but such updates aren't very interesting anyway:

Proposition 3.1.   *Under the standard semantics, any update U: insert ω where ϕ is equivalent to insert reduce(ω, ϕ) where ϕ.*

Proof of Proposition 3.1.   If ϕ is false in a model M, then $U_1(M) = U_2(M)$. Otherwise, let M' be a member of $U_1(M)$. Then reduce(ω, ϕ) is true in M, so rule 1 in the standard semantics definition of *insert* is true for U_2. Rule 2 is also satisfied, because any atoms present in U_2 but not U_1 have the same truth valuation in M and M'. Similar arguments hold if M' is taken to be a member of $U_2(M)$. We conclude that $U_1(M) = U_2(M)$, and by MB3 U_1 and U_2 are equivalent.

Once the updates being tested for equivalence have been reduced, little work remains:

Theorem 3.2.   *Let U_1 and U_2 be null-free updates under the standard semantics:*

U_1:   *insert ω_1 where ϕ,*
U_2:   *insert ω_2 where ϕ.*

U_1 and U_2 are equivalent iff

(1)   *ϕ is unsatisfiable; or*
(2)   *ω_1 and ω_2 are unsatisfiable; or*
(3)   *reduce(ω_1, ϕ) and reduce(ω_2, ϕ) contain the same data atoms and are logically equivalent.*

Example 3.7.   If U_1 is *insert g* and U_2 is *insert $g \vee \mathsf{T}$*, then these two updates
are reduced. Since g is not logically equivalent to $g \vee \mathsf{T}$, the two updates must not
be equivalent; they differ on producing models where g is false. For updates *insert
g where $g \wedge f$* and *insert f where $g \wedge f$*, in both cases ω is replaced by T during
reduction, and the two updates become identical. Theorem 3.2 will proclaim these
two updates equivalent.

Proof of Theorem 3.2.   By Proposition 3.1, it suffices to prove this theorem
for the case where ω_1 and ω_2 are already reduced with respect to ϕ. Assume that
ϕ, ω_1, and ω_2 are satisfiable, as otherwise the theorem follows immediately. By
Theorem 3.1, we need only show that when none of conditions (1)–(3) hold, the
updates are not equivalent.

Suppose first that ω_1 and ω_2 are not logically equivalent, so that, say, $\omega_1 \wedge \neg \omega_2$
is satisfiable. Let M be a model having null substitution σ, such that ϕ is true in
M and every atom g such that $(g)_\sigma$ does not occur in $(\phi)_\sigma$ is false in M. Then
there is a relational theory Theory(M). Also, $U_1(M)$ contains a model M' where
$\omega_1 \wedge \neg \omega_2$ holds, and M' cannot be a member of $U_2(M)$. Therefore U_1 and U_2
cannot be equivalent.

Now suppose that ω_1 and ω_2 are logically equivalent but do not contain the same
data atoms. Let g be a data atom appearing in, say, U_1 but not U_2. Then either ω_1
$\wedge g$ and $\phi \wedge \neg g$ are both consistent, or else $\omega_1 \wedge \neg g$ and $\phi \wedge g$ are both consistent,
by the definition of reduction; assume the former, and a similar argument will hold
for the latter. Let M be a model with null substitution σ, in which $\phi \wedge \neg g$ holds,
and in which all atoms f such that $(f)_\sigma$ does not occur in $(\omega_1)_\sigma$ are false. Then
there is a relational theory Theory(M). $U_1(M)$ contains a model in which g is true,
but $U_2(M)$ does not. We conclude that U_1 and U_2 are not equivalent.

Theorem 3.2 gives sufficient but not necessary conditions in the case
where the pair of updates contains nulls, as the following example shows.

Example 3.8.   Let U_1 be *insert $P(\epsilon_1) \wedge \epsilon_1 = \epsilon_2$*, and let U_2 be *insert $P(\epsilon_2) \wedge \epsilon_1 = $*
ϵ_2*. These two formulas are logically equivalent but do not contain the same data
atoms, and U_1 and U_2 are equivalent.

A necessary condition for update equivalence for updates containing nulls
must ensure that the two updates are equivalent *under all null substitutions*.
Equivalence can be verified by checking that the pair of updates satisfies
Theorem 3.2 whenever a portion of a null substitution containing the nulls
of the updates is appended to the formulas being inserted. In fact it is not
necessary to consider all the different possible null substitutions; [Winslett
86c] describes a more efficient test.

Under the standard semantics, what conditions govern update equivalence when two updates have different selection clauses ϕ? If U_1 and U_2 are

two equivalent null-free updates with selection clauses ϕ_1 and ϕ_2, respectively, then U_1 must not make any changes in any model where ϕ_2 is false, and vice versa.

Theorem 3.3.   *Let U_1 and U_2 be two null-free updates under the standard semantics:*

U_1:   *insert ω_1 where ϕ_1,*
U_2:   *insert ω_2 where ϕ_2.*

Then U_1 and U_2 are equivalent iff

(1)   *insert ω_1 where $\phi_1 \wedge \phi_2$ is equivalent to insert ω_2 where $\phi_1 \wedge \phi_2$;*
(2)   *$\phi_1 \wedge \neg\phi_2$ logically entails ω_1 and $\phi_2 \wedge \neg\phi_1$ logically entails ω_2; and*
(3)   *If $\phi_1 \wedge \neg\phi_2$ is satisfiable, then ω_1 is uniquely satisfiable[9]; and if $\phi_2 \wedge \neg\phi_1$ is satisfiable, then ω_2 is uniquely satisfiable.*

Proof of Theorem 3.3.   For sufficiency, if M is a model where $\phi_1 \wedge \phi_2$ is true, condition (1) guarantees that $U_1(M) = U_2(M)$. If $\phi_1 \wedge \neg\phi_2$ is true in M, then $U_2(M) = \{M\}$, and, by conditions (2) and (3), $U_1(M) = \{M\}$. If $\phi_2 \wedge \neg\phi_1$ is true in M, or $\neg\phi_1 \wedge \neg\phi_2$, again the sole result model is M. We conclude that conditions (1)–(3) guarantee equivalence.

For necessity, the need for condition (1) is immediate. To see that conditions (2) and (3) are necessary, let M be a model with null substitution σ, where, say, $\phi_1 \wedge \neg\phi_2$ is true, and where every atom f such that $(f)_\sigma$ does not occur in $(\phi_1 \wedge \neg\phi_2)_\sigma$ is false. Then there is a relational theory Theory(M), of which M is a model. Since $U_2(M) = \{M\}$, if U_1 and U_2 are equivalent then it must be the case that ω_1 is already true in M (condition (2)). Further, because U_1 is null-free, the cardinality of $U_1(M)$ under the standard semantics is equal to the number of truth valuations that satisfy ω_1. Therefore ω_1 must be uniquely satisfiable (condition (3)).

3.6. The Minimal-Change Semantics

An obvious alternative to the standard semantics is a semantics for updates where the third main desideratum that determined the standard semantics, namely:

> The information in ω is to represent the *most exact and most recent state of knowledge obtainable* about those atoms; and that information is to *override all previous information* about those atoms,

---

[9]   A ground formula α is *uniquely satisfiable* if there exists exactly one truth valuation v for all the atoms of α such that α is true under v.

is replaced by the following:

> An alternative world of T where ϕ is true should be changed *as little as possible* to make ω true.

The meaning of "as little as possible" is subject to interpretation, as shown in Chapter 2. For our purposes, "as little as possible" means that if one set of changes to an alternative world A is a proper subset of another set of changes, and both sets of changes will make ω true in the updated version of A, then the larger set of changes should not be performed.

To pin down the notion of "as little as possible," we begin by defining the difference between a pair of predicate interpretations. Informally, the difference between a pair of predicate interpretations is the set of tuples that appear in only one of the two interpretations.

Definition. *The difference between a predicate symbol interpretation in a pair of models M_1 and M_2, written diff(P, M_1, M_2), is a relation containing the set of tuples $(P_1 - P_2) \cup (P_2 - P_1)$, where P_1 is the interpretation of P in M_1, and P_2 is the interpretation of P in M_2.*

Definition. *Let M be a model of a relational theory T and U an update insert ω where ϕ under the minimal-change semantics. Then $U(M)$, the set of models obtained by updating M, contains every model M' with the same constant interpretations as M, such that*

(1)   *ω is true in M'; and*

(2)   *there is no model M'' such that*

    (a)   *ω is also true in M''; and*

    (b)   *for each predicate symbol P, diff(P, M, M'') is a subset of diff(P, M, M'); and*

    (c)   *for some predicate symbol P, diff(P, M, M'') is a proper subset of diff(P, M, M').*

The alternative worlds produced by an update under the minimal-change semantics are always a subset of those produced under the standard semantics, as the minimal-change semantics is more restrictive than the standard semantics.

Example 3.9. Suppose that T has an empty body, and U is the update *insert* Emp(Chien, CS) $\vee$ Emp(Chien, EE). Then the effect of this update on the alternative world of T will be to create two new alternative worlds, one in which Chien is in CS and one in which she is in EE. Under the standard semantics, an additional world in which Chien was in both departments would also be produced; to avoid producing that world under the standard semantics, one would have to phrase the update as, say, *insert* Emp(Chien, ϵ) $\land$ (ϵ=CS $\lor$ ϵ=EE).

Under the minimal-change semantics, insertion of a tautology will not change the worlds of a theory, as tautologies are already true in all models. More generally, as shown in Theorem 2.4, there is no way to express a minimal-change insertion update that will simply add additional alternative worlds to the set of worlds of a theory. In other words, one cannot use minimal-change insertions to move to a situation where less is known about the state of the world than formerly. Expression of such updates requires the introduction of additional update operators that mask or screen out previously known information about atom truth valuations, just as can be done under the standard semantics by insertion of a tautology. An appropriate definition of such a "forget" operator for the minimal-change semantics is, for update U: *forget* ω,

$$U(M) = \{M\} \cup U'(M),$$

where U' is the minimal-change update *insert* $\neg\omega$. This definition of *forget* says that we should also consider possible those closest worlds in which ω is false.

Sufficient conditions for update equivalence are simple under the minimal-change semantics:

Theorem 3.4.   *Let U_1 and U_2 be two updates under the minimal-change semantics:*

U_1:   *insert* ω_1 *where* ϕ_1,
U_2:   *insert* ω_2 *where* ϕ_2.

Then U_1 and U_2 are equivalent if

(1)   *if $\phi_1 \land \phi_2$ is satisfiable, then ω_1 and ω_2 are logically equivalent; and*
(2)   *$\phi_1 \land \neg\phi_2$ logically entails ω_1, and $\phi_2 \land \neg\phi_1$ logically entails ω_2.*

Proof of Theorem 3.4.   First note that condition (1) implies that *insert* ω_1 *where* $\phi_1 \land \phi_2$ is equivalent to *insert* ω_2 *where* $\phi_1 \land \phi_2$. Also note that by condition (2), if $\phi_1 \land \neg\phi_2$ is true in a model M, then $U_1(M) = \{M\} = U_2(M)$. A similar line of reasoning holds if $\phi_2 \land \neg\phi_1$ is true in M. We conclude that conditions (1) and (2) are sufficient for equivalence.

Necessary and sufficient conditions for equivalence under the minimal-change semantics are surprisingly complex, due to the potential for interactions between ϕ and ω. Exact conditions are given in [Winslett 86c].

3.7. Handling Equality

None of the model-based update semantics we have presented allow revision of beliefs held about the equality of objects. For example, temporarily dropping the unique names assumption, if the formula "President = Reagan" appears in T, then no model-based semantics can be used to insert the new piece of information that, say, "President = Bush." This follows from the fact that M and members of $U(M)$ must all have the same constant interpretations. Because of this, an update can only narrow the range of possible interpretations for a null; it cannot change the set of possible interpretations for a null to a new and disjoint set. For example, if we insert the formula $\epsilon_1 =$Reagan $\lor$ $\epsilon_1 =$Bush, then a later insertion of $\epsilon_1 =$Carter will make T inconsistent.

In complex applications, such as those of artificial intelligence, one often needs functions other than constants in L. For example, one might need to say "President(USA) = Bush," where "President" is a unary function rather than a constant. If in the definition of update semantics, one requires that M and members of $U(M)$ have the same function interpretations, then updates cannot alter which terms of the language are equal in M.

To allow changes in facts about equality, one must first drop the restriction that M and members of $U(M)$ have the same constant and function interpretations. The definition of the difference between a pair of models must then be reexamined. The appropriate change is, in brief, that when computing the difference between a pair of models, one must consider the set of equality atoms on which the two models differ, and also the difference between the universes of the two models. This provides a simple means of reasoning about changes in equality that can be adapted to any model-based semantics. For details, the reader is referred to [Winslett 90].

CHAPTER FOUR

UPDATE ALGORITHMS FOR MODEL-BASED SEMANTICS

As truth is gathered, I rearrange
  inside out
  outside in
Perpetual change. —Yes, *Perpetual Change*

The semantics presented in Chapter 3 describe the effect of an update on the *models* of a theory; the semantics give no hints whatsoever on how to translate that effect into changes in the relational theory. An algorithm for performing updates cannot proceed by generating models from the theory and updating them directly; this is because the number of standard models may be exponential in the size of the theory, and it may be very difficult to find even one model, as that is equivalent to testing the satisfiability of the theory.

In the sections of this chapter, we consider algorithmic means of accomplishing successively more complicated updates, beginning with updates under the standard semantics, without nulls and selection clauses, operating under an open-world assumption, in Section 4.1. Section 4.2 extends this approach to updates with nulls, and Section 4.3 shows how to process selection clauses correctly. Section 4.4 shows how to enforce the closed-world assumption.

Section 4.5 shows that these algorithms are correct in the sense that the alternative worlds produced under the algorithms are the same as those produced by updating each alternative world individually.

Section 4.6 discusses the computational complexity of the algorithms. For relational theories and updates without nulls, the algorithms have the same asymptotic cost as for an ordinary complete-information database update, but may increase the size of the relational theory. For updates involving nulls, the increase in size will be severe if many data atoms in the theory unify with those in the update. Chapter 6 is devoted to a discussion of a means of preventing excessive growth in the theory.

Section 4.7 gives an update algorithm for the minimal-change semantics, and shows its correctness.

4.1. Simple Updates

Suppose that neither T nor U contain nulls, and that therefore any uncertainty present in T is disjunctive in nature. In addition, let us assume that the selection clause ϕ of U is simply T, so that U is to be applied to all alternative worlds. Finally, let us temporarily adopt the open-world assumption, so that atoms not occurring in T may be either true or false in the models of T, and we need not keep completion axioms. This is the simplest possible scenario, and is a good place to begin our investigation.

Intuitively, we need to replace T by a theory T' in which ω, the formula to be inserted, is true. We cannot simply add ω to T, however, because ω and T may contradict one another, as when we try to insert Emp(Chien, English) into the theory whose body is ¬Emp(Chien, English) (i.e., is the set containing that single formula). Evidently those parts of T that contradict ω must be removed before ω is added to T; in this case it would suffice to simply remove the formula ¬Emp(Chien, English).

But suppose that the body of T contains more complicated pieces of data, formulas such as

(Mgr(Nilsson, CS) ∨ ¬Emp(Chien, English)) ∧

    ¬(Mgr(Nilsson, CS) ∧ ¬Emp(Chien, English) ∧ Emp(Lopez, English)).

One cannot simply excise ¬Emp(Chien, English) or replace it by a truth value without changing the models for the remaining atoms of T; but by the semantics for updates, no atom truth valuation except that of Emp(Chien, English) can be affected by the requested update.

One can remove the offending atoms using the following procedure [Weber 86]: If f is a data atom of ω that occurs in α, then replace α by $(\alpha)_T^f \vee (\alpha)_F^f$, and the new formula will have the same models (restricted to atoms other than f) as did the old. For example, we can take the formula

(Mgr(Nilsson, CS) ∨ ¬Emp(Chien, English)) ∧

    ¬(Mgr(Nilsson, CS) ∧ ¬Emp(Chien, English) ∧ Emp(Lopez, English)),

and substitute in truth values for Emp(Chien, English). In this example, the resulting formula simplifies to T.

When applying this approach to all of T rather than to just a single formula, formulas where f does not occur can be moved outside the scope of the substitution, and the remaining formulas conjoined, stripped of f, and then logically simplified. This approach works very well when f occurs only a few times in T, and is perfect for the common case where f occurs as a separate formula of T. As such, it is a good choice for the cornerstone of a practical implementation of update semantics.

However, the worst-case behavior of this scheme is unappealing, and it has serious flaws for more complicated updates involving nulls and selection clauses. In the worst case, Weber's scheme will multiply the space required to store the theory by a factor that is exponential in the number of atoms in the update. For those reasons, we wish to have a fall-back approach, to be applied in those instances where Weber's scheme is too expensive. This approach will also be used in calculating the worst-case time requirements for the update algorithms.

The situation calculus, proposed for use in artificial intelligence applications, offers potential here. In situation calculus, each atom in a theory is "tagged" with an additional argument indicating the "situation" or state of the world to which it applies. For example, a situation calculus database to describe a world where Nilsson was manager of the English department until he left for a position at CS might have the body

Manager(Nilsson, English, situation0)
Manager(Nilsson, CS, situation1)
¬Manager(Nilsson, English, situation1),

with an implicit ordering between situations 0 and 1. A fact can be implicitly assumed to be true until superceded by information about its truth in a later situation. To perform updates under this paradigm, one could simply label the atoms of ω with a new situation number, insert the labeled ω into T, and rely heavily on the query-answering mechanism to determine what facts now hold.

In situation calculus, one maintains complete information about all previous states of the world. In traditional database applications, information about past world states will not be relevant to future queries, will slow answering of future queries, and will waste storage space. A less wasteful approach is to introduce historical information into T only when necessary (e.g., when Weber's approach is too expensive), and to assume by default that unlabeled atoms refer to the most recent situation. We call our labeled atoms *history atoms*; they are the special-purpose predicates mentioned in Chapter 3.

To "remove" a data atom f of ω from T, then, it suffices to replace all occurrences of f in T by a history atom f_U, where U is the update identifier constant assigned to the current update, the equivalent of the "situation" argument used in situation calculus. For ease of notation, the history predicate symbol for an n-ary predicate P will also be P, but with arity $n + 1$. For example, if f is the atom Mgr(Nilsson, CS), then f_U would be Mgr(Nilsson, CS, U). The process of replacing all data atoms f of ω by history atoms is accomplished by replacing all occurrences of f by f_U.

Once this is done, ω can be added to T, and the update is complete. The "worst case" algorithm can be summarized as follows:

1. Perform the history substitution σ_H: for each data atom f that occurs in ω, replace every occurrence of f in the body of T by f_U.
2. Then add ω to the body of T.

Example 4.1.   Let the body of T be
Mgr(Nilsson, CS)
and let U_1 be the update
insert ¬Mgr(Nilsson, CS) ∨ (Mgr(Nilsson, CS) ∧ Emp(Chien, CS)).

We first show how U_1 affects the data predicate interpretations of a sample model M. Before the update, let the interpretation of Emp in M be the empty relation, and let Mgr have an interpretation with the single tuple
[Nilsson, CS].

$U_1(M) = \{M_1, M_2, M_3\}$. In M_1, both Emp and Mgr are interpreted as empty relations. In M_2, Mgr is
[Nilsson, CS]
and Emp is
[Chien, CS].
In M_3, Mgr is the empty relation; and Emp is
[Chien, CS].

After update, the body of T will contain the two formulas
Mgr(Nilsson, CS, U_1)
¬Mgr(Nilsson, CS) ∨ (Mgr(Nilsson, CS) ∧ Emp(Chien, CS)).

4.2. Selection Clauses

So far, we have assumed that U took the form *insert* ω *where* T. When the selection clause ϕ is more complicated than simply T, we must change the update algorithm accordingly.

The purpose of ϕ is to select those worlds where the update is to take place. Worlds where ϕ is false should not be changed at all by the update. In other words, rather than simply adding ϕ to the body of T, we need to add a formula along the lines of $\phi \rightarrow \omega$; and to make sure that worlds where ϕ is false are unaffected by U, we will also have to add to T something like $\neg\phi \rightarrow$ "don't change anything."

A bit of analysis will reveal the correct formulas to add. After the update, ω is to be true in all worlds where ϕ was true *before* the update. Once the history substitution σ_H has been performed, those are exactly the worlds where $(\phi)_{\sigma_H}$ is true (Lemma 5.1). To make ω true in those worlds, we simply add $(\phi)_{\sigma_H} \rightarrow \omega$ to the body of T after performing the history substitution.

The worlds where ϕ was false before the update are those where $\neg(\phi)_{\sigma_H}$ now holds. In those worlds, an atom should be true after the update iff it was true before the update. In other words, an atom f should hold in those worlds iff f_U holds there once the history substitution is performed. In other words, for updates not involving nulls,

$$\neg(\phi)_{\sigma_H} \rightarrow (f \leftrightarrow f_U) \tag{4.1}$$

is the needed formula, for each atom f occurring in σ_H. Our update algorithm now has three steps:

1.   Perform the history substitution σ_H: for each data atom f that occurs in ω, replace every occurrence of f in the body of T by f_U.
2.   Then add $(\phi)_{\sigma_H} \rightarrow \omega$ to the body of T.
3.   Finally, for each data atom f occurring in σ_H, add the formula

$$\neg(\phi)_{\sigma_H} \rightarrow (f \leftrightarrow f_U) \tag{4.1}$$

to the body of T.

Example 4.2.   Let the body of T be
Mgr(Nilsson, CS) $\vee$ Mgr(Nilsson, EE),
and let U_2 be the update
insert Emp(Chien, CS) *where* Mgr(Nilsson, CS).

We first show how U_2 affects the data predicate interpretations of sample models M_1 and M_2. Before the update, both models have empty relations as the interpretation of Emp. As the interpretation of Mgr, M_1 has the single tuple

[Nilsson, EE],

and M_2 has the single tuple

[Nilsson, CS].

$U_2(M_1) = \{M_1\}$, and $U_2(M_2) = \{M_3\}$, where M_3's interpretation of Mgr is the single tuple

[Nilsson, CS],

and of Emp is the single tuple

[Chien, CS].

As Emp(Chien, CS) does not occur in the body of T, the history substitution of Step 1 does not change T. After the update, the body of T will contain the three formulas

Mgr(Nilsson, CS) $\vee$ Mgr(Nilsson, EE)

Mgr(Nilsson, CS) $\rightarrow$ Emp(Chien, CS)

$\neg$Mgr(Nilsson, CS) $\rightarrow$ [Emp(Chien, CS) $\leftrightarrow$ Emp(Chien, CS, U_2)].

Note that the desired result models will be produced, even though Emp(Chien, CS, U_2) and $\neg$Emp(Chien, CS) might both hold in a model before U_2 takes place, a seemingly contradictory situation.

Example 4.3. Let the body of T be the result theory produced by Example 4.2, i.e.,

Mgr(Nilsson, CS) $\vee$ Mgr(Nilsson, EE)

Mgr(Nilsson, CS) $\rightarrow$ Emp(Chien, CS)

$\neg$Mgr(Nilsson, CS) $\rightarrow$ [Emp(Chien, CS) $\leftrightarrow$ Emp(Chien, CS, U_2)],

and let U_3 be the update

insert Mgr(Nilsson, CS) $\wedge$ $\neg$Mgr(Nilsson, EE) *where* Mgr(Nilsson, EE).

After update, the body of T will contain the formulas

Mgr(Nilsson, CS, U_3) $\vee$ Mgr(Nilsson, EE, U_3)

Mgr(Nilsson, CS, U_3) $\rightarrow$ Emp(Chien, CS)

$\neg$Mgr(Nilsson, CS, U_3) $\rightarrow$ [Emp(Chien, CS) $\leftrightarrow$ Emp(Chien, CS, U_2)]

Mgr(Nilsson, EE, U_3) $\rightarrow$ [Mgr(Nilsson, CS) $\wedge$ $\neg$Mgr(Nilsson, EE)]

$\neg$Mgr(Nilsson, EE, U_3) $\rightarrow$ [Mgr(Nilsson, CS) $\leftrightarrow$ Mgr(Nilsson, CS, U_3)]

$\neg$Mgr(Nilsson, EE, U_3) $\rightarrow$ [Mgr(Nilsson, EE) $\leftrightarrow$ Mgr(Nilsson, EE, U_3)].

4.3. Nulls

The presence of nulls in ω or in the body of T will require changes in steps

1 and 3 of the algorithm developed so far. The first difficulty is that the history substitution, as defined so far, may leave some information in T about the atoms of ω. For example, when inserting ¬Mgr(Nilsson, CS) into the theory with body Mgr(Nilsson, ϵ) $\wedge$ ϵ=CS, clearly Mgr(Nilsson, ϵ) must also take part in the history substitution. The solution is simply to extend the history substitution to all atoms in the body of T that unify with an atom of ω, so that, for example, Mgr(Nilsson, ϵ) $\wedge$ ϵ=CS becomes Mgr(Nilsson, ϵ, U) $\wedge$ ϵ=CS.

The inclusion of unifying atoms in the history substitution in turn leads to problems with formula 4.1 in step 3. For example, suppose that the formula being inserted is Mgr(Nilsson, CS), and T already contains the formula ¬Mgr(Nilsson, ϵ). Consider a model where ϵ=EE, i.e., where EE is the department that Nilsson does not manage. Nilsson should still not manage EE in any world in $U(M)$. In other words, because Mgr(Nilsson, ϵ) and Mgr(Nilsson, CS) do not unify under the null substitution of M, the truth valuation of Mgr(Nilsson, ϵ) should not change during the update. To accomplish this, the left-hand side of formula 4.1 must be strengthened, as described in step 3 below:

1.   Perform the history substitution σ_H, replacing by f_U each occurrence of a data atom f in the body of T that unifies with a data atom of ω.

2.   Then add $(\phi)_{\sigma_H} \to \omega$ to the body of T.

3.   Finally, for each data atom f occurring in σ_H, let Σ be the set of all most general substitutions σ under which f unifies with an atom of ω. Add the formula

$$\neg((\phi)_{\sigma_H} \wedge \bigvee_{\sigma \in \Sigma} \sigma) \to (f \leftrightarrow f_U) \qquad (4.2)$$

to the body of T.

Example 4.4.   Let the body of T be

Mgr(Nilsson, ϵ_1),

and let U_4 be the update

insert ¬Mgr(Nilsson, CS).

We first show how U_1 affects the data predicate interpretations of sample models M_1 and M_2. The null substitution for M_1 includes ϵ_1=English, and that for M_2

and M_3 includes $\epsilon_1 = CS$. Before the update, all predicate interpretations are the empty relation, except for Mgr, which contains the tuple

[Nilsson, English]

in M_1, and

[Nilsson, CS]

in M_2. $U_4(M_1) = \{M_1\}$; and $U_4(M_2) = \{M_3\}$, where M_3 has empty predicate interpretations.

Mgr(Nilsson, CS) unifies with Mgr(Nilsson, ϵ_1) under most general substitution $\epsilon_1 = CS$. Therefore after update, the body of T will contain the formulas

Mgr(Nilsson, ϵ_1, U_4)

T $\rightarrow$ ¬Mgr(Nilsson, CS)

¬(T $\wedge$ $\epsilon_1 = CS$) $\rightarrow$ [Mgr(Nilsson, ϵ_1) $\leftrightarrow$ Mgr(Nilsson, ϵ_1, U_4)].

4.4. The Closed-World Assumption

So far we have assumed that T did not contain any completion axioms, so that we could operate under the open-world assumption. If the open-world assumption is appropriate for the application at hand, then the algorithm as constructed so far will perform updates correctly [Winslett 86a]. When, as we assume in the remainder of this chapter, a closed-world assumption is required, the presence of completion axioms will require modification of the update algorithms.

First consider the case where T and U contain no nulls. It may be that ω and ϕ contain data atoms that do not occur in T and therefore are not represented in T's completion axioms. For example, T may have an empty body, and we may be attempting to insert the fact Mgr(Nilsson, CS). The completion axioms of T rule out the possibility of new atoms such as Mgr(Nilsson, CS) being true, and therefore those axioms must be changed. The needed change is simply to represent all new data atoms of ω and ϕ in the appropriate completion axioms, and then add $\neg f$, for each new data atom f, to the body of T. Though the addition of $\neg f$ is not strictly necessary, it has the advantage of leaving the models of T unaffected by the change in completion axioms. In addition, this technique works correctly when the completion axioms are not stored explicitly but rather are computable on demand from the body of T.

If nulls are present in U or T, then a more complex approach is required. For example, in inserting Mgr(Nilsson, CS), it may be the case that Mgr(Nilsson, ϵ) $\wedge$ $\epsilon = CS$ already occurs in T. Adding ¬Mgr(Nilsson, CS) to the body would make T inconsistent.

More generally, suppose that f is a data atom occurring in U but not in the body of T. If f does not unify with any atom of T, then f is false in all models of T, and adding $\neg f$ to T will not change the models of T. For example, if Mgr(Nilsson, CS) does not unify with any atom of T, then we can represent it in the completion axioms and add $\neg$Mgr(Nilsson, CS) to the body of T without changing the models of T. If, however, f does unify with a single atom g of T, then f can only be true in a model of T in which g holds and in which in addition a substitution holds under which f unifies with g. For example, if f is Mgr(Nilsson, CS), and f unifies with a single atom Mgr(Nilsson, ϵ) of the body of T, then adding $\neg$Mgr(Nilsson, CS) to T might change the models of T. The correct formula to add is Mgr(Nilsson, CS) $\rightarrow$ (ϵ=CS). If the atom Mgr(ϵ_1, ϵ_2) also appeared in T, the appropriate formula would be Mgr(Nilsson, CS) $\rightarrow$ [(ϵ=CS) $\vee$ (ϵ_1=Nilsson $\wedge$ ϵ_2=CS)].

Stating the above principle more precisely, we have the following approach to maintaining the completion axioms: for each data atom g that occurs in U but not in T, let Σ_0 be the set of the substitutions σ such that for some atom f in the body of T, f unifies with g under most general substitution σ. If Σ_0 is the empty set, then add $\neg g$ to the body of T; otherwise, add the formula

$$g \; \rightarrow \; \bigvee_{\sigma \in \Sigma_0} \sigma \tag{4.3}$$

to the body of T. Then for every data atom g of T not represented in the completion axioms, add a disjunct representing g to those axioms.

Once the completion axioms are repaired, the update proper can begin, using the algorithms described in the previous sections.

Example 4.5.   Let us reconsider Example 4.4, using the closed-world assumption. The body of T is

Mgr(Nilsson, ϵ_1),

and U_4 is *insert* $\neg$Mgr(Nilsson, CS). The completion axioms of T:

$\forall x \forall y \; \neg$Emp$(x, y)$
$\forall x \forall y \; [$Mgr$(x, y) \rightarrow (x$=Nilsson $\wedge \; y$=$\epsilon_1)]$.

After update, the body of T will contain the formulas

Mgr(Nilsson, CS, U_4) $\rightarrow \epsilon_1$=CS
Mgr(Nilsson, ϵ_1, U_4)
$\top \rightarrow \neg$Mgr(Nilsson, CS)

$\neg(\mathsf{T} \wedge \epsilon_1{=}\mathsf{CS}) \rightarrow [\mathrm{Mgr}(\mathrm{Nilsson}, \epsilon_1) \leftrightarrow \mathrm{Mgr}(\mathrm{Nilsson}, \epsilon_1, U_4)]$
$\neg(\mathsf{T} \wedge \mathsf{T}) \rightarrow [\mathrm{Mgr}(\mathrm{Nilsson}, \mathrm{CS}) \leftrightarrow \mathrm{Mgr}(\mathrm{Nilsson}, \mathrm{CS}, U_4)],$

and will have completion axioms

$\forall x \forall y \; \neg\mathrm{Emp}(x, y)$
$\forall x \forall y \; [\mathrm{Mgr}(x, y) \rightarrow ((x{=}\mathrm{Nilsson} \wedge y{=}\epsilon_1) \vee (x{=}\mathrm{Nilsson} \wedge y{=}\mathrm{CS}))].$

4.5. Summary

The complete version of the Update Algorithm described in the previous sections:

The Update Algorithm (Version I)
Input. A relational theory T and an update U.
Output. T', an updated version of T.
Procedure. A sequence of four steps:
Step 1. Maintain the closed-world assumption. To maintain the closed-world assumption, all data atoms in ω and ϕ must be represented in the completion axioms of T. First change the body of T to reflect the new completion axioms: for each data atom g that occurs in ω or ϕ but not in T, let Σ_0 be the set of substitutions σ such that for some atom f in the body of T, f unifies with g under most general substitution σ. If Σ_0 is the empty set, then add $\neg g$ to the body of T; otherwise, add the formula

$$ g \; \rightarrow \; \bigvee_{\sigma \in \Sigma_0} \sigma \tag{4.3} $$

to the body of T. Then for every data atom g of T not represented in the completion axioms, add a disjunct representing g to those axioms. Call the resulting theory T'.
Step 2. Make history. For each data atom f in T' that unifies with an atom of ω, replace all occurrences of f in the body of T' by the history atom f_U.
Step 3. Define the scope of the update. Add the formula $(\phi)_{\sigma_H} \rightarrow \omega$ to T'.
Step 4. Restrict the scope of the update. For each data atom f in σ_H, let Σ be the set of all most general substitutions σ under which f unifies

with an atom of ω. Add the formula

$$\neg((\phi)_{\sigma_H} \wedge \bigvee_{\sigma \in \Sigma} \sigma) \rightarrow (f \leftrightarrow f_U) \tag{4.2}$$

to T'. Intuitively, for f an atom that might possibly have its truth valuation changed by update U, formula 4.2 says that the truth valuation of f can change only in a model where ϕ was true originally, and further that in any model so created, f must be unified with an atom of ω.

Example 4.6.   Let the body of T be
$\neg\text{Emp}(\text{Chien, CS}) \wedge \text{Emp}(\text{Chien, English}) \wedge \text{Mgr}(\text{Nilsson}, \epsilon_1)$,
and let U_5 be the update
insert $\text{Emp}(\text{Chien}, \epsilon_1) \wedge \epsilon_1 \neq \text{EE}$.
Then the alternative worlds of T initially consist of all worlds where Chien is in English and Nilsson manages some one department, either a known department or ϵ_1. After the update, the alternative worlds should be those where Chien is in English and Chien is in a department managed by Nilsson, and that department is not EE.

   Step 1. Add the formula $\text{Emp}(\text{Chien}, \epsilon_1) \rightarrow (\epsilon_1 = \text{CS} \vee \epsilon_1 = \text{English})$ to the body of T, and the corresponding disjunct to the completion axiom. Note that Step 1 does not change the worlds of T.

   Step 2. Replace $\text{Emp}(\text{Chien, CS})$, $\text{Emp}(\text{Chien, English})$, and $\text{Emp}(\text{Chien}, \epsilon_1)$ by $\text{Emp}(\text{Chien, CS}, U_5)$, $\text{Emp}(\text{Chien, English}, U_5)$, and $\text{Emp}(\text{Chien}, \epsilon_1, U_5)$, respectively. The body of T' now contains the two formulas
$\neg\text{Emp}(\text{Chien, CS}, U_5) \wedge \text{Emp}(\text{Chien, English}, U_5) \wedge \text{Mgr}(\text{Nilsson}, \epsilon_1)$
$\text{Emp}(\text{Chien}, \epsilon_1, U_5) \rightarrow (\epsilon_1 = \text{CS} \vee \epsilon_1 = \text{English})$.

   Step 3. Add the formula $(\phi)_{\sigma_H} \rightarrow \omega$ (i.e., $\mathsf{T} \rightarrow (\text{Emp}(\text{Chien}, \epsilon_1) \wedge \epsilon_1 \neq \text{EE})$) to the body of T'.

   Step 4. Add to T' the three formulas
$\neg(\mathsf{T} \wedge \mathsf{T}) \rightarrow (\text{Emp}(\text{Chien}, \epsilon_1) \leftrightarrow \text{Emp}(\text{Chien}, \epsilon_1, U_5))$
$\neg(\mathsf{T} \wedge \epsilon_1 = \text{CS}) \rightarrow (\text{Emp}(\text{Chien, CS}) \leftrightarrow \text{Emp}(\text{Chien, CS}, U_5))$
$\neg(\mathsf{T} \wedge \epsilon_1 = \text{English}) \rightarrow (\text{Emp}(\text{Chien, English}) \leftrightarrow \text{Emp}(\text{Chien, English}, U_5))$.
   Examination of Worlds(T') shows that T' accomplishes U_5.

   The models of T' produced by the Update Algorithm always represent exactly the alternative worlds that U is defined to produce from T:

Theorem 4.1.   *Given a relational theory T and an update U, the relational theory T' produced by the Update Algorithm Version I accomplishes U under the standard semantics.*

In other words, Worlds$(T') = \bigcup_{M \in \text{Models}(T)} \text{Worlds}(U(M))$. Theorem 4.1 will not be proven here, as it follows immediately from Theorem 5.1.

4.6. Computational Complexity of the Update Algorithm

Let the *size* of a formula be defined as the number of occurrences of atoms in the formula, and let the size of an update U be the sum of the sizes of ϕ and ω. Let U be an update of size k; and let R be the maximum number of distinct atoms of T over the same data predicate. When T and U contain no nulls, the Update Algorithm will process U in time $O(k \log R)$ (the same asymptotic cost as for ordinary database updates) and increase the size of T by $O(k)$ worst case. This is not to say that an $O(k \log R)$ implementation of updates is the best choice; rather, it is advisable to devote extra time to heuristics for minimizing the length of the formulas to be added to T. Nonetheless, a worst-case time estimate for the algorithm is informative, as it tells us how much time must be devoted to the algorithm proper. The implementation assumptions necessary for this estimate to be achieved are described in the chapter on implementation, Chapter 9. Further, we assume that the schema is fixed, i.e., that the number of predicates is a constant.

When nulls occur in T or in U, the controlling factor in costs is the number of atoms of T that unify with atoms of U. If n atoms of T each unify with one atom of U, then T will grow by $O(n + k)$. In the worst case, *every* atom of T may unify with *every* atom of U, in which case after a series of m updates, the number of occurrences of atoms in T may *multiply* by $O(mk)$. Theorem 4.2 summarizes these properties.

Theorem 4.2. *Let T be a relational theory containing n different data atoms (not occurrences of data atoms) having nulls as arguments. Let k be a constant that is an upper bound on the size of updates. Then after a series of m updates not containing nulls is performed by the Update Algorithm, in the worst case the size of T will increase by $O(nmk)$. Under a series of m updates containing nulls, in the worst case the size of T will increase by $O(nmk + m^2 k^2)$.*

Proof of Theorem 4.2. We show the space requirements for each step of the Update Algorithm.

Let g be a data atom of U, the first of the m updates. If g already occurs in T, then nothing is added to T for g in Step 1. Otherwise, g does not occur in T, and the number of atoms in T that unify with g determines the size of Σ_0 in Step 1.

By assumption, g unifies with at most n atoms of T. Each substitution σ in Σ_0 is of size bounded by a constant. Therefore at most $O(nk)$ occurrences of atoms are added to T for U. Under a series of m updates not containing nulls, Step 1 can add as many as $O(nmk)$ occurrences of atoms to T'. If the updates contain nulls, then each update can add k data atoms containing nulls to T, so that the first update after U may have a Σ_0 of size $n + k$, the second may have size $n + 2k$, and so on. As there may be k choices of Σ_0 for each update, after m updates the size of this compounding factor is $O(m^2 k^2)$.

Step 2 does not change the size of T'. Step 3 adds $O(k)$ occurrences of atoms to T'.

For Step 4 of update U, a trick is helpful to keep down the size of formula 4.2. It can be quite expensive to repeatedly add $(\phi)_{\sigma_H}$ to T' for every choice of f in formula 4.2. Much more efficient is to add a single formula $H(U) \leftrightarrow (\phi)_{\sigma_H}$ to T' before Step 4, and then use $H(U)$ in place of $(\phi)_{\sigma_H}$ in all instantiations of formula 4.2. ($H(U)$ is an atomic formula over the unary history predicate H, not occurring elsewhere in T'.) We assume that this measure is taken, incurring a cost of $\mathcal{O}(k)$ atoms per update.

If U does not contain nulls, there are at most $n + 1$ atoms in T' that unify with an atom of ω, giving a maximum of $n+1$ choices for f in formula 4.2. (If U contains nulls, there may be as many as $n + k$ such atoms in T'.) Let g be a data atom in T' that unifies with an atom of ω. The size of formula 4.2 for g is $O(k)$ worst case, so the cost of instantiating formula 4.2 for U will be $O(nk)$ (or $O((n + k)k)$, if U contains nulls). Therefore under a series of m updates not containing nulls, Step 4 will add up to $O(nmk)$ occurrences of atoms to T'. If the updates contain nulls, then each update can add k data atoms to T, so that again a compounding factor of $O(m^2 k^2)$ appears.

As for the time complexity of the Update Algorithm, let us assume that an indexing scheme is available that enables any atom to be located in T in $O(\log R)$ time. Then the running time of the Update Algorithm is $O(kn \log R)$ worst case. This estimate assumes that the history step (Step 2) is optimized through special data structures (see Chapter 9): the body of the relational theory must be represented as a set of logical relationships between *pointers*. All occurrences of a single data atom in the body are linked together in a chain of pointers; only the head of the chain points to the stored record for the actual data atom.

Happily, a large class of common types of updates—those with very simple ω and ϕ—can be performed in $O(k \log R)$ time per update; Abiteboul and Grahne have examined a subset of these simple updates [Abiteboul 85]. For the general case, however, potential growth of $O(nmk)$ in the size of T is much too large, yet is unavoidable if the effect of the update is to be represented directly in the relational theory, for every data atom of T that unifies with an atom of the update *must* be changed in some way in T. In some sense the information content of a single update is no more than its size, k, and so growth of more than $O(mk)$ after m updates is too much. We can achieve growth of no more than $O(mk)$ by simply storing the updates without incorporating them into T. However, since query answering presupposes some means of integrating updates with the rest of the database to allow satisfiability testing, a means of at least temporary incorporation must be offered. We have devised a scheme of delayed evaluation and simplification of expensive updates, by bounding the permissible number of unifications for the atoms of an incoming update. This lazy evaluation technique is discussed in Chapter 6.

An interesting question is how the history predicates affect the complexity of query answering. Of course query answering will be at least as hard as satisfiability testing, and the exact difficulty will depend on the query language allowed [Vardi 86]. Query answering is $\mathcal{NP}$-hard in the number of history atoms present in the relational theory, but we conjecture that the time taken up by computations on history atoms can be bounded by a function of the complexity of the database before those atoms were introduced. It is difficult to estimate the average-case impact of history predicates on query answering, though Chapter 9 gives some preliminary indications.

4.7. An Update Algorithm for the Minimal-Change Semantics

To adapt the Update Algorithm to work with the minimal-change semantics, only the formula of Step 4 need be modified. Recall that in Step 4 of the Update Algorithm using the standard semantics,

$$\neg((\phi)_{\sigma_H} \wedge \bigvee_{\sigma \in \Sigma} \sigma) \rightarrow (f \leftrightarrow f_U) \tag{4.2}$$

is added to T' for every data atom f of T' that unifies with an atom of ω. For example, if U is *insert* Emp(Chien, EE) $\vee$ Emp(Chien, CS) and there are no nulls in T, then this means that T' gets the two new formulas

$\neg(\mathsf{T} \wedge \mathsf{T}) \rightarrow [\text{Emp}(\text{Chien, EE}) \leftrightarrow \text{Emp}(\text{Chien, EE}, U)]$
$\neg(\mathsf{T} \wedge \mathsf{T}) \rightarrow [\text{Emp}(\text{Chien, CS}) \leftrightarrow \text{Emp}(\text{Chien, CS}, U)],$

both of which are logically equivalent to T. To move to the minimal-change semantics, one needs to add the two formulas

[Emp(Chien, EE, U) ∨ Emp(Chien, CS, U) ∨ Emp(Chien, CS)] →
    [Emp(Chien, EE)↔Emp(Chien, EE, U)]
[Emp(Chien, EE, U) ∨ Emp(Chien, CS, U) ∨ Emp(Chien, EE)] →
    [Emp(Chien, CS)↔Emp(Chien, CS, U)].

These formulas say that the truth valuation of Emp(Chien, EE) can only change in an alternative world if Chien is in neither department before the update and Chien is not in CS in that alternative world after the update. If Emp(Chien, EE) and/or Emp(Chien, CS) are already true in an alternative world, then they remain true there; and otherwise, Chien is put into exactly one of those two departments.

In the general case, formula 4.2 needs to contain extra terms that are true exactly when f is part of a set of minimal changes that makes ω true in an alternative world. To capture those states, one must know which atoms of ω are already true in each model M. Unfortunately, when nulls occur in ω, we may need to know more: in particular, if two data atoms of ω unify with one another, one may also need part of the information contained in M's null substitution, as the following example shows.

Example 4.7.   Consider the update
insert Emp(Chien, CS) ∨ (Emp(Chien, ϵ_1) ∧ Emp(Chien, EE)),
applied to a model M where all three data atoms are false. If $\epsilon_1 \neq$ CS is true in M, then one minimal change that will make ω true is to make both Emp(Chien, ϵ_1) and Emp(Chien, EE) true. If $\epsilon_1 =$ CS is true in M, however, then this is not a minimal change, as making just Emp(Chien, ϵ_1) true will satisfy ω.

Only part of the information in M's null substitution will be needed to interpret an update. To that end, let atoms(ω) be the set containing all data and equality atoms of ω plus all atoms occurring in most general substitutions under which two data atoms of ω unify. For example, in Example 4.7 atoms(ω) is
{Emp(Chien, CS), Emp(Chien, ϵ_1), Emp(Chien, EE), ϵ_1=CS, ϵ_1=EE, ⊤}.
The minimal changes in M that make ω true will depend on which members of atoms(ω) are true in M.

Let valuations(U) be the set of all truth valuations for all the members of atoms(ω). We say that a subset v' of the data atom truth valuations of a valuation $v \in$ valuations(U) *defines a minimal change for v and U* if

(1)   if all data atom truth valuations of v except those of v' are negated, then ω is consistent with the revised version of v; and

(2)   no proper superset of v' within v has property (1).

In Example 4.7, one member v of valuations(U) is (in wff form[9])

$\neg$Emp(Chien, CS) $\wedge$ Emp(Chien, ϵ_1) $\wedge$ Emp(Chien, EE) $\wedge$
$\quad$ $\epsilon_1 \neq$CS $\wedge$ $\epsilon_1 =$EE.

In any model M in which this choice of v is true, ω will also be true. Therefore the only minimal change for v and U, i.e., the only choice for v', is the set of all data atom truth valuations of v. This means that no data atom can change its truth valuation in M when U is performed. Whenever ω is unsatisfiable, then there will be no choice of v' that defines a minimal change for v and U.

Let minChanges(v, U) be the set of all v' that define a minimal change for v and U; in the current example, minChanges(v, U) is

$\{\neg$Emp(Chien, CS) $\wedge$ Emp(Chien, ϵ_1) $\wedge$ Emp(Chien, EE)$\}$.

Then, intuitively, the truth valuation of a data atom f of ω in a model M can only change as a result of U if there is a $v \in$ valuations(U) such that v is true in M and a $v' \in$ minChanges(v, U), such that f does not occur in v'. More precisely, in any result model $M' \in U(M)$, every data atom f must have the same truth valuation as in M unless the following all hold:

(1) Let Σ be the set of all most general substitutions under which f unifies with an atom of ω. Then some $\sigma \in \Sigma$ must be true in M';

(2) There must be a valuation $v \in$ valuations(U) that is true in M; and

(3) There must be a valuation $v' \in$ minChanges(v, U) such that v' is true in M', and $(f)_\sigma$ does not occur in $(v')_\sigma$.

These three conditions combine to form formula 4.4, which will be added to T' in Step 4 of the Update Algorithm for the minimal-change semantics:

$$\neg\Big((\phi)_{\sigma_H} \wedge \bigvee_{\substack{\sigma \in \Sigma \\ v \in \text{valuations}(U) \\ v' \in \text{minChanges}(v,U) \\ (f)_\sigma \text{ does not occur in } (v')_\sigma}} (\sigma \wedge (v)_{\sigma_H} \wedge v')\Big) \rightarrow (f \leftrightarrow f_U) \quad (4.4)$$

It is possible for the disjunction in formula 4.4 to be empty, in which case it should be replaced by F. In the insertion of a tautology, minChanges(v,

---

[9] A truth valuation v can be written in wff form as the conjunction of the truth value T and a set of literals, such that the atom α is a conjunct of v in wff form iff α receives the truth valuation T under v, and $\neg\alpha$ is a conjunct of v in wff form iff α receives the truth valuation F under v. The wff form of the empty set of truth valuations can be written as T.

U) will contain one member, v', consisting of all the data atom truth valuations of v. In this case, the restriction that $(f)_\sigma$ not occur in $(v')_\sigma$ will never hold, and the disjunction of 4.4 will be empty. In inserting an unsatisfiable formula, minChanges(v, U) will be empty, again leading to an empty disjunction in formula 4.4. That disjunction will also be empty if, for example, f is Emp(Chien, English) and U is

insert Emp(Nilsson, CS) $\wedge$ (Emp(Chien, English) $\vee$ ¬Emp(Chien, English)).

Example 4.8.   Again consider the update

U: *insert* Emp(Chien, CS) $\vee$ (Emp(Chien, ϵ_1) $\wedge$ Emp(Chien, EE)).

The set atoms(ω) is {T, ϵ_1=CS, ϵ_1=EE, Emp(Chien, CS), Emp(Chien, ϵ_1), Emp(Chien, EE)}. As the size of valuations(U) grows exponentially with the size of U, valuations(U) already contains very many members v. However, for almost all choices of v, minChanges(v, U) contains all the data atoms of ω, meaning that ω is already true in a model where v holds. As mentioned earlier, the disjunction of formula 4.4 will be empty in all these cases. In other cases, v is unsatisfiable, which is again uninteresting. The remaining six members of valuations(U) are, listing only the true equality and data atoms under the valuation,

(1)   all false;
(2) $\epsilon_1 = $ EE;
(3) $\epsilon_1 = $ CS;
(4)   Emp(Chien, ϵ_1);
(5)   Emp(Chien, EE);
(6)   Emp(Chien, EE) and $\epsilon_1 = $ CS.

The corresponding values for minChanges(v, U):

(1)   { {¬Emp(Chien, CS)},
        {¬Emp(Chien, ϵ_1), ¬Emp(Chien, EE)} }
(2)   { {¬Emp(Chien, CS)},
        {¬Emp(Chien, ϵ_1), ¬Emp(Chien, EE)} }
(3)   { {¬Emp(Chien, EE)} }
(4)   { {¬Emp(Chien, CS), Emp(Chien, ϵ_1)},
        {Emp(Chien, ϵ_1), ¬Emp(Chien, EE)} }
(5)   { {¬Emp(Chien, CS), Emp(Chien, EE)},
        {¬Emp(Chien, ϵ_1), Emp(Chien, EE)} }
(6)   { {Emp(Chien, EE)} }

In the case where f is Emp(Chien, ϵ_1), there are three choices for σ in formula 4.4:

$\Sigma = \{$T, ϵ_1=CS, ϵ_1=EE$\}$.

The disjunction in formula 4.4 for this choice of f is, in condensed format and with unsatisfiable disjuncts eliminated,

$(T \wedge \epsilon_1 \neq CS \wedge \epsilon_1 \neq EE \wedge \neg Emp(Chien, CS, U) \wedge \neg Emp(Chien, \epsilon_1, U) \wedge \neg Emp(Chien, EE, U) \wedge \neg Emp(Chien, CS)) \vee$

$(T \wedge \epsilon_1 \neq CS \wedge \epsilon_1 \neq EE \wedge \neg Emp(Chien, CS, U) \wedge \neg Emp(Chien, \epsilon_1, U) \wedge \neg Emp(Chien, EE, U) \wedge \neg Emp(Chien, \epsilon_1)) \wedge \neg Emp(Chien, EE)) \vee$

$(T \wedge \epsilon_1 \neq CS \wedge \epsilon_1 \neq EE \wedge \neg Emp(Chien, CS, U) \wedge Emp(Chien, \epsilon_1, U) \wedge \neg Emp(Chien, EE, U) \wedge \neg Emp(Chien, CS) \wedge Emp(Chien, \epsilon_1)) \vee$

$(T \wedge \epsilon_1 \neq CS \wedge \epsilon_1 \neq EE \wedge \neg Emp(Chien, CS, U) \wedge Emp(Chien, \epsilon_1, U) \wedge \neg Emp(Chien, EE, U) \wedge Emp(Chien, \epsilon_1) \wedge \neg Emp(Chien, EE)) \vee$

$(T \wedge \epsilon_1 \neq CS \wedge \epsilon_1 \neq EE \wedge \neg Emp(Chien, CS, U) \wedge \neg Emp(Chien, \epsilon_1, U) \wedge Emp(Chien, EE, U) \wedge \neg Emp(Chien, CS) \wedge Emp(Chien, EE)) \vee$

$(T \wedge \epsilon_1 \neq CS \wedge \epsilon_1 \neq EE \wedge \neg Emp(Chien, CS, U) \wedge \neg Emp(Chien, \epsilon_1, U) \wedge Emp(Chien, EE, U) \wedge \neg Emp(Chien, \epsilon_1) \wedge Emp(Chien, EE)) \vee$

$(\epsilon_1 = CS \wedge \epsilon_1 = CS \wedge \epsilon_1 \neq EE \wedge \neg Emp(Chien, CS, U) \wedge \neg Emp(Chien, \epsilon_1, U) \wedge \neg Emp(Chien, EE, U) \wedge \neg Emp(Chien, EE)) \vee$

$(\epsilon_1 = CS \wedge \epsilon_1 = CS \wedge \epsilon_1 \neq EE \wedge \neg Emp(Chien, CS, U) \wedge \neg Emp(Chien, \epsilon_1, U) \wedge Emp(Chien, EE, U) \wedge Emp(Chien, EE)) \vee$

$(\epsilon_1 = EE \wedge \epsilon_1 \neq CS \wedge \epsilon_1 = EE \wedge \neg Emp(Chien, CS, U) \wedge \neg Emp(Chien, \epsilon_1, U) \wedge \neg Emp(Chien, EE, U) \wedge \neg Emp(Chien, CS)) \vee$

$(\epsilon_1 = EE \wedge \epsilon_1 \neq CS \wedge \epsilon_1 = EE \wedge \neg Emp(Chien, CS, U) \wedge \neg Emp(Chien, \epsilon_1, U) \wedge \neg Emp(Chien, EE, U) \wedge \neg Emp(Chien, \epsilon_1) \wedge \neg Emp(Chien, EE)).$

We now present the new version of Step 4 of the Update Algorithm Version I that implements the minimal-change semantics:

Step 4′. Restrict the scope of the update. For each data atom f in σ_H, let Σ be the set of all most general substitutions σ under which f unifies with an atom of ω. Add the formula

$$\neg\left((\phi)_{\sigma_H} \wedge \bigvee_{\substack{\sigma \in \Sigma \\ v \in \text{valuations}(U) \\ v' \in \text{minChanges}(v, U) \\ (f)_\sigma \text{ does not occur in } (v')_\sigma}} (\sigma \wedge (v)_{\sigma_H} \wedge v')\right) \rightarrow (f \leftrightarrow f_U) \quad (4.4)$$

to T'. When the disjunction in formula 4.4 is empty, it should be replaced by F. Intuitively, for f an atom that might possibly have its truth valuation changed by update U, formula 4.4 says that the truth valuation of f can change only in a model where ϕ was true originally, and further that in any model so created, f must be unified with an atom of ω, and must be part of a minimal change in that model to make ω true.

Example 4.9.   For the update *insert* Emp(Chien, EE) $\vee$ Emp(Chien, CS), applied to a theory not containing nulls, there is one choice of σ in formula 4.4, and four choices of v. For f the atom Emp(Chien, EE), the formula added in Step 4' is

$\neg[\mathsf{T} \wedge$
$(\mathsf{T} \wedge \neg$Emp(Chien, EE, $U) \wedge \neg$Emp(Chien, CS, $U) \wedge \mathsf{T} \wedge \neg$Emp(Chien, CS))]
$\quad \rightarrow$ (Emp(Chien, EE) $\leftrightarrow$ Emp(Chien, EE, U)).

For f the atom Emp(Chien, CS), the formula added in Step 4' is

$\neg[\mathsf{T} \wedge$
$(\mathsf{T} \wedge \neg$Emp(Chien, EE, $U) \wedge \neg$Emp(Chien, CS, $U) \wedge \mathsf{T} \wedge \neg$Emp(Chien, EE))]
$\quad \rightarrow$ (Emp(Chien, CS) $\leftrightarrow$ Emp(Chien, CS, U)).

The style of formula 4.4 was chosen for clarity rather than efficiency: using it as written will cause a greater increase in the size of T than is necessary, as Example 4.8 illustrated. For example, one need only consider satisfiable combinations of σ, v, v', and ϕ in the disjunction of formula 4.4. Also, the single disjunction of 4.4 can be replaced by a sequence of nested disjunctions, so that σ is not repeated for every choice of v and v'. Repeated conjuncts should also be eliminated.

Theorem 4.3.   *Given a relational theory T and an update U, the result theory T' produced by the Update Algorithm Version I, with Step 4 replaced by 4', accomplishes U under the minimal–change semantics.*

Proof of Theorem 4.3.   This new algorithm produces a set of alternative worlds that is a subset of those produced by the Update Algorithm Version I, as formula 4.4 logically entails formula 4.2. Therefore the proof of Theorem 5.1 can be used to show that the new algorithm is correct and complete, with one exception: we must show that all models produced by the algorithm are in fact minimally changed, and we must show that all minimally changed models are in fact produced.

First, let M be a model of T where ϕ is true, and let M_4' be a model in $U(M)$. Let M_4 be a model identical to M_4', except that for all data atoms $f \in \sigma_H$, f_U in M_4 is given the truth valuation of f in M. The proof of Theorem 5.1 shows that M_4 satisfies all formulas of T' except possibly formula 4.4. Consider a particular data atom f that occurs in σ_H. Let v be the truth valuation in valuations(ω) that is true in M. Then $(v)_{\sigma_H}$ is true in M_4. Let v' be the maximal subset of the data atom truth valuations of v such that v' is true in M_4. Then v' must be a member of minChanges(v, U). If f has a different truth valuation in M and M_4, then $(f)_\sigma$ cannot occur in $(v')_\sigma$, so formula 4.4 is true in M_4. We conclude that M_4 is a model of T'.

Now let M_4 be a model of T_4 where $(\phi)_{\sigma_H}$ is true; let σ_4 be the null substitution for M_4; and let M be defined exactly as in the proof of Theorem 5.1. We must show that M_4 is minimally changed from M. By formula 4.4, for every data atom f having a different truth valuation in M and M_4, there is a choice of σ, v, and v' in formula 4.4 such that $\sigma \wedge (v)_{\sigma_H} \wedge v'$ is true in M_4 and $(f)_\sigma$ does not occur in $(v')_\sigma$. Let M_4' be a model identical to M_4, except that every history atom h receives the same truth valuation in M_4' as it does in M. If $M_4' \notin U(M)$, then there must be a model $M' \in U(M)$, with null substitution σ_4, such that diff(P, M, M') is a subset of diff(P, M, M_4') for all predicate symbols P, and is a proper subset for some choice of P. Let S be the subset of v whose data atoms have the same truth valuations in M and M_4', and let S' be the subset of v whose data atoms have the same truth valuations in M and M'. Then S must be a proper subset of S'. Let f be a data atom of ω that occurs in S' but not in S. Then T_4 contains an instance of formula 4.4 for f, in which each data atom α of ω that occurs in S also occurs in v'. By the definition of v', then, it is not possible for S to be a proper subset of S', contradicting our earlier assumption. Therefore M_4' must be a member of $U(M)$. Since World$(M_4') =$ World(M_4), the theorem follows.

As defined, the set of formulas added to T' in Step 4$'$ will always have size exponential in the number of atoms in U and linear in the number of data atoms of T that unify with data atoms of ω. Though a size increase in T that is exponential in the size of U is unavoidable in the worst case, this estimate is greatly exaggerated for the typical theory and update. For example, for simple ω formulas such as conjunctions and disjunctions of literals, a much smaller size increase—linear and quadratic, respectively, in the size of U—is possible for ground theories and updates, with commensurate savings when nulls are present. Therefore, rather than applying the worst-case formulas blindly and adding their instantiations directly to T, the heuristic size minimization procedures described earlier, in addition to logical simplification of formulas, should be applied first to reduce the length of the formulas. In addition, Weber's procedure for avoiding the introduction of history atoms (after adaptation for the presence of nulls) provides another helpful heuristic for size minimization in the case where no data atom of ϕ unifies with an atom of ω.

CHAPTER FIVE

UPDATES WITH VARIABLES

In traditional data manipulation languages, variables can occur in updates. Typically, these updates only cause changes in a single tuple; the variables are used as placeholders for don't-care values in that tuple. For example, in updating an employee's salary, variables can be used for all the irrelevant attributes of the employee record, and only the employee ID and the new salary specified in the update request.

To speed query processing in a relational theory, it may be desirable to restrict the body of the theory to ground formulas, as we did in the preceding chapters. In this case, to perform an update U containing variables, one must first find all the bindings σ of variables to data values such that the selection clause $(\phi)_\sigma$ of U might be satisfied by some model of the theory. (In general, we expect all variables in ω to also appear in ϕ.) Each such set of bindings transforms U into a ground update $(U)_\sigma$. The task of the update algorithm is then to perform all the ground updates $(U)_\sigma$ simultaneously, as described in Section 5.1. The cost of an update containing variables will be a function of the number of bindings σ for its variables, just as in ordinary relational databases.

If, on the other hand, the body of the relational theory is not restricted to ground formulas, updates with variables are very easy to perform, as shown in Section 5.2.

As usual, we confine our attention to *insert* requests: *insert ω where ϕ*. The only change required in update syntax is that variables may now occur in ϕ and ω.

5.1. Semantics of Updates Containing Variables

As when defining the semantics of ground updates, we would like the extended semantics to agree with traditional semantics for relational data manipulation language updates with variables, in the case where T has a single alternative world. To meet this criterium, we will treat an update U containing variables as a set of ground updates, derived by binding data constants and nulls to all the variables of U. If we apply every possible binding to the variables of U, then the result of applying U to a relational theory T should be that of simultaneously applying all the updates in the (probably infinite) set just generated.

To rephrase this definition more formally, let U: *insert ω where ϕ* be an update possibly containing variables. Let M be a model of a relational theory T, and let σ be the null substitution for M. Let Σ_v be the desired set of substitutions σ_v for all the variables of ϕ and ω. Our goal is to perform all the updates *insert $(\omega)_{\sigma_v}$ where $(\phi)_{\sigma_v}$* simultaneously, for all $\sigma_v \in \Sigma_v$. Let Ω be the set of all formulas $(\omega)_{\sigma_v}$ such that σ_v is in Σ_v and $(\phi)_{\sigma_v}$ is true in M. Then Ω contains exactly the formulas that we would like to make true in M as a result of the update.

Definition. *Let U be an update, let M be a model of a relational theory T with null substitution σ, and let Σ_v and Ω be as defined above. Then under the standard semantics, $U(M)$ contains every model M' with the same constant interpretations as M, such that*

(1)   *All members of Ω are true in M'; and*
(2)   *M' agrees with M on the truth valuations of all atoms α such that $(\alpha)_\sigma$ does not occur in any member of $(\Omega)_\sigma$.*

In the case where U does not contain variables, Ω contains just ω, and the new semantics coincides with the definition of the standard semantics in Chapter 3.

Updates under the minimal-change semantics can be defined by making analogous changes in the variable-free definition of minimal change given in Chapter 3. Update algorithms for the minimal-change semantics can be crafted in the same manner. We will not consider the minimal-change semantics further in this chapter.

A relational theory T' accomplishes $U(T)$ if $\text{Worlds}(T') = \bigcup_{M \in \text{Models}(T)} \text{Worlds}(U(M))$.

Example 5.1.   Consider the following three updates, to be applied to a relational theory T with body $\text{Emp}(\text{Pratt}, \epsilon_1)$:
1. *insert* $\text{Emp}(\text{Pratt}, x)$ *where* $\neg\text{Emp}(\text{Pratt}, x)$
2. *insert* $\text{Emp}(\text{Pratt}, \epsilon_1)$ *where* $\neg\text{Emp}(\text{Pratt}, \epsilon_1)$
3. *insert* $\text{Emp}(\text{Pratt}, \epsilon_2)$ *where* $\neg\text{Emp}(\text{Pratt}, \epsilon_2)$

The first update applied to a model M of T makes Pratt an employee of all departments in M'. The second update does not change the worlds of T at all; and the third update produces all worlds where Pratt is in one or two different departments.

If U is a ground update and ω is satisfiable, $U(M)$ will be nonempty. Once variables occur in U, this ceases to be true. For example, the update *insert* $R(x) \wedge \neg R(y)$ *where* $x \neq y$ will probably be ill-advised when applied to a theory containing $R(a) \wedge R(b)$, because it asks for $R(a)$ and $R(b)$ to be both true and false: $R(a) \wedge \neg R(b)$, and $R(b) \wedge \neg R(a)$. We will not provide any syntactic means of avoiding conflicting updates; in our system, conflicting updates simply eliminate models where a conflict arises.

5.2. An Update Algorithm: No Variables in Body

Once again we face the problem of turning a model-based update semantics into an effective procedure for performing updates. The first problem is that of constructing Σ_v. One possible choice for Σ_v is to include in Σ_v *every* substitution of data constants and nulls for variables of U. But in typical updates, most of the substitutions σ_v in Σ_v would be such that $(\phi)_{\sigma_v}$ was false in all models of T; in other words, $(U)_{\sigma_v}$ would not change the models of T, and hence there is no point in including σ_v in Σ_v. In any case, Σ_v must be finite to be of use in query and update processing.

Intuitively, the ideal choice of Σ_v is the answer to the query ϕ, i.e., all the bindings of variables of ϕ to constants such that the bound ϕ may be true in some model of T. (We do *not* require that $(\phi)_{\sigma_v}$ actually be true in some model of T, as such a condition is equivalent to testing satisfiability, and hence might require exponential time to verify. The generation of Σ_v should require time polynomial in the size of the relational theory and exponential in the length of the update request.) One could therefore generate Σ_v by calling the database query processor on query ϕ. However, that query may not have a finite answer (e.g., $\neg\text{Emp}(x, \text{CS})$), in which case Σ_v would still be infinite.

The method traditionally used in database data manipulation languages to guarantee a finite Σ_v is the use of safe selection clauses [Ullman 88]. An adaptation of the concept presented there to the incomplete information situation might be to include a substitution σ_v in Σ_v iff σ_v substitutes data constants and nulls *already occurring in T or U* for all the variables of U. A domain completion axiom can be employed to this end. Another technique would be to require typed selection clauses, that is, to have type axioms restricting which constants can appear as values for each argument of a predicate, and require that the selection clause specify the types of all variables; INGRES [Stonebraker 85] and System R [Chamberlin 76] use a variant of this technique. We choose not to dictate the choice of a safe query mechanism, but rather operate on the assumption that one way or another, the query and update processor knows how to reduce an update with variables to a finite set of ground updates. In practice in today's database management systems, determination of Σ_v is typically initiated via index lookup on selection and join attributes. As is true in ordinary databases when variables occur in updates, an update with variables may require more changes in the relational theory than a ground update does, because each instantiation of variables represents an additional change to be made in the theory.

We now present an extension of the Update Algorithm Version I to handle updates with variables. (Note that Version I is a special case of Version II.) The new algorithm must take into account that an atom of T may be affected simultaneously in several different ways by different instantiations of the variables in an update.

The Update Algorithm (Version II)

Input. A relational theory T, an update U and a nonempty set Σ_v of substitutions σ_v for all the variables of U. (If U is ground, then Σ_v will contain just the empty substitution.)

Output. T', an updated version of T.

Procedure. A sequence of four steps:

Step 1. Maintain the closed-world assumption. To maintain the closed-world assumption, all atoms in $(\omega)_{\sigma_v}$ and $(\phi)_{\sigma_v}$, for all $\sigma_v \in \Sigma_v$, must be represented in the completion axioms of T. First change the body of T to reflect the new completion axioms: for each data atom g that occurs in some $(\omega)_{\sigma_v}$ or $(\phi)_{\sigma_v}$ but not in T, let Σ_0 be the set of substitutions σ such that for some atom f of the body of T, f unifies with g under most general substitution σ. If Σ_0 is the empty set, then add $\neg g$ to the body of

T; otherwise, add the formula

$$g \rightarrow \bigvee_{\sigma \in \Sigma_0} \sigma \tag{5.1}$$

to the body of T. Then for every data atom g that occurs in the body of T and is not represented in the completion axioms, add a disjunct representing g to those axioms. Call the resulting theory T'.

Step 2. Make history. For each atom f of the body of T' that unifies with an atom of $(\omega)_{\sigma_v}$ for some $\sigma_v \in \Sigma_v$, replace all occurrences of f in the body of T' by the history atom f_U.

Step 3. Define the scope of the update. For every σ_v in Σ_v, add the formula $((\phi)_{\sigma_v})_{\sigma_H} \rightarrow (\omega)_{\sigma_v}$ to T'.

Step 4. Restrict the scope of the update. For each σ_v and each data atom f in σ_H, let $\Sigma(\sigma_v, f)$ be the set of substitutions σ such that f unifies with an atom of $(\omega)_{\sigma_v}$ under the most general substitution σ. For each data atom f in σ_H, add the formula

$$\neg[\bigvee_{\substack{\sigma_v \in \Sigma_v \\ \sigma \in \Sigma(\sigma_v, f)}} \left(((\phi)_{\sigma_v})_{\sigma_H} \wedge \sigma\right)] \rightarrow (f \leftrightarrow f_U) \tag{5.2}$$

to the body of T'. Intuitively, for f a data atom that might possibly have its truth valuation changed by update U, formula 5.2 says that the truth valuation of f can change only in a model where $(\phi)_{\sigma_v}$ (for some σ_v) was true originally, and further that in any model so created, f must be unified with an atom of $(\omega)_{\sigma_v}$ for that same σ_v.

Example 5.2. Let U be *insert* $\neg\text{Emp}(\text{Chien}, x)$ *where* $\text{Emp}(\text{Chien}, x)$, when the body of T is $\text{Emp}(\text{Chien}, \text{CS}) \wedge \text{Emp}(\text{Chien}, \epsilon_1)$. The alternative worlds of T initially consist of all worlds where Chien is in CS and possibly one other department, and all other data atoms are false. After the update, T' should have one alternative world, in which everything is false. Let the set of substitutions Σ_v contain the two substitutions $x=\text{CS}$ and $x=\epsilon_1$.

Step 1. No actions are required, as all data atoms occurring in $(\omega)_{\sigma_v}$ are already in T.

Step 2. Upon application of σ_H, the body of T' becomes

$\text{Emp}(\text{Chien}, \text{CS}, U) \wedge \text{Emp}(\text{Chien}, \epsilon_1, U)$.

Step 3. Two formulas are added to the body of T':

Emp(Chien, CS, U) $\rightarrow$ ¬Emp(Chien, CS)
Emp(Chien, ϵ_1, U) $\rightarrow$ ¬Emp(Chien, ϵ_1).

Because U is a simple update, at this point T' already has the correct alternative worlds, and Step 4 is superfluous.

Step 4. Add to T' the following two formulas:

¬[(Emp(Chien, CS, U) $\wedge$ T) $\vee$ (Emp(Chien, ϵ_1, U) $\wedge$ (ϵ_1 = CS))] $\rightarrow$
    (Emp(Chien, CS) $\leftrightarrow$ Emp(Chien, CS, U))
¬[(Emp(Chien, CS, U) $\wedge$ (ϵ_1=CS)) $\vee$ (Emp(Chien, ϵ_1, U) $\wedge$ T)]$\rightarrow$
    (Emp(Chien, ϵ_1) $\leftrightarrow$ Emp(Chien, ϵ_1, U)).

Theorem 5.1. *For any relational theory T and update U possibly containing variables, the relational theory T' produced by the Update Algorithm Version II accomplishes U under the standard semantics.*

Readers not interested in a formal proof of correctness for the Update Algorithm should skip to the next section. To prove Theorem 5.1, we will use a lemma showing that Step 1 of the Update Algorithm does not change the models of T.

Lemma 5.1. *Let T be a relational theory containing a completion axiom α for an n-ary predicate R, and let g be a data atom $R(c_1, \ldots, c_n)$. Let Σ_0 be the set of all σ such that for some atom f in the body of T, f unifies with g under most general substitution σ. Let T' be the theory created from T by adding the new disjunct $(x_1=c_1 \wedge \cdots \wedge x_n=c_n)$ to α, and then adding ¬g to the body of T if Σ_0 is the empty set or adding*

$$g \rightarrow \bigvee_{\sigma \in \Sigma_0} \sigma \tag{5.1}$$

otherwise. Then $Models(T) = Models(T')$.

Proof of Lemma 5.1. Let α' be α with the disjunct added to represent g, and let β be the formula $g \rightarrow (\bigvee_{\sigma \in \Sigma_0} \sigma)$. First consider the case where Σ_0 is nonempty.

Let M be a model of T with null substitution σ. M satisfies all formulas of T' other than α' and β, since all other formulas also are formulas of T. But $\alpha \rightarrow \alpha'$, so M satisfies α'. As for β, if g is false in M then β is satisfied. If g is true in M, then $(g)_\sigma$ must be represented by some disjunct of $(\alpha)_\sigma$. Let f be the atom represented by that same disjunct in α. Then g and f unify under substitution σ, and therefore β is satisfied in M. We conclude that M is a model of T'.

For the reverse implication, let M' be a model of T' and let σ be the null substitution for M'. M' satisfies all the formulas of T except possibly α. But if α is false in M', it must be because for some binding to the variables of α', the disjunct representing g is true in M', i.e., that g is true in M'. But then by β there exists a data atom f of T such that f unifies with g under σ. Since f is represented in α, M' satisfies α. Therefore M' is a model of T.

Now consider the case where Σ_0 is the empty set, i.e., where g is false in all models of T. Let M be a model of T. Then $\alpha \rightarrow \alpha'$, and g is false in M, so M is also a model of T'.

Conversely, if M' is a model of T', then M' satisfies all formulas of T except possibly α. But if α is false in M' for some instantiation of the variables of α, it must be because the disjunct representing g in α' is true in M'. But we know that g is false in M'. Therefore M' is a model of T.

Proof of Theorem 5.1.   For simplicity of reference, let T be the original relational theory, T_1 be the theory produced by Step 1 of the Update Algorithm, T_2 be the theory produced by Step 2, and so on. M will always refer to a model of the original theory, M_1 to a model of T_1, and so on. We first show that the Update Algorithm produces a subset of the correct set of alternative worlds.

Suppose that M_4 is a model of T_4 having a null substitution σ_4. Our goal is to show that $\text{World}(M_4) \in \text{Worlds}(U(M))$, for some model M of T. It suffices to show that T_1 has such a model M, because by Lemma 5.1, the models of T and T_1 are the same.

Let M be a model identical to M_4, except that for all data atoms f occurring in σ_{H_1}, let f be true in M iff f_U is true in M_4. To show that M is actually a model of T_1, let α be a formula of the body of T_1. The descendant of α in T_4 is $(\alpha)_{\sigma_H}$. Since M and M_4 agree on the truth assignments to all atoms of $(\alpha)_{\sigma_H}$, therefore $(\alpha)_{\sigma_H}$ must be true in M. This implies that α will be true in M if every data atom f occurring in σ_H and in α has the same truth assignment in M as does f_U in M and M_4. But this is true by definition. As the completion axioms are the same in both theories, we conclude that M is a model of T_1 and T.

It remains to show that U applied to M produces the alternative world of M_4. Let Σ_ϕ be the set of all σ_v in Σ_v such that $(\phi)_{\sigma_v}$ is true in M. By the previous argument, $((\phi)_{\sigma_v})_{\sigma_H}$ is true in M_4 iff $\sigma_v \in \Sigma_\phi$. By the formula of Step 3, it follows that $(\omega)_{\sigma_v}$ is true in M_4 for all $\sigma_v \in \Sigma_\phi$, so rule 1 of the definition of *insert* is satisfied by M_4. For rule 2, if the truth valuation of a data atom f is different in M and M_4, then $(f)_{\sigma_4}$ occurs in $(\sigma_H)_{\sigma_4}$, and therefore f unifies with an atom of $(\omega)_{\sigma_v}$ for some set of $\sigma_v \in \Sigma_v$. By formula 5.2, there must be one such σ_v and a choice of $\sigma \in \Sigma(\sigma_v, f)$ such that σ and $(\phi)_{\sigma_v}$ are true in M. Therefore rule 2 is satisfied for the data atoms of M_4. We conclude that $\text{World}(M_4) \in \text{Worlds}(U(M))$.

We have shown that the Update Algorithm produces only correct alternative worlds; we now turn to the question of completeness: does the Update Algorithm produce every alternative world that should be derived under U?

Let M be a model of T, and let σ_1 be the null substitution for M. By Lemma 5.1, M is also a model of T_1.

Let Σ_ϕ be the set of all substitutions $\sigma_v \in \Sigma_v$ such that $(\phi)_{\sigma_v}$ is true in M. Then Ω is the set of all $(\omega)_{\sigma_v}$ such that $\sigma_v \in \Sigma_\phi$. Let e be a truth valuation for all the equality atoms of $(\Omega)_{\sigma_1}$, such that e is true in M. Let v be a truth valuation for all the data atoms of $(\Omega)_{\sigma_1}$, such that $v \wedge e \wedge ((\omega)_{\sigma_v})_{\sigma_1}$ is satisfiable for all $(\omega)_{\sigma_v} \in \Omega$. If no such v exists, then U produces no alternative worlds from M, and the theorem follows.

Let M_4 be the model that is identical to M except that (1) M_4 agrees with v on all atom valuations of v; and (2) f_U is true in M_4 iff f is true in M, for all data atoms f in σ_H. Then World(M_4) is an arbitrary alternative world that should be produced by U from M, and we claim that M_4 is a model of T_4.

Let σ_v be a substitution in Σ_v. First, M_4 satisfies the completion axioms of T_4, as every data atom of $(\omega)_{\sigma_v}$ already occurs in T_1, and T_4 and T_1 have identical completion axioms. For data atoms f in $(\omega)_{\sigma_v}$, since f_U has the same truth valuation in M_4 as does f in M, it follows that M_4 satisfies $(\beta)_{\sigma_H}$, where β is a formula of the body of T_1, to which σ_H was applied in Step 2. Since $(\omega)_{\sigma_v}$ is true in M_4 if $\sigma_v \in \Sigma_\phi$, the formulas $((\phi)_{\sigma_v})_{\sigma_H} \rightarrow (\omega)_{\sigma_v}$ added to T_4 in Step 3 are satisfied in M_4. There is only one remaining class of formulas of T_4 that M_4 might not satisfy: formula 5.2 from Step 4.

Let f be a data atom occurring in σ_H. If f and f_U have the same truth valuations in M_4, then formula 5.2 is satisfied. If f and f_U have different truth valuations in M_4, then $(f)_{\sigma_1}$ must occur in v, and therefore also in $((\omega)_{\sigma_v})_{\sigma_1}$ for some $\sigma_v \in \Sigma_\phi$. Therefore $(\phi)_{\sigma_v}$ must be true in M, and $((\phi)_{\sigma_v})_{\sigma_H}$ must be true in M_4. This implies that formula 5.2 is satisfied, since $((\phi)_{\sigma_v})_{\sigma_H} \wedge \sigma_1$ is true in M_4. We conclude that M_4 is a model of T_4, and World(M_4) is produced by the Update Algorithm.

It remains to verify that T_4 is a relational theory. T_4 has disjuncts in its completion axioms for exactly the data atoms in its body. The body of T_4 is still finite and contains no variables.

The computational complexity of Version II of the Update Algorithm depends on the size of Σ_v. In particular, if V is the number of members of Σ_v, then the number of atoms that are added to T' will be as much as V times greater than that added by the same steps in Version I. Of course the same relationship holds between ordinary relational database insertions with and without variables. The time complexity of Version II will likewise by multiplied by a factor of V worst case: $O(V \log R(nmk + m^2k^2))$.

5.3. An Update Algorithm: Variables in Body

This section presents an update algorithm for use with relational theories with arbitrary formulas in the theory body. Having variables in the theory body makes more work for the query processor, but as we will see, makes life much easier for the update processor.

First, the definitions given earlier for relational theories, substitution, unification, etc., need to be modified slightly. These modified definitions are in effect for the remainder of this chapter only. The changes needed are as follows:

- Substitutions: A variable may be substituted for another variable. For example, the atomic formulas Emp(Chien, x) and Emp(y, z) now unify under substitution Chien=y $\wedge$ x=z.

- Data atoms may now contain variables. For example, Emp(Chien, x) and Emp(y, z) are now both data atoms.

- A relational theory is now a finite set of sentences. As before, only standard models will be considered.

What happened to the completion axioms? Since quantifiers are now permitted in theory bodies, there is no reason to separate the completion axioms from the rest of the theory. To implement a closed-world assumption for a predicate R, it suffices to include the formula $\forall x_1 \cdots \forall x_n \neg R(x_1, \ldots, x_n)$ in the body at the inception of the theory. Subsequent updates will maintain the closed-world assumption automatically, by modifying that formula. The examples given after the presentation of the new update algorithm will illustrate this technique.

Though the definitions of relational theories and other technical terms are changed slightly for this section, update syntax and semantics remain exactly as presented in Sections 5.1 and 5.2.

With these formalities out of the way, we now show that a very simple version of the Update Algorithm accomplishes updates containing variables. This algorithm, Version III, adds only $O(k)$ atomic formulas to the size of the theory, where k is the size of the update. This is in contrast to Version II, which depends directly on the number of instantiations of variables in Σ_v (given to Version II as part of its input), and on the number of atoms in the theory that unify with atoms in the update. Further, this independence from Σ_v means that Version III works correctly even for updates with unsafe selection clauses—e.g., an infinite number of relevant instantiations of variables.

Input. A relational theory T and an update U containing variables $y_1, \ldots, y_n$.

Output. T', an updated version of T.

Procedure. A sequence of three steps:

Step 1. Make history. Let σ_H be the substitution that replaces each data atom f of T and U that unifies with an atom of ω by its history atom f_U. Then replace all occurrences of f in T by f_U. Call the resulting theory T'.

Step 2. Define the scope of the update. Add the formula $\forall y_1 \cdots \forall y_n \, ((\phi)_{\sigma_H} \to \omega)$ to T'.

Step 3. Restrict the scope of the update. For each n-ary data predicate R that appears in ω, let $x_1, \ldots, x_n$ be variables not occurring in U, and let Σ_v be the set containing all substitutions σ such that $R(x_1, \ldots, x_n)$ unifies with an atom of ω under most general substitution σ. Add the formula

$$\forall x_1 \cdots \forall x_n \left[\neg \exists y_1 \cdots \exists y_n \left((\phi)_{\sigma_H} \wedge \bigvee_{\sigma \in \Sigma_v} \sigma \right) \to \left(R(x_1, \ldots, x_n) \leftrightarrow R(x_1, \ldots, x_n, U) \right) \right]$$

to T'.

Example 5.3. Let T contain the single formula

$\forall z_1 \forall z_2 \, \neg \mathrm{Emp}(z_1, z_2),$

and let U be the update

insert $\mathrm{Emp}(\mathrm{Chien}, \mathrm{CS})$ *where* $\mathrm{Emp}(\mathrm{Chien}, \mathrm{EE})$.

As there are no employees initially in T, this update should not change any atom truth valuations. Step 1 changes T to the formula

$\forall z_1 \forall z_2 \, \neg \mathrm{Emp}(z_1, z_2, U);$

Step 2 adds the formula

$\mathrm{Emp}(\mathrm{Chien}, \mathrm{EE}, U) \to \mathrm{Emp}(\mathrm{Chien}, \mathrm{CS});$

and Step 3 adds the formula

$\forall x_1 \forall x_2 \, [\neg (\mathrm{Emp}(\mathrm{Chien}, \mathrm{EE}, U) \wedge (x_1 = \mathrm{Chien}) \wedge (x_2 = \mathrm{CS})) \to (\mathrm{Emp}(x_1, x_2) \leftrightarrow \mathrm{Emp}(x_1, x_2, U))].$

There are still no employees after the update.

Example 5.4. Let T contain the single formula

$\forall z_1 \forall z_2 \, [\mathrm{Emp}(z_1, z_2) \to (z_1 = \mathrm{Chien}) \wedge (z_2 = \epsilon_1)].$

The models of this theory have either no employees or just one employee, Chien, in some one department. Let U be the update *insert* Emp(Chien, CS) *where* Emp(Chien, EE).

This update should change all models where Chien is in EE so that Chien is now also in CS. Step 1 changes T to the formula

$\forall z_1 \forall z_2 \ [\text{Emp}(z_1, z_2, U) \rightarrow (z_1 = \text{Chien} \land z_2 = \epsilon_1)]$.

Step 2 adds the formula

Emp(Chien, EE, U) $\rightarrow$ Emp(Chien, CS);

and Step 3 adds the formula

$\forall x_1 \forall x_2 \ [\ \neg(\text{Emp}(\text{Chien}, \text{EE}, U) \land (x_1 = \text{Chien}) \land (x_2 = \text{CS})) \rightarrow$
$(\text{Emp}(x_1, x_2) \leftrightarrow \text{Emp}(x_1, x_2, U))]$.

Again the correct models are obtained.

Example 5.5.   Let T be the three formulas

Emp(Chien, CS)
Emp(Liu, EE)
$\forall z_1 \forall z_2 \ [\text{Emp}(z_1, z_2) \rightarrow$
$(((z_1 = \text{Chien}) \land (z_2 = \text{CS})) \lor$
$((z_1 = \text{Liu}) \land (z_2 = \text{EE})))$.

Let U be the update *insert* Emp(y_1, CS) *where* Emp(y_1, EE). After this update is completed, T should have one alternative world, in which Chien is in CS and Liu is in CS and EE. After the history substitution step, T' contains the three formulas

Emp(Chien, CS, U)
Emp(Liu, EE, U)
$\forall z_1 \forall z_2 \ [\text{Emp}(z_1, z_2, U) \rightarrow$
$(((z_1 = \text{Chien}) \land (z_2 = \text{CS})) \lor$
$((z_1 = \text{Liu}) \land (z_2 = \text{EE})))]$.

Step 2 adds the formula

$\forall y_1 \ [\text{Emp}(y_1, \text{EE}, U) \rightarrow \text{Emp}(y_1, \text{CS})]$

to T; and Step 3 contributes the formula

$\forall x_1 \forall x_2 \ [\neg \exists y_1 \ (\text{Emp}(y_1, \text{EE}, U) \land (x_1 = y_1) \land (x_2 = \text{CS})) \rightarrow$
$(\text{Emp}(x_1, x_2) \leftrightarrow \text{Emp}(x_1, x_2, U))]$.

Theorem 5.2.   *Let T be a theory, let U be an update possibly containing variables, and let T' be the theory produced from T and U by the Update Algorithm Version III. Then T' accomplishes U under the standard semantics.*

Proof of Theorem 5.2.   We begin by showing that the Update Algorithm Version III produces a subset of the correct set of alternative worlds.

Suppose that M_3 is a model of T_3, the theory produced by Step 3 of the Update Algorithm. Let σ_3 be the null substitution for M_3. Our goal is to show that U should produce M_3 from some model M of T.

Let M be a model identical to M_3, except that if f is a data atom occurring in σ_H, and b is a substitution of constants for all the variables of f, $(f)_b$ is true in M iff $(f_U)_b$ is true in in M_3.

To show that M is actually a model of T, let α be a formula of T. The descendant of α in T_3 is $(\alpha)_{\sigma_H}$. For any substitution b of constants for all the variables of $(\alpha)_{\sigma_H}$, M and M_3 agree on the truth assignments to all atoms of $((\alpha)_{\sigma_H})_b$, and therefore $(\alpha)_{\sigma_H}$ must be true in M. This implies that $(\alpha)_b$ will be true in M if for every data atom f that occurs in both σ_H and α, the atom $(f)_b$ has the same truth assignment in M as does $(f_U)_b$ in M and M_3. But this is true by definition. We conclude that M is a model of $(T)_{\sigma_3}$ and T.

It remains to show that U applied to M produces the alternative world of M_3. Let Σ_ϕ be the set containing all substitutions b of constants for all the variables of U such that $(\phi)_b$ is true in M. By the previous argument, $((\phi)_b)_{\sigma_H}$ is satisfied by M_3 iff $b \in \Sigma_\phi$. By the formula of Step 3, it follows that $(\omega)_b$ is true in M_3 for all $b \in \Sigma_\phi$, so rule 1 of the definition of *insert* is satisfied by M_3. For rule 2, suppose that f is a ground data atom such that $(f)_{\sigma_3}$ does not occur in any member of $(\Omega)_{\sigma_3}$ (recall that Ω is the set of all $(\omega)_{\sigma_v}$ such that $\sigma_v \in \Sigma_\phi$). If f does not unify with an atom of ω, then f has the same truth valuation in M and M_3, and rule 2 of the definition of *insert* is satisfied for f. Otherwise, let R be the predicate of f, and let $x_1, \ldots, x_n$ be the arguments of f. Then in the formula of Step 3, the left hand side of the implication is true in M for this choice of $x_1, \ldots, x_n$. By this same formula, then, $f \leftrightarrow f_U$ holds in M_3. We conclude that U produces the alternative world of M_3 from M.

We have shown that the Update Algorithm produces only correct alternative worlds; we now turn to the question of completeness: does the Update Algorithm produce every alternative world that should be derived under U?

Let M be a model of T, and let σ be the null substitution for M. Let Σ_ϕ be the set of all substitutions b of constants for all the variables of U such that $(\phi)_b$ is true in M. Let e be the truth valuation for all the equality atoms of $((\omega)_b)_\sigma$, for all $b \in \Sigma_\phi$, such that e holds in M. Select one particular set v of truth valuations for the data atoms of $((\omega)_b)_\sigma$, for all $b \in \Sigma_\phi$, such that $((\omega)_b)_\sigma \wedge v \wedge e$ is satisfiable for all $b \in \Sigma_\phi$. If no such v exists, then U produces no alternative worlds from M, and the theorem follows.

Let M_3 be a model identical to M except that M_3 agrees with v on all atom valuations of v, and $(f_U)_b$ is true in M_3 iff $(f)_b$ is true in M, for all atoms f in σ_H and substitutions b of constants b for all the variables of f. Then M_3 is a model of an arbitrary alternative world that should be produced by U from M, and we claim that M_3 is a model of T_3.

For atoms f in ω, since f_U has the same truth valuation in M_3 as does f in M, it follows that M_3 satisfies $(\beta)_{\sigma_H}$, for every formula β in T to which σ_H was applied in Step 1. Let b be a substitution of constants for all the variables of U. Since $(\omega)_b$ is true in M_3 if $b \in \Sigma_\phi$, the formula $\forall y_1 \cdots \forall y_n\ [(\phi)_{\sigma_H} \rightarrow \omega]$ added to T_3 in Step 2 is satisfied in T_3. There is only one remaining class of formulas of T_3 that M_3 might not satisfy: the formula from Step 3.

Let f be an atomic formula, and let b be a substitution of constants for all the variables of f. If $((f)_\sigma)_b$ and $((f_U)_\sigma)_b$ have the same truth valuations in M_3, then the formula of Step 3 is satisfied when x_1 through x_n are bound to the corresponding arguments of f and R is the predicate of f. If f and f_U have different truth valuations in M_3, then $(f)_\sigma$ must occur in $(\sigma_H)_\sigma$, and $((f)_b)_\sigma$ must occur in v, and therefore also in $((\omega)_{b'})_\sigma$ for some $b' \in \Sigma_\phi$. This implies that the formula of Step 3 is satisfied for f, since $((\phi)_{b'})_\sigma$ is true in M_3. We conclude that M_3 is a model of T_3, and the alternative world of M_3 is produced by the Update Algorithm. This concludes the proof of correctness for the Update Algorithm.

CHAPTER SIX

LAZY EVALUATION OF UPDATES

Delayed, but nothing altered. —Shakespeare, Romeo and Juliet *i.*4

When nulls occur in a relational theory T, updates to T will cause excessive growth in the size of T if many data atoms of T unify with atoms occurring in the updates. This chapter proposes a scheme of lazy evaluation for updates that strictly bounds the growth of T caused by each update, via user-specified limits on permissible size increases. Under lazy evaluation, an overly-expensive update U will be stored away rather than executed, with the hope that new information on costly null values will reduce the expense of executing U before the information contained in U is needed for an incoming query. If an incoming query unavoidably depends on the results of an overly expensive portion of an update, the query must be rejected, as there is no way to reason about the information in the update other than by incorporating it directly in the relational theory. When a query is rejected, the originator of the query is notified of the exact reasons for the rejection. The query may be resubmitted once the range of possible values of the troublesome nulls has been narrowed down. The bottom line for an efficient implementation of updates, however, is that null values should not be permitted to occur as attribute values for attributes heavily used in update selection clauses—particularly those used as join attributes.

The cost of an update can be measured as a function of the increase in the size of T that would result from execution of the update, and by measures of the expected time to execute the update and to answer subsequent queries. Once a database administrator has established a policy on when an update is too expensive, the techniques of this chapter can be used to recognize and defer or reject too-expensive updates and queries. This involves use of a lazy evaluation technique to delay execution of expensive updates as long as possible. Our discussion will be based on the standard semantics for updates; the techniques are also applicable to other choices of semantics.

Recall from Theorem 4.2 that when T contains n atoms containing nulls, a series of m updates of size k each may cause the size of T to grow by $O(nmk + m^2k^2)$. This potential growth is much too large, yet large growth (at least $O(nm)$) is unavoidable if the effect of an update is to be represented directly in the relational theory, for in the worst case every data atom of T that unifies with an atom of the update *must* be changed in some way in T. In some sense the information content of a single update is no more than its size, k, and so growth of more than $O(mk)$ after m updates is too much. We can achieve growth of no more than $O(mk)$ by simply storing the updates without incorporating them into T. However, since the usual means of query answering presupposes some means of integrating updates with the rest of the database to allow satisfiability testing, a means of at least temporary incorporation must be offered. This chapter puts forth a scheme of delayed evaluation and simplification of expensive updates based on bounding the permissible number of unifications for the atoms of an incoming update. We begin with a general overview and a series of examples.

6.1. Overview and Motivation

The first element of a system for cost reduction of too-expensive updates is a cost estimation function, so that we can decide which updates are too expensive to execute. If an incoming update U is determined to be too expensive, we will not execute U, but instead set U aside in the hopes that either no queries will be asked that require processing U completely, or intervening updates will reduce the cost of U sufficiently before it must be executed.

As the main data structure for this *lazy evaluation scheme*, we propose to use a *lazy graph*, a directed acyclic graph that keeps track of data dependencies between updates. The lazy graph helps minimize the amount of updating that must be performed before executing an incoming query Q, and keeps track of relevant update sequencing information. Some examples will clarify the potential benefits.

Example 6.1.   The effect of the two updates *insert* Emp(Pratt, CS) and *insert* ¬Emp(Pratt, CS) is dependent upon the order in which they are executed; if these two are stored away for lazy execution, we must make sure that any eventual

Figure 6.1. Example of lazy evaluation.

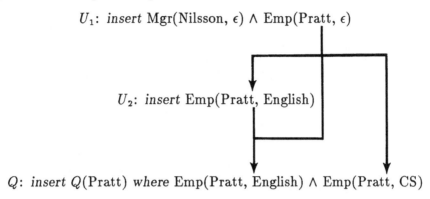

U_1: *insert* Mgr(Nilsson, ϵ) $\wedge$ Emp(Pratt, ϵ)

U_2: *insert* Emp(Pratt, English)

Q: *insert* Q(Pratt) *where* Emp(Pratt, English) $\wedge$ Emp(Pratt, CS)

processing of them is done in the order in which they were received. On the other hand, neither of these two conflicts with the update *insert* Emp(Pratt, English), which could be performed before, after, or between the other two.

This example suggests a parallel between lazy evaluation sequencing control and concurrency control [Papadimitriou 86]. The main difference is that in database concurrency control, any execution equivalent to some serial execution is correct, while sequencing control requires that the execution be equivalent to the original update input order.

Example 6.2.   Suppose the update U': *insert* ϵ=CS is received while the update U: *insert* Emp(Pratt, ϵ) is still unexecuted. Unlike information about the truth valuations of data atoms, information about the bindings of nulls is permanent and once asserted can never be refuted, only refined. (For example, if the user follows U' by the update *insert* ϵ=English then T will become inconsistent.) This property of permanence allows us to use the new information in U' about the value of ϵ to simplify not only T, but also the pending update U: U can now be reduced to *insert* Emp(Pratt, CS), which may well be affordable enough to execute directly even if *insert* Emp(Pratt, ϵ) is not.

Example 6.3.   Another potentially useful feature is the ability to execute only part of an update, leaving the more expensive part for later incorporation. For example, suppose the update U: *insert* Emp(Pratt, ϵ) $\wedge$ Mgr(Nilsson, CS) is too expensive only because Emp(Pratt, ϵ) unifies with too many data atoms of T. If a user later asks a query involving only Mgr(Nilsson, CS), it is advantageous to split U into the two updates U_1: *insert* Mgr(Nilsson, CS) and U_2: *insert* Emp(Pratt, ϵ) and only execute U_1 before processing the query.

Example 6.4.   Suppose an update U_1: *insert* Mgr(Nilsson, ϵ) $\wedge$ Emp(Pratt, ϵ) arrives in the system, followed by the update U_2: *insert* Emp(Pratt, English). Then U_2 and possibly U_1 as well contain new information about the truth valuation of Emp(Pratt, English); both of these updates may write new information about Emp(Pratt, English) into T. In the language of concurrency control, there is a *write/write conflict* between Emp(Pratt, ϵ) in U_1 and Emp(Pratt, English) in U_2; the lazy graph of Figure 6.1 depicts these relationships. Suppose that the query Q: *insert* Q(Pratt) *where* Emp(Pratt, English) $\wedge$ Emp(Pratt, CS) arrives next. (We have not formally defined queries yet; think of them as establishing a new relation Q that gives a view of the current database.) A *read/write conflict* occurs when one update "reads" an atom (i.e., the atom occurs in ϕ) that a later update "writes." There are read/write conflicts between Emp(Pratt, English) of Q and Emp(Pratt, ϵ) of U_1 and Emp(Pratt, English) of U_2, and between Emp(Pratt, CS) of Q and Emp(Pratt, ϵ) of U_1, as depicted in Figure 6.1.

Assuming that both Emp(Pratt, ϵ) and Mgr(Nilsson, ϵ) in U_1 cause U_1 to be too expensive to execute because they unify with too many atoms of T, the best procedure is first to split Mgr(Nilsson, ϵ) out of U_1, as depicted in Figure 6.2, creating updates U_3 and U_4. Then U_4 needs to be split on the two substitutions ϵ=English and ϵ=CS, creating updates U_5, U_6, and U_7, depicted in Figure 6.3. At this point Q and the updates Q depends upon are more likely to be affordable.

With the algorithm and data structures presented in this chapter, if a query is rejected due to excessive expense, exact reasons for the high cost can be made available to the caller, so that assertions about the possible values for nulls may be used to reduce the amount of uncertainty in the database and render the query affordable. Furthermore, any new information on null values can be used to reduce the size of the relational theory, in effect retroactively reducing the cost of all earlier updates that contained those nulls.

These examples should suffice to give a flavor of the possible advantages of a lazy evaluation scheme. We now turn to the details of lazy evaluation, beginning with a definition of queries. The lazy graph data structure is then presented formally, followed by an algorithm for adding incoming updates and queries to the lazy graph. After a presentation of the Lazy Algorithm, the remainder of the chapter is devoted to a discussion of splitting techniques. The chapter concludes with a measure of the benefits afforded by lazy evaluation.

6.2. Queries

We define a query as a temporary materialized view, to wit, a short-lived

Figure 6.2. Lazy evaluation horizontal split.

U_3: *insert* Mgr(Nilsson, ϵ)

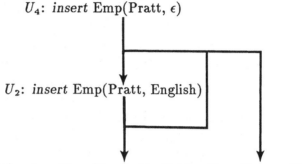

U_4: *insert* Emp(Pratt, ϵ)

U_2: *insert* Emp(Pratt, English)

Q: *insert* Q(Pratt) *where* Emp(Pratt, English) $\wedge$ Emp(Pratt, CS)

Figure 6.3. Lazy evaluation vertical split.

U_3: *insert* Mgr(Nilsson, ϵ)

U_7: *insert* Emp(Pratt, ϵ) *where* ($\epsilon{\neq}$English) $\wedge$ ($\epsilon{\neq}$CS)

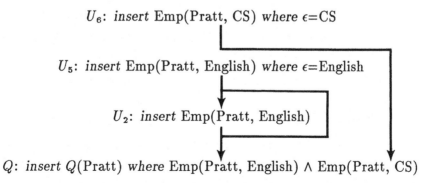

U_6: *insert* Emp(Pratt, CS) *where* ϵ=CS

U_5: *insert* Emp(Pratt, English) *where* ϵ=English

U_2: *insert* Emp(Pratt, English)

Q: *insert* Q(Pratt) *where* Emp(Pratt, English) $\wedge$ Emp(Pratt, CS)

relation. In keeping with our emphasis on mechanism rather than policy, we do not define what the user should actually "see" as output from a query.

A user interface routine will be in charge of optimizing and reformulating the view relation produced by the query execution mechanism into a format judged acceptable for human or programmatic consumption. We will consider only the process of creation of that view relation, not its presentation.

Syntactically, queries take the form *insert* $Q(c_1, \ldots, c_n)$ *where* ϕ, where ϕ is a formula of the language L not containing history atoms or variables, Q is an n-ary predicate symbol not in L, and c_1 through c_n are data constants or nulls of L. Note that Q cannot contain variables. Of course, in any database application, queries almost always contain variables, so this may seem a peculiar choice of definition for Q. The goal of this chapter, however, is to explore the issues arising in lazy evaluation and to present mechanisms for the basic tasks of lazy evaluation, much as the goal of Chapters 3 and 4 was to introduce a semantics for updates and to explain the basic technique for implementing such a semantics in polynomial time. Here, as in those chapters, the presence of variables in the operations under consideration would only obscure the principles at play. As the incorporation of variables into updates in Chapter 5 did not require major departures from the paradigms laid down in Chapters 3 and 4, so will the generalization of lazy evaluation to queries and updates containing variables not involve radical changes in the techniques proposed here.

When query Q arrives, the first step in handling Q is to add the new predicate symbol Q to L and the completion axiom $\forall x_1 \cdots \forall x_n \ \neg Q(x_1, \ldots, x_n)$ to T. (Q and its completion axiom can be flushed from the system once the user interface routine is done with it.) Q is then added to the lazy graph like any ordinary update request (Section 6.5). In fact, the only major difference between a query and an ordinary update request is that query Q must be either executed or rejected right away. The Lazy Algorithm (Section 6.6) will determine whether to accept or reject Q.

6.3. Cost Estimation

The first element of a system for lazy evaluation of too-expensive updates is a cost estimation function, so that we can decide which updates are too expensive to execute. Recall that one precious commodity in the system is the space required for relational theory storage. In fact, in the update algorithms discussed in previous chapters, the time to execute an update was just a logarithmic factor higher than the amount of additional space that the update added to T. In lazy evaluation, the time required to answer a query will be traded off against the amount of space occupied by the relational theory; with lazy evaluation a large number of unexecuted updates may require attention before a query can be answered. The techniques proposed in this chapter have the goal of minimizing storage space, necessarily to the detriment of query response time. In other words, in this discussion of lazy evaluation, an expensive update is one which adds too many atoms to the relational theory.[10]

The 80/20 rule says that in an ordinary database, 80% of the queries reference at most 20% of the data; 80% of that 80% (i.e., 64%) only reference at most 20% of that 20% (i.e., 4%); and so forth. Because of the 80/20 rule, we assume that, once executed, updates are permanently incorporated into T. The alternative is to integrate the update with T during query execution, but then abort the update at the end of query execution to save space in T. However, the 80/20 rule implies that if an update requires execution once, it will probably require execution again, and we might as well save the recomputation costs. This conclusion is, however, based on a particular tradeoff between computation and storage costs, and one might take a different view in a system where processing was affordable and storage was expensive.

The amount of space consumed by an update U is proportional to the number of *relevant* (in a sense to be made precise later) unifications of atoms in T with atoms of U. To control the amount of space consumed by U, lazy evaluation defines the estimated cost of an update as the estimated number of atoms added to T by each step of the Update Algorithm while U is being executed, and refuses to execute U if this estimate is excessive, i.e., if it exceeds the cost bound given for that update.

The cost estimate and cost bound for an incoming update or query are to be computed by functions supplied by the database administrator. The cost functions must satisfy the following requirements:

1. The cost estimation function may overestimate but never underestimate the costs (as defined by the database administrator) associated with executing a set of updates.

2. The cost estimation function and cost bound function must be computable from the information stored in the lazy graph (described in the following section).

---

[10] If query response time is a problem, then over-zealous lazy evaluation algorithms may be curbed by introducing constraints on the lazy graph (e.g., restrictions on height, flexible update cost limits, etc.).

The cost-related information provided in the lazy graph includes an estimate of the number of data atoms in T that unify with atoms of ω, as these unifications cause most of the expense incurred when executing an update. The cost estimation function will presumably rely heavily on this unification count. One can compute an exact unification count by using index lookup and null instantiation until either no more relevant unifications are found or the cost of the unifications found so far exceeds the cost bound. An estimate of the unification count can be computed from estimates of the number of null attribute values, using statistical techniques.

Queries also have associated storage costs, for their temporary view relations. The cost bound function might well choose to allot much more space to queries than to updates, since that space will only be used temporarily.

Unification counting and cost estimation should be performed with a bit of optimization, and that is where the phrase "relevant unifications" comes into play. The algorithms below use a test for satisfiability of bounded-length formulas to determine relevance. Other optimizations are also possible: an efficient implementation of the cost estimation procedure given below might do a much more thorough job of detecting spurious unifications. For example,   although Emp(Pratt, CS) unifies with Emp(ϵ, CS), there is no need to count that unification if the formula where Emp(ϵ, CS) occurs in T is Emp(ϵ, CS) $\wedge$ ϵ=Nilsson; that unification is not relevant, because it will not materialize in any model of T. Such optimizations will be part of the heuristic component of an implementation of the Update Algorithm, and will be important also for any user interface routine for query answering. The choice of optimizations beyond that required by algorithms given here is left to the implementor.

6.4. The Lazy Graph

The lazy graph is the data structure needed for lazy evaluation. In the lazy graph, nodes represent the atoms of updates. *Update hyperedges* group atoms into updates. *Family hyperedges* associate updates that are descended via splitting from the same original update. In addition, there is a directed arc between two nodes if the atom labels of the two nodes unify and cause one update to become dependent upon the results of the other. More formally, the lazy graph contains the following information:

1.   A set of *nodes*. Each node is labeled with a data or history atom, and cost information.

2. A set of *update hyperedges*. Each node is on one update hyperedge. Each update hyperedge is labeled with an update or query, such as U: *insert* Emp(ϵ, CS), and flagged as being either unexecuted (hereafter called *pending*) or executed.

3. A set of *family hyperedges*. Each node and update hyperedge is contained in one family hyperedge. Each family hyperedge is labeled with an update or query, such as U: *insert* Emp(ϵ, CS) $\wedge$ Mgr(Nilsson, CS), and flagged as being either an update or query. In addition, each family hyperedge has an associated cost bound.

4. A set of directed *labeled arcs* between nodes. Each arc is labeled with a substitution. These arcs represent dependencies between updates.

5. A set of directed *unlabeled arcs* between nodes. These arcs represent implied dependencies, such as that between ω of an update and ϕ of the same update.

We have chosen not to store cost estimate information for equality atoms, and hence they are not included in the lazy graph. This choice was made because equality atoms will be instrumental in reducing the size of the relational theory by eliminating nulls, and we therefore felt that an actual and estimated cost of zero was most appropriate for any optimized implementation of the Update Algorithm.

The main expense in an update is typically due to data atoms in ω. For example, if U_1 is the update *insert* Emp(Pratt, CS) $\vee$ Emp(Pratt, English), and U_2 is the update *insert* ϵ=CS $\vee$ ϵ=English, then these two updates have the same size. Yet a count of the formulas added by the Update Algorithm shows that U_1 will cost *at least* 5 times as much as U_2 under the Update Algorithm—and that minimum is attained if no data atom of ω of U_1 unifies with an atom of T. Therefore it seems reasonable for non-data atoms to be assigned much lower cost estimates than other types of atoms in ω. For atoms g that occur only in ϕ, again a lower estimate would be appropriate. Only if Step 1 of the Update Algorithm is required for g will g add more to T than would a non-data atom.

In this chapter, we distinguish between update and query *execution*, which is the incorporation of an update or query into the relational theory; update and query *processing*, which is the act of reforming the lazy graph to make a particular update or query executable; and update and query *addition*, which is the act of adding a new update or query to the lazy graph. These three phases are the topics of the next three sections.

6.5. Adding Updates and Queries to the Lazy Graph

The NAP algorithm will be used in two scenarios: When an update or query U arrives in the system, the NAP algorithm adds U to the lazy graph as the first member of a new update family. If U needs to be incorporated into the relational theory, we then process and execute U. In addition, when an update is split into two subupdates, the NAP algorithm is called to add those subupdates to the lazy graph. In this case, the split-off updates are members of the same update family as the original update.

The NAP algorithm allows the possibility of updates containing history atoms. Users still cannot mention history atoms in updates; history atoms only creep in when an update is split. We will use the notation ϕ_U to designate the selection clause of an update U, and ω_U to designate the formula being inserted by U. Any mysterious terminology in what follows will be explained in Section 6.7.

A helpful example of the operation of the NAP algorithm appears in Figure 6.4.

The NAP (Node Addition Procedure) Algorithm
Input: A lazy graph G and a request U, flagged as an update or query; and the preexisting update family to which U belongs, if any.
Output: A new lazy graph G' containing U.
Procedure: A sequence of three steps:
Step 1. Add nodes and hyperedges. For each non-equality atom g of U, add a node labeled g to G. Add a new update hyperedge to G containing exactly the new nodes, and label that hyperedge with U. If U defines a new history atom, also add a node labeled with that atom to the hyperedge. Mark the update hyperedge as pending. If U is to be part of a preexisting update family, then add its nodes to the hyperedge for that family; otherwise (1) create a new family hyperedge, labeled with U, (2) mark the family hyperedge as a query or update, as appropriate, and (3) compute the family hyperedge cost bound. Call the new graph G'.
Step 2. Add relevant arcs. *Intra-update arcs.* Let n and n' be two different nodes on the update hyperedge for U. If n is in ω of U and n' is in ϕ_U, then add an unlabeled arc from n' to n. These arcs represent the fact that the truth valuations for the atoms in ω after U is executed will depend upon the truth valuations for the atoms of ϕ at the time U is executed.

History atom definition arcs. If a history atom h of U also is the label of a node of a pending update U', then add an unlabeled arc from h in U' to the node h of U. This ensures that history atoms are defined before they are used.

Inter-update arcs. If any update hyperedges other than U are pending, then the effect of executing U may depend upon the results of those other updates. Let U' be a pending update hyperedge of G' other than U. Let f be the label of a node on the update hyperedge U', and g the label of a node on the update hyperedge U. Place a directed arc labeled σ from node f to node g if

(1) f unifies with g under most general substitution σ; and

(2) $\sigma \wedge \phi_U$ and $\sigma \wedge \phi_{U'}$ are both satisfiable; and

(3)   if ϕ_U logically entails a formula α containing only equality atoms, then $\phi_{U'} \wedge \alpha$ is satisfiable; and either

(4a)   (write/read conflict) f occurs in $\omega_{U'}$ and g occurs in ϕ_U; or

(4b)   (read/write conflict) f occurs in $\phi_{U'}$ and g occurs in of ω_U; or

(4c)   (write/write conflict) f occurs in $\omega_{U'}$ and g occurs in ω_U.

Explanations and examples of these tests appear after the algorithm.

Step 3. Record cost information. As input to the cost estimation function, cost information must be recorded for each node of U that is labeled with an atom g. Record whether g occurs in T or is the label of any ancestor of g in the lazy graph. (In the latter case, g would occur in T by the time U is executed.) Also record an estimate of the number of different atoms occurring in T or on labels of ancestors of g that unify with g, up to a preset limit l.

In Step 2 of the NAP algorithm, tests (1), (2), and (3) ensure that the conflict is relevant. If test (1) is failed, then there can be no conflict between U and U' due to f and g, because those two atoms do not even unify. For example, Emp(Pratt, CS) and Mgr(Nilsson, CS) cannot by themselves cause a conflict.

Test (2) of Step 2 ensures that the unification under which the conflict occurs can actually materialize in some model. For example, let U be *insert* Emp(Pratt, ϵ) *where* Mgr(Nilsson, ϵ) $\wedge$ (($\epsilon = $ EE) $\vee$ ($\epsilon = $ English)), and let U' be *insert* Emp(Pratt, CS). Then σ is $\epsilon = $ CS, and U and U' can only conflict in models where ϵ is CS. But in any model where ϵ is CS, the selection clause ϕ_U must be false. Therefore U and U' cannot conflict.

Test (3) ensures that U' and U can take place in "overlapping" sets of alternative worlds. Test (3) is a useful heuristic for reducing the number of arcs in the lazy graph without incurring much additional expense. For

Figure 6.4. Lazy graph example.

U_1:   *insert* Emp(Pratt, ϵ_1) $\vee$ Mgr(Nilsson, ϵ_2)
    pending

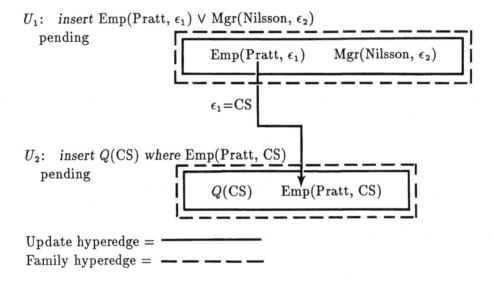

Update hyperedge $=$ ——————
Family hyperedge $=$ — — — — —

example, suppose U_1 is *insert* Emp(Pratt, CS) *where* $\epsilon =$ CS and U_2 is *insert* Emp(Pratt, CS) *where* $\epsilon =$ EE. Without test (3), a write/write conflict would be recorded between these two updates, even though in fact the updates must take place in disjoint sets of alternative worlds. Including this unnecessary write/write arc in the lazy graph would force extra serialization. Test (3) considers only equality atoms, because the truth valuations of data atoms might be changed by intervening updates.

Example 6.5.   Suppose the lazy graph contains the pending update U_1: *insert* Emp(Pratt, ϵ_1) $\vee$ Mgr(Nilsson, ϵ_2), and the update U_2: *insert* Q(CS) *where* Emp(Pratt, CS) arrives. Figure 6.4 shows the new lazy graph minus cost information.

All nulls and history atoms occurring in a pending update U are *pinned* in T until U has completed execution. This means that database optimization routines cannot remove those nulls and formulas from the database, even if they are no longer logically necessary. For example, if the database system discovers that $\epsilon=$Pratt, at least the single formula "$\epsilon=$Pratt" must remain in T until all pending updates containing ϵ have been executed. (Alternatively, one might prefer to substitute the newly discovered values into the pending updates that reference them; for simplicity we do not consider this method.) If these atoms were not pinned, then errors might occur in execution. For example, suppose a user requests the update U_1: *insert* Emp(Pratt, ϵ) as soon as it becomes known that Pratt is definitely a member of some department. Suppose that U_1 is too expensive to execute, and that U_1 is still pending when the user discovers that Pratt is in CS, that is, that $\epsilon = $ CS. This new update *insert* $\epsilon = $ CS is probably affordable, so assume that it is executed immediately. If all mention of ϵ is subsequently removed from the theory, and then U_1 is finally executed, U_1 will not add the fact that Pratt is in CS; rather, U_1 will erroneously declare that Pratt is in some unknown and unrestricted department. For this reason, history atoms and atoms containing nulls must be pinned.

It is important to show that the lazy graph does capture the information needed to process incoming updates correctly with the Update Algorithm. The arcs and hyperedges of the lazy graph induce a directed acyclic graph whose "nodes" are update hyperedges, and in which an arc goes from update U to U' if there is an arc in the lazy graph between a node of U and a node of U'. The original lazy graph and the induced update graph contain no cycles, because when an update U is added to the lazy graph using the NAP algorithm, all new arcs go to nodes of U from nodes of preexisting updates. Therefore the lazy graph induces a partial order on updates, and one can use this ordering to sort the updates topologically. Recall that a topological sort of a directed acyclic graph is constructed by repeatedly selecting a root in the graph and deleting it and its incident arcs from the graph. If $U_1 \cdots U_n$ is a topological sort, then call the sequence $U_n \cdots U_1$ a *reverse* topological sort.

Theorem 6.1. *Let $U_1 \cdots U_n$ be a sequence of updates and queries, and let T be a relational theory. Let G be the lazy graph created by sequentially inserting U_1 through U_n into an initially empty lazy graph. Let Toposort be any reverse topological sort of all the updates in G. Then Worlds(Toposort(T)) = Worlds($U_n(\cdots(U_1(T))\cdots)$).*

The proof of Theorem 6.1 uses a bit of new terminology:

Definition. *Let n and n' be nodes in a lazy graph. Then n is an ancestor of n' if there is a directed path from n to n' in the lazy graph. If U and U' are update hyperedges, then U is an ancestor of U' if there is a directed path from a node of U to a node of U' in the lazy graph.*

Proof of Theorem 6.1.   First, the sequence $S_1 = U_n \cdots U_1$ is a reverse topological sort of the lazy graph, because when an update or query U is inserted into the lazy graph with the NAP algorithm, no new ancestors are created for any update except U. Let Toposort be a reverse topological sort other than S_1. There must be a rightmost position on which the two sorts differ; counting from the right, say that S_1 and Toposort agree on positions 1 through $i - 1$, but differ in the ith position, where S_1 has U_i and Toposort has U_j. Let S_2 be the sequence $U_n \cdots U_{j+1} U_{j-1} \cdots U_i U_j U_{i-1} \cdots U_1$. Since Toposort is a reverse topological sort, U_j must not have any ancestors in the sequence $U_{j-1} \cdots U_i$. In particular, U_{j-1} must not be an ancestor of U_j. Applying Lemma 6.1, Worlds($U_n \cdots U_{j+1} U_{j-1} U_j U_{j-2} \cdots U_1(T)$) = Worlds($U_n \cdots U_1(T)$). By induction, Worlds($S_2(T)$) = Worlds($S_1(T)$). By induction, it follows that Worlds(Toposort(T)) = Worlds($S_1(T)$).

Lemma 6.1.   *Let T be a relational theory, and let U_1 and U_2 be updates or queries:*
U_1:   *insert ω_1 where ϕ_1,*
U_2:   *insert ω_2 where ϕ_2,*
such that if first U_1 and then U_2 are inserted into a lazy graph G using the NAP algorithm, U_1 is not an ancestor of U_2. Then Worlds($U_2(U_1(T))$) = Worlds($U_1(U_2(T))$).

Proof of Lemma 6.1.   Let M be a model of T with null substitution σ. Suppose that ϕ_1 is not true in M. Let M_2 be a model in $U_2(M)$. If ϕ_1 is true in M_2, then there must be non-equality atoms f in ϕ_1 and g in ω_2 such that f unifies with g under σ. Further, f and g pass test (1) of Step 2 of the NAP algorithm. For test (2), $\sigma \wedge \phi_1$ is true in M_2, and $\sigma \wedge \phi_2$ is true in M, so both formulas are satisfiable. For test (3), suppose ϕ_2 logically entails α, where α consists of equality atoms. Then α is true in M, and therefore also in M_2. As ϕ_1 is true in M_2, α must be consistent with ϕ_1. Therefore if ϕ_1 is true in M_2, then U_1 must be an ancestor of U_2 in the lazy graph, which we have assumed not to be the case. We conclude that ϕ_1 is false in all members of $U_2(M)$, and that Worlds($U_2(U_1(M))$) = Worlds($U_1(U_2(M))$). The proof is symmetric if ϕ_2 is false in M, if ϕ_1 is false in a member of $U_2(M)$, or if ϕ_2 is false in a member of $U_1(M)$. We conclude that in all these cases, the lemma holds.

Now suppose that ϕ_1 and ϕ_2 are true in M, that ϕ_1 is true in all members of $U_2(M)$, and ϕ_2 is true in all members of $U_1(M)$. Suppose that ω_1 and ω_2 contain non-equality atoms f and g, respectively, that unify under substitution σ. Then f and g satisfy the three tests of Step 2 of the NAP algorithm: (1) f and g do unify; (2) $\sigma \wedge \phi_1$ and $\sigma \wedge \phi_2$ are both satisfied, by assumption; and as ϕ_1 and ϕ_2 are both true in M, test (3) is also satisfied. This means that there is a write/write conflict between U_1 and U_2, a contradiction. We conclude that no non-equality

Figure 6.5. Determining whether an update is affordable.

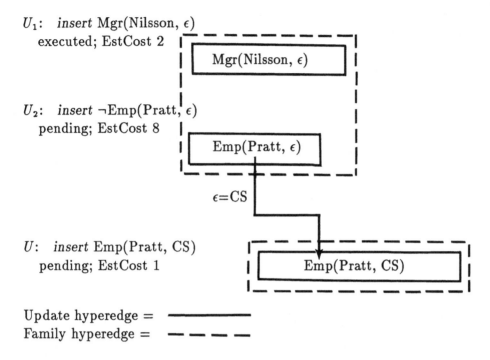

U_1: *insert* Mgr(Nilsson, ϵ)
   executed; EstCost 2

U_2: *insert* ¬Emp(Pratt, ϵ)
   pending; EstCost 8

U: *insert* Emp(Pratt, CS)
   pending; EstCost 1

Update hyperedge = ————————
Family hyperedge = — — — — —

atoms of ω_1 and ω_2 unify under σ. But then $(\omega_1)_\sigma$ and $(\omega_2)_\sigma$ are over disjoint sets of non-equality atoms, so any model in $U_2(U_1(M))$ is also in $U_1(U_2(M))$.

6.6. The Lazy Algorithm

When can a pending update U be executed? The rule is that U may be executed now if *U is affordable and all its ancestors in the lazy graph have been executed.* This determination is made by examining each update family in the lazy graph G. For U to be affordable, within each update family of G, the costs of the ancestors of U plus the costs of previously executed members of the family cannot exceed the cost limit for the family.

For example, let U be the incoming update *insert* Emp(Pratt, CS). Suppose the relevant portion of the lazy graph is as in Figure 6.5. Summing estimated costs (actual costs may be used for U_1 if available), it appears that no splits will be needed in this lazy graph if the cost limit l is at least

10. If the cost limit is less than 10, a split of U_2 is the most appropriate course of action.

As another example, the update *insert* $\epsilon =$ CS must be a root in its lazy graph, since it contains no data or history atoms; if its estimated cost is zero, then it may be executed at any time.

The test for affordability may be described more formally as follows.

Definitions.   *Let S be a set of updates and/or queries in a lazy graph. For each family F with an update or query in S, let $S(F)$ be the set of all updates or queries in family F that are in S or have already been executed. Then S is* affordable *if for each family F with an update or query in S,*

$$CostLimit(F) \quad \geq \quad \sum_{U \in S(F)} EstCost(U),$$

i.e., if the amount spent on executed updates and queries of F plus the amount estimated for updates and queries of F that are in S is no more than the cost limit for F. If S is not affordable, then S is expensive.

The Lazy Algorithm non-deterministically processes a query or update U of the lazy graph, working U into an executable position by splitting its ancestors to reduce their costs.

The Lazy Algorithm
Input. A lazy graph G with one particular update hyperedge, U, that is to be processed. Initially all update hyperedges of G are marked as being *unexamined*.
Output. An equivalent version of G and either an ACCEPT or REJECT verdict. If the verdict is ACCEPT, then all ancestors of U in G are now affordable. If the verdict is REJECT, then the cause of the rejection is also returned.
Procedure. A sequence of three steps:
Step 1. Accept U. If the set of all ancestors of U in G is affordable, then terminate with an ACCEPT verdict.
Step 2. Reject U. If all ancestors of U have been examined and any of them are expensive, send the user a REJECT verdict along with information on the reason for the rejection. This information can take the form of the family and update hyperedge labels and all family cost information for every

update and query on any path from an expensive ancestor to U. Then restore the lazy graph to its original state and terminate execution.

Step 3. Split ancestors. Choose a nearest[11] pending unexamined ancestor update U' of U. Guess a sequence of splits for U', and perform them using the Splitting Algorithm. Mark U' as examined, if it still exists; otherwise mark the updates split off from U' as examined. Go back to Step 1.

If the Lazy Algorithm accepts node U, then to execute U, choose an affordable pending ancestor update U' whose ancestor updates in the induced update graph have all been executed. Execute U', afterwards marking its hyperedge as executed. Repeat until U itself has been executed and so marked. If every update hyperedge in a family hyperedge has been executed, then all nodes, hyperedges, and incident arcs of that family can be removed from G.

In the case of a REJECT verdict, the Lazy Algorithm may return a great deal of information to the user. This is because there are many possible ways to make an update cheaper, including retroactively reducing the cost of previously executed members of an update family. To make the best choice for cost reduction, the user may need all that information.

For the Lazy Algorithm to work according to expectations, it must satisfy a number of requirements. First, if the Lazy Algorithm accepts an update or query U, then no family cost bounds may be exceeded during execution of the ancestors of U. Fortunately, this follows immediately from Step 1 and the fact that the cost estimate function is guaranteed not to underestimate costs as defined by the database administrator.

Second, we must show that the splits performed in Step 3 of the Lazy Algorithm map one correct lazy graph into another "equivalent" graph. The following section presents a large repertoire of splitting techniques and proves that they meet this requirement.

Finally, Theorem 6.1 guarantees that the relational theory will reach a correct final state as long as the updates in the lazy graph are executed in topological sort order. However, we need a characterization of the *intermediate* state of the relational theory, in particular, of the state of the relational theory when a query U and all its ancestors have just been executed; for that is the state that the user glimpses. Intuitively, for U a

---

[11] A *nearest ancestor* of U with property P, if one exists, is an ancestor U' of U with property P such that no other ancestor of U with property P has a shorter path to U than U' does.

leaf of the lazy graph, at an intermediate stage the alternative worlds of the relational theory are correct *when projected onto just the atoms in the update or query U*.

To explore this last point more formally, new terminology is in order. We distinguish the case where ω contains the equality predicate or is unsatisfiable (an *assertion*). Assertions are different from other updates in that they may eliminate some alternative worlds of a theory to which they are applied. Updates that are not assertions, on the other hand, cannot eliminate any alternative worlds of a theory: for if ω is satisfiable and does not contain the equality predicate, an insertion always produces some model from any model to which it is applied. If ω is satisfiable but contains the equality predicate, then the update may eliminate some models by conflicting with their null substitutions. For example, *insert* $\epsilon = $ CS will eliminate all models where ϵ is not mapped to CS. The distinction between these types of updates is important because most users will want execution of queries to force execution of all[12] pending assertions, because assertions may affect the answer to the query by eliminating the alternative worlds where some potential answers to the query are true. In other words, assertions reduce the amount of incomplete information, allowing answers to queries to be more precise and therefore more useful.

Definition. *Let S be a set of atoms, T a relational theory, and M a model of T with null substitution σ. Then* World(M) *restricted to S (written World(M)$|S$) is the wff form[13] of the truth valuations in M of atoms in $(S)_\sigma$. Further,*

$$Worlds(T)|S \;=\; \bigcup_{M \in \text{Models}(T)} \{World(M)|S\}.$$

Theorem 6.2. *Suppose the updates and queries of a lazy graph G formed by the NAP algorithm have topological sort $U_1 \cdots U_n Q$. Let S be the set containing all atoms of Q, and let T be a relational the-*

---

[12] Well, up to the limits imposed by the user's patience.

[13] A truth valuation v can be written in wff form as a conjunction of literals, such that the atom a is a conjunct of v in wff form iff a receives the truth valuation T under v, and $\neg a$ is a conjunct of v in wff form iff a receives the truth valuation F under v.

ory. If Toposort is a reverse topological sort of the ancestors of Q, then $Worlds(Toposort(T))|S \subseteq Worlds(Q(U_n(\cdots U_1(T) \cdots)))|S$. Further, if A is a reverse topological sort of Q and the assertions in G, and all their ancestors, then $Worlds(Q(U_n(\cdots U_1(T) \cdots)))|S = Worlds(A(T))|S$.

Proof of Theorem 6.2. Choose a particular topological sort F of all the updates and queries of G. Let A be derived from F by deleting all updates and queries of F that are not assertions or ancestors of Q. Let Toposort be derived from A by deleting all updates and queries that are not assertions, ancestors of assertions, Q, or ancestors of Q. Then by Theorem 6.1, $Worlds(F(T)) = Worlds(Q(U_n(\cdots U_1(T) \cdots)))$. It therefore suffices to show that $Worlds(F(T))|S = Worlds(A(T))|S$, and $Worlds(Toposort(T))|S \subseteq Worlds(F(T))|S$.

There must be a rightmost position in which A and F contain different updates or queries. Suppose that the occupant of that position is U in F. Then U does not appear in A. Therefore U is not Q, an ancestor of Q, an assertion, or an ancestor of an assertion. Let M be a model of T with null substitution σ. When U is applied to M, it may change the alternative world of M but it cannot eliminate that world, as ω_U must be satisfiable. If ϕ_U is false in M, then U does not change the alternative world of M, and so eliminating U from F would not change the alternative worlds eventually produced from M. If ϕ_U is true in M, then U may change the alternative world of M. However, U is not an ancestor of Q. If $(U)_\sigma$ has no atoms in common with any member of $(Left(U))_\sigma$, that is, the sequence of queries and updates $Q \cdots U'$ appearing to the left of U in F, then $Worlds(Left(U)(U(M)))|S = Worlds(Left(U)(M))|S$. If a data or history atom f of ω_U unifies under σ with an atom g of U', for U' any member of $Left(U)$, then it must be the case that test (2) or (3) of Step 2 of the NAP algorithm is violated for f and g, i.e., that $\phi_{U'}$ is false in M and in all descendants of M. In this case, when U' is executed, it cannot change the alternative world of M or any descendant of M. Therefore eliminating U from F cannot change the effect of U'. We conclude that U can be removed from F without changing the alternative worlds of $F(T)$ restricted to S. By induction, $Worlds(F(T))|S = Worlds(A(T))|S$. By the same argument, $Worlds(Toposort(T))|S \subseteq Worlds(A(T))|S$, so it follows that $Worlds(Toposort(T))|S \subseteq Worlds(A(T))|S$.

Theorem 6.2 implies that unless all assertions are executed, a query may give less precise answers than is otherwise possible. In particular, it may report that a sentence α is true in some alternative worlds and false in others when, if all assertions were executed, it would be known that in fact α had the same truth valuation in all alternative worlds.

6.7. Update Splitting

To reduce the cost of the ancestors of a query or update that needs to be executed, the Lazy Algorithm makes use of a formalization of the *splitting techniques* illustrated in Section 6.1. There are two varieties of *splits*, or divisions of an update U into a sequence of updates: *horizontal splits*, in which disjuncts, conjuncts, or atoms of ω or ϕ are removed from U, generating a sequence of two updates to replace U; and *vertical splits*, in which U is split into multiple updates by conjoining a substitution or other formula ϕ to one version of U and $\neg\phi$ to the other. When an update is split, the resulting updates belong to the same family as did the original, and hence apply to the same cost bound as did the original. In addition, there are certain logical manipulations of ϕ and ω that can be useful, and they will be discussed also.

There are many ways to split an update. Given an update or query U in the lazy graph to process, in the worst case the best way to split the ancestors of U will not be at all obvious. In fact, in a deterministic version of the Lazy Algorithm, one can easily spend time exponential in the size of the lazy graph (assuming $\mathcal{P} \neq \mathcal{NP}$) just trying to decide how to split U's ancestors; the update split that initially looks most advantageous may turn out to cause an unacceptable increase in the costs of that update's ancestors. This plethora of possibilities does not lead to nice theorems telling when the Lazy Algorithm will accept U, or even to a nice algorithm for trying out all the possibilities. For that reason, we present a large repertoire of splits but only present a characterization of the performance of the Lazy Algorithm for a small subset of these splits.

6.7.1. A Repertoire of Splits

In a horizontal split, selected atoms are removed from ϕ or ω of an update U. Horizontal splits can be helpful when U is an ancestor of the incoming query Q, and some expensive part of U is not actually relevant to Q at all. For example, in *insert $\alpha \vee g$ where ϕ*, if g is expensive and not needed for the execution of Q, it will be advantageous to split g off, because the estimated cost of *insert α where ϕ* will doubtless be lower than that for U. It is possible to split between conjuncts of ω or disjuncts of ω or ϕ, and also to remove individual atoms from ω. These four types of splits will be covered in Splitting Rules 1 through 4, which map an update U into an *equivalent* sequence of updates:

Definition.   *If S_1 and S_2 are two sequences of updates over a language L, then S_1 and S_2 are* equivalent *under a particular update algorithm if for every relational theory T over L, Worlds($S_1(T)$) = Worlds($S_2(T)$) when the updates are performed under that algorithm.*

One obstacle to splitting an update U into U_1 and U_2 is that when U_2 is executed, U_2 must have some means of locating those alternative worlds where U is not yet completed. For example, suppose that U is *insert ω where ϕ*, to be split into U_1 and U_2, where U_1 is *insert ω_1 where ϕ*. Then in general U_2 cannot also use selection clause ϕ, because ω_1 may have changed the truth valuations for atoms in ϕ. A more promising candidate for U_2's selection clause is $(\phi)_{\sigma_{HU_1}}$, where σ_{HU_1} is the history substitution for U_1. However, there are two drawbacks to the use of $(\phi)_{\sigma_{HU_1}}$ in U_2. First, a future update with ancestor U may need to write some of the atoms in $(\phi)_{\sigma_{HU_1}}$, and there will be a read/write conflict between U_2 and that update, forcing sequential execution. Second, U may be split many times before it is fully executed. Every split-off update will incur costs associated with ϕ. Even if ω is very simple, the added expense of dealing with $(\phi)_{\sigma_{HU_1}}$, $((\phi)_{\sigma_{HU_1}})_{\sigma_{HU_2}}$, etc. may push the total cost for U beyond the cost limit, and force rejection of queries.

The solution to this difficulty is to make ϕ_{U_2} as short as possible. The technique for doing so has been presented once before, in the discussion of computational complexity of the Update Algorithm Version I in Chapter 4. There the goal was to minimize the amount of space required for formula 4.2, by defining a new history atom $H(U)$ via the formula $H(U) \leftrightarrow \phi$, and adding this formula to T just after Step 1 of the Update Algorithm. This is adapted to the current case as follows.

Definition.   *If an update U: insert ω where ϕ is split into U_1 and U_2, then U_1* defines $H(U)$ *if $H(U)$ is a new[13] history atom and during the execution of U_1, after Step 1 of the Update Algorithm, the formula $H(U) \leftrightarrow \phi$ is added to T.*

Once defined, $H(U)$ can be used by subsequent updates; $H(U)$ is just a history atom that will be true in a model M iff ϕ was true in the precursor to that model just before U_1 was executed. $H(U)$ is an inexpensive way of marking the models where ϕ is true so that one can come back later and

---

[13] A *new* history atom is one which does not unify with any history atom in T or in a pending update.

finish U easily. In many of our splitting rules, U_1 will define a history atom that is subsequently used by U_2. In the previous example, U_2 can use $H(U)$ as its selection clause rather than $(\phi)_{\sigma_{HU_1}}$. By this means, history atoms can now appear in split-off updates.

Please note that if U defines a history atom and U is itself to be split into U_1 and U_2, then U_1 inherits the job of defining that history atom.

Splitting Rule 1.   *Splits between conjuncts of ω. If no data or history atom in ω_1 unifies with an atom of ω_2, then the update U: insert $\omega_1 \wedge \omega_2$ where ϕ is equivalent under the Update Algorithm to the sequence of updates*

U_1:   *insert ω_1 where ϕ,*
U_2:   *insert ω_2 where $H(U)$,*

where U_1 defines $H(U)$.

When U is split into U_1 and U_2, if ϕ is T, then the expense of defining $H(U)$ is unnecessary. It is preferable in this case not to define $H(U)$ at all. This will be done in the examples of this chapter.

Example 6.6.   insert Emp(Pratt, CS) $\wedge$ Emp(Pratt, EE) is equivalent to the sequence of updates

insert Emp(Pratt, CS),
insert Emp(Pratt, EE).

Proofs of correctness for these splitting rules are collected in Section 6.7.2.

Selection clauses are not the only places where extra history atoms are useful for marking models where updating is to be completed later. The case where ω is a disjunction, e.g., $R(a) \vee R(b)$, is a good illustration. If we want to insert just $R(a)$ for now and complete the disjunction later, then there must be some way of identifying the models where $R(b)$ should be inserted later. A new history atom is the best solution.

Splitting Rule 2.   *Splits between disjuncts of ω. If no data or history atom in ω_1 unifies with an atom of ω_2, then the update U: insert $\omega_1 \vee \omega_2$ where ϕ is equivalent under the Update Algorithm to the sequence of updates*

U_1:   *insert $\omega_1 \vee H(U_1)$ where ϕ,*
U_2:   *insert $H(U_1) \leftrightarrow \omega_2$ where $H(U)$,*

where $H(U_1)$ is a new history atom, and U_1 defines $H(U)$.

Please note that in Splitting Rule 2, U_1 does not *define* $H(U_1)$, but merely uses it.

Example 6.7. The update U: *insert* Emp(Pratt, CS) $\vee$ Emp(Pratt, ϵ) is equivalent to the sequence of updates
insert Emp(Pratt, CS) $\vee$ $H(U_1)$,
insert $H(U_1) \leftrightarrow$ Emp(Pratt, ϵ).

Splitting Rule 2 would not work if the Update Algorithm treated history atoms as it does data atoms. For if it did, then U_2 would change the truth valuation of $H(U_1)$, rather than using it to identify the models where the update is incomplete. The proofs of these Splitting Rules will show that nothing in the Update Algorithm or in its proof of correctness prevents the use of history atoms in certain situations within updates; the system may as well make internal use of history atoms whenever this is convenient and correct.

To see the necessity of the restriction in Splitting Rules 1 and 2 that atoms of ω_1 and ω_2 must not unify, consider the update *insert* Emp(Pratt, CS) $\vee$ Emp(Pratt, CS). This update is not equivalent to the sequence of updates
insert Emp(Pratt, CS) $\vee$ $H(U)$,
insert Emp(Pratt, CS) $\leftrightarrow H(U)$,
because those two updates may create alternative worlds where Emp(Pratt, CS) is false. For example, if T has an empty body, then U_1 will produce a model M where Emp(Pratt, CS) is true and $H(U)$ is false, and U_2 will make Emp(Pratt, CS) false in M. A similar problem occurs with the update *insert* Emp(Pratt, CS) $\wedge \neg$ Emp(Pratt, CS).

Using DeMorgan's laws and Splitting Rules 1 and 2, one can completely pick apart many ωs, using no more splits than there are conjunctions and disjunctions[13] in ω. Splitting Rules 1 and 2 only apply when ω takes a special form, however, and even when ω is in that form, at times it may be annoying to have to dissect ω just to get at one important data atom. Splitting Rule 3 allows a one-step isolation of any set of data atoms in ω; however, it may require the use of more history atoms than would be needed if Splitting Rules 1 and 2 were repeatedly applied.

Though ω_{U_2} in Splitting Rule 3 is intimidating, the intent is simple. If f is an atom of U to be removed from ω, then replace f by a history atom f_F in ω. Call this history substitution σ_F. Then let U_1 insert $(\omega)_{\sigma_F}$, and

---

[13] Express any other binary operations in ω in terms of $\wedge$, $\vee$, and $\neg$.

let U_2 insert $f \leftrightarrow f_F$. The alarming second term of ω_{U_2} in Splitting Rule 3 is vacuously true unless f unifies with an atom of $(\omega)_{\sigma_F}$—the same case that caused restrictions in Splitting Rules 1 and 2. The second conjunct of ω_{U_2} in Splitting Rule 3 says that in models where f unifies with an atom of $(\omega)_{\sigma_F}$, U_2 cannot change the truth valuation of f. Just how U_2 accomplishes that is a bit mysterious: $(f)_{\sigma_{HU_2}}$ is an atom from U_2's *own* history substitution.

Splitting Rule 3.   *Removal of selected atoms from ω. Let U be the update insert ω where ϕ. Let F be a subset of the data atoms that occur in ω. Let σ_F be the history substitution that replaces every atom f in F by a history atom f_F.[14] Then U is equivalent under the Update Algorithm to the sequence of updates*

$$U_1 : \quad \text{insert } (\omega)_{\sigma_F} \text{ where } \phi,$$

$$U_2 : \quad \text{insert } \bigwedge_{f \in F} \Big((f \leftrightarrow f_F) \wedge$$

$$\Big((\bigvee_{\sigma \in \Sigma} \sigma) \quad \rightarrow (f \leftrightarrow (f)_{\sigma_{HU_2}}) \Big) \Big) \text{ where } H(U),$$

where U_1 defines $H(U)$, σ_{HU_2} is the history substitution for the update in which it occurs, and Σ is the set containing the formula F and all substitutions σ such that for some atom g in $(\omega)_{\sigma_F}$, f unifies with g under most general substitution σ.

Intuitively, this type of split is useful when the atoms in F are too expensive or else need to be isolated from the other atoms of ω to facilitate vertical splitting of ω. U_1 leaves placeholders for those atoms in ω, in the form of history atoms. When the atoms of F become affordable later on, their truth valuations can be tied to those of the history atoms in σ_F through update U_2.

Example 6.8.   Let U be the update *insert* $(\neg R(a) \vee R(b)) \wedge (R(c) \vee \neg R(b))$, and let Q be the query *insert* $Q(b)$ *where* $R(b)$. Suppose that U is expensive, and the only conflict preventing execution of Q is the write/read dependency on $R(b)$. Then $R(b)$ can be split out of U in one step by creating the two updates

U_1:   *insert* $(\neg R(a, F) \vee R(b)) \wedge (R(c, F) \vee \neg R(b))$,

---

[14] By analogy to U in f_U, F in f_F is a unique constant not previously used in any history atom, so that f_F does not unify with any preexisting history atom.

U_2: *insert* $(R(a) \leftrightarrow R(a, F)) \wedge (R(c) \leftrightarrow R(c, F))$.

Example 6.9. Let U be the update *insert* $(\epsilon = a) \wedge R(\epsilon) \wedge \neg R(a)$. As ω is unsatisfiable, this update should eliminate all alternative worlds of any theory to which it is applied. Splitting U with Splitting Rule 3 produces

U_1: *insert* $(\epsilon = a) \wedge R(\epsilon) \wedge \neg R(a, F)$,
U_2: *insert* $(R(a) \leftrightarrow R(a, F)) \wedge ((\epsilon = a) \rightarrow (R(a, F) \leftrightarrow R(a, U_2))))$.

Without this final conjunct of ω in U_2, U_1 and U_2 applied to a relational theory with empty body would produce an alternative world in which $R(a)$ is false. The additional conjunct correctly eliminates all alternative worlds.

Splitting Rule 4. *Splits between disjuncts of ϕ. The update U: insert ω where $\phi_1 \vee \phi_2$ is equivalent under the Update Algorithm to the sequence of updates*

U_1: *insert* ω *where* ϕ_1,
U_2: *insert* ω *where* $(\phi_2)_{\sigma_{HU_1}}$,

where σ_{HU_1} is the history substitution for U_1.

Example 6.10. The update *insert* Emp(Pratt, CS) *where* Emp(Pratt, EE) $\vee$ Mgr(Nilsson, ϵ) is equivalent to the sequence of updates

U_1: *insert* Emp(Pratt, CS) *where* Emp(Pratt, EE),
U_2: *insert* Emp(Pratt, CS) *where* Mgr(Nilsson, ϵ).

Though Splitting Rule 4 shows that it is possible to split between disjuncts of ϕ, in general it is not possible to split between conjuncts of ϕ, as all conjuncts of ϕ are needed to determine whether an alternative world is to be affected by the update.

We now turn to an examination of vertical splitting. In Splitting Rule 5 below, typically ϕ' will be a substitution σ, and there will be an update or query Q that depends on the results of U for some pair of atoms of Q and U that unify under substitution σ. It may be much cheaper to execute U only in those models where σ is true, rather than in all models where ϕ is true. This typically occurs if nulls in the updates U and U_2 cause the unacceptable expense in U. For example, if U is *insert* Mgr(Nilsson, ϵ) *where* Emp(Pratt, ϵ), and Q is *insert* Q(Nilsson) *where* Mgr(Nilsson, CS), then Q has a write/read dependency on U. However, this dependency only materializes in models where $\epsilon = $ CS. If U is split into U_1: *insert* Mgr(Nilsson, ϵ) *where* Emp(Pratt, ϵ) $\wedge \epsilon = $ CS and U_2: *insert* Mgr(Nilsson,

ϵ) where $\text{Emp}(\text{Pratt}, \epsilon) \wedge \epsilon \neq \text{CS}$, then U_1 may well be affordable though U is not. U_2 can be executed later, as it will not be an ancestor of Q.

Splitting Rule 5.   *Vertical Splits. Let U be the update insert ω where ϕ. If ϕ' is a ground formula, then U is equivalent under the Update Algorithm to the sequence of updates*

U_1:   *insert ω where $\phi \wedge \phi'$ and*
U_2:   *insert ω where $H(U) \wedge \neg(\phi')_{\sigma_{HU_1}}$,*

where U_1 defines $H(U)$.

Example 6.11.   Let U be the update *insert* $\text{Emp}(\text{Pratt}, \epsilon)$, and let U' be the update *insert* $\text{Emp}(\text{Pratt}, \text{CS})$ *where* $\text{Mgr}(\text{Nilsson}, \text{CS})$. There is a write/write dependency between U and U'; but this dependency only occurs for models where ϵ is bound to CS. If U is too expensive, try splitting U into

U_1:   *insert* $\text{Emp}(\text{Pratt}, \epsilon)$ *where* $\epsilon = \text{CS}$,
U_2:   *insert* $\text{Emp}(\text{Pratt}, \epsilon)$ *where* $\epsilon \neq \text{CS}$.

Then U' does not depend on U_2, and U_1 may well be affordable.

   Sometimes two updates are guaranteed not to depend on one another by virtue of the fact that they take place in disjoint sets of alternative worlds. For example, the updates

insert $\text{Emp}(\text{Pratt}, \epsilon)$ *where* $\epsilon = \text{CS}$ and
insert $\neg\text{Emp}(\text{Pratt}, \epsilon)$ *where* $\epsilon \neq \text{CS}$

will produce the same effect no matter which update is executed first. The NAP algorithm takes advantage of any such opportunities created by vertical splitting, by eliminating dependencies of this sort between updates. However, it is not sufficient that the selection clauses of the two updates be mutually exclusive; for example, the effect of the two updates

insert $\text{Emp}(\text{Pratt}, \text{CS})$ *where* $\neg \text{Emp}(\text{Pratt}, \text{CS})$ and
insert $\neg\text{Emp}(\text{Pratt}, \text{CS})$ *where* $\text{Emp}(\text{Pratt}, \text{CS})$

depends upon the order in which they are executed.

   Logical massage of ϕ and ω can be used to reduce the cost of Step 1 of the Update Algorithm, by removing atoms from U that do not occur in T or in pending ancestors of U. By applying a substitution σ to ϕ or ω, sometimes the resulting atoms in ϕ and ω already occur in T even though the original atoms did not. Of course, this sword cuts both ways: applying σ may turn an atom that did occur in T into one requiring expenditures during Step 1.

Splitting Rule 6.   *Logical massage. The four updates*

U_1: insert ω where $\phi \wedge \sigma$,
U_2: insert $(\omega)_\sigma$ where $\phi \wedge \sigma$,
U_3: insert ω where $(\phi)_\sigma \wedge \sigma$,
U_4: insert $(\omega)_\sigma$ where $(\phi)_\sigma \wedge \sigma$,

where σ is a ground substitution, are all equivalent.

Of course the splits and rearrangements presented in the preceding splitting rules are not the only possible manipulations of updates; for example, U can be replaced by any other equivalent update.

6.7.2. Correctness Proofs for Splits

Readers not interested in formal proofs of correctness for the splits of the previous section should proceed to Section 6.7.3.

Proof of Splitting Rule 1.   Let M be a model of relational theory T with null substitution σ. Let M_{U_1} be a model of $U_1(T)$, such that World$(M_{U_1}) \in$ Worlds$(U_1(M))$. Let M_{U_2} be a model of $U_2(U_1(T))$, such that World$(M_{U_2}) \in$ Worlds$(U_2(M_{U_1}))$. Then ϕ is true in M iff $H(U)$ is true in M_{U_1}, by the arguments of Theorem 5.1. If ϕ is true in M, then $\omega_1 \wedge \omega_2$ is true in M_{U_2}, because $(\omega_1)_\sigma$ and $(\omega_2)_\sigma$ have no data or history atoms in common. Therefore World$(M_{U_2}) \in$ Worlds$(U(M))$.

If ϕ is false in M, then $H(U)$ is false in M_{U_1}, and World$(M_{U_2}) \in$ Worlds$(U(M))$. The reverse implication is symmetric.

Proof of Splitting Rule 2.   This proof follows the outline of the proof of Splitting Rule 3, with significant differences only in the forward and reverse proofs of correctness for Step 3. The revised forward and reverse proofs for Step 3 follow:

In the definition of M_U and M_{U_2}, also define the truth valuation of $H(U_1)$: let $H(U_1)$ be true in M_{U_2} iff ω_2 is true in M_U.

Consider those formulas added to $U_2(U_1(T))$ during Step 3 of U_1 or U_2. By definition M_{U_2} satisfies $(\phi)_{\sigma_{HU}} \rightarrow (\omega_1 \vee \omega_2)$. We must show that M_{U_2} satisfies $((\phi)_{\sigma_{HU_1}})_{\sigma_{HU_2}} \rightarrow ((\omega_1)_{\sigma_{HU_2}} \vee H(U_1))$ and $((\phi)_{\sigma_{HU_1}})_{\sigma_{HU_2}} \rightarrow (H(U_1) \leftrightarrow \omega_2)$. The latter formula is true by definition of the truth valuation of $H(U_1)$ in M_{U_2}. For the other formula, since no data or history atom of ω_1 unifies with an atom of ω_2, it follows that $(\omega_1)_{\sigma_{HU_2}}$ is identical to ω_1. But then by definition of M_{U_2}, $((\phi)_{\sigma_{HU_1}})_{\sigma_{HU_2}} \rightarrow ((\omega_1)_{\sigma_{HU_2}} \vee H(U_1))$ is satisfied in M_{U_2}.

For the reverse implication, consider the formula added to $U(T)$ during Step 3 of U: $(\phi)_{\sigma_{HU}} \to \omega$. We know M_U satisfies

$$((\phi)_{\sigma_{HU_1}})_{\sigma_{HU_2}} \to ((\omega_1)_{\sigma_{HU_2}} \vee H(U_1))$$

and

$$((\phi)_{\sigma_{HU_1}})_{\sigma_{HU_2}} \to (\omega_2 \leftrightarrow H(U_1)).$$

Again, because no data or history atom of ω_1 unifies with an atom of ω_2, it follows that $(\omega_1)_{\sigma_{HU_2}}$ is identical to ω_1. Therefore the latter two formulas together logically imply that $((\phi)_{\sigma_{HU_1}})_{\sigma_{HU_2}} \to (\omega_1 \vee \omega_2)$ is true in M_U. Then by the definition of M_U, $(\phi)_{\sigma_{HU}} \to (\omega_1 \vee \omega_2)$ is true in M_U.

Proof of Splitting Rule 3. Let σ_{HU}, σ_{HU_1}, and σ_{HU_2} be the history substitutions for U, U_1, and U_2, respectively. First we show that any world produced by U under the Update Algorithm is also produced by U_1 followed by U_2.

Let M_U be a model of $U(T)$. Let M_{U_2} be a model identical to M_U except that for every data atom f, the history atoms f_{U_1}, f_{U_2}, and f_F are given the following truth valuations in M_{U_2}:[14]

$H(f, U_1)$ gets the same valuation as $H(f, U)$

$H(f, F)$ gets the same valuation as f

$H(f, U_2)$ gets the same valuation as f, if $\exists g \mid g \in (\omega)_{\sigma_F}$ and $f \sim_{\sigma'} g$

$H(f, U_2)$ gets the same valuation as $H(f, U)$, otherwise.

In addition, let $H(U)$ be true in M_{U_2} iff ϕ is true in M. Note that $H(U)$ is true in M_{U_2} iff $((\phi)_{\sigma_{HU_1}})_{\sigma_{HU_2}}$ is true in M_{U_2}; this correspondence will be used throughout the formulas in this proof without special notice, by replacing occurrences of $H(U)$ by an equivalent expression over ϕ.

Clearly M_U and M_{U_2} represent the same alternative world. To show that World(M_{U_2}) $\in$ Worlds($U_2(U_1(M))$), we will consider all the possible reasons that a particular formula might be in $U_2(U_1(T))$, and show that in each case, M satisfies that formula.

---

[14] For α a formula, theory, or substitution, and g an atom, the notation $g \in \alpha$ means "g occurs in α." If α is a hyperedge or set of nodes in a graph, then the notation $g \in \alpha$ means that the node g is on the hyperedge or in the set of nodes α. The notation $f \sim_\sigma g$ means that f unifies with g under most general substitution σ.

First suppose α is a formula of the body of T. Then under the Update Algorithm, $U_2(U_1(T))$ contains the formula $((\alpha)_{\sigma_{HU_1}})_{\sigma_{HU_2}}$. M_{U_2} satisfies $(\alpha)_{\sigma_{HU}}$, and by definition therefore also satisfies $((\alpha)_{\sigma_{HU_1}})_{\sigma_{HU_2}}$.

Now consider the formulas added to T during Step 1 of update U_1. If f is an atom of $(\omega)_{\sigma_P}$, then $U_2(U_1(T))$ contains the formula

$$((f \to \bigvee_{\substack{g \in T \\ f \sim_\sigma g}} \sigma)_{\sigma_{HU_1}})_{\sigma_{HU_2}}. \tag{6.1}$$

Since $U(T)$ contains the formula

$$(f \to \bigvee_{\substack{g \in T \\ f \sim_\sigma g}} \sigma)_{\sigma_{HU}}, \tag{6.2}$$

it follows by definition that formula 6.1 is satisfied by M_{U_2}. If f is an atom in F, then $U_2(U_1(T))$ also contains the formula

$$(f \to (\bigvee_{\substack{g \in T \\ f \sim_\sigma g}} \sigma \vee \bigvee_{\substack{g \notin T, g \in (\omega)_{\sigma_F} \\ f \sim_\sigma g}} \sigma))_{\sigma_{HU_2}}. \tag{6.3}$$

Since formula 6.2 implies formula 6.3 under the definition of M_{U_2}, it follows that formula 6.3 is satisfied by M_{U_2}.

Now consider those formulas added to $U_2(U_1(T))$ during Step 3 of U_1 or U_2. We first show that $(\phi)_{\sigma_{HU}}$ is true in M_{U_2} iff $((\phi)_{\sigma_{HU_1}})_{\sigma_{HU_2}}$ is true in M_{U_2}.

If $(\phi)_{\sigma_{HU}}$ is true in M_{U_2}, then $((\phi)_{\sigma_{HU_1}})_{\sigma_{HU}}$ must also be true there, by definition of the truth valuations of $(f)_{\sigma_{HU_1}}$. Conversely, if an atom f of ϕ occurs in σ_{HU_2} but not σ_{HU_1}, then it must be the case that f unifies with an atom of F and does not unify with any atom of $(\omega)_{\sigma_P}$. But then by definition the truth valuation of f_U is the same as that of $(f)_{\sigma_{HU_2}}$. It follows that $(\phi)_{\sigma_{HU}}$ is true in M_{U_2} iff $((\phi)_{\sigma_{HU_1}})_{\sigma_{HU_2}}$ is also true there.

By definition M_{U_2} satisfies $(\phi)_{\sigma_{HU}} \to \omega$. We must show that M_{U_2} satisfies the formula $((\phi)_{\sigma_{HU_1}})_{\sigma_{HU_2}} \to ((\omega)_{\sigma_P})_{\sigma_{HU_2}}$, introduced during Step 3 of U_1. If $((\phi)_{\sigma_{HU_1}})_{\sigma_{HU_2}}$ is true in M_{U_2}, then $(\phi)_{\sigma_{HU}}$ is also true, and therefore ω is true in M_{U_2}. By definition of M_{U_2}, it follows that $((\omega)_{\sigma_P})_{\sigma_{HU_2}}$ is true in M_{U_2}. We must also show that

$$((\phi)_{\sigma HU_1})_{\sigma HU_2} \rightarrow \bigwedge_{f \in F} ((f \leftrightarrow f_F) \wedge ((\bigvee_{\sigma \in \Sigma} \sigma) \rightarrow (f \leftrightarrow (f)_{\sigma HU_2})))$$

is satisfied in M_{U_2}. But both conjuncts of this formula are true, by definition of Σ. Therefore M_{U_2} satisfies the formulas added during Step 3.

Now consider those formulas added to $U_2(U_1(T))$ during Step 4 of U_1 or U_2. M_{U_2} satisfies the formula of $U(T)$

$$\neg((\phi)_{\sigma HU} \wedge \bigvee_{\substack{g \in \omega \\ f \sim_\sigma g}} \sigma) \rightarrow (f \leftrightarrow f_U), \tag{6.4}$$

for each atom f in $U(T)$ that unifies with an atom of $(\omega)_{\sigma F}$ or F.

If f in $U_2(U_1(T))$ unifies with an atom of $(\omega)_{\sigma F}$, then $U_2(U_1(T))$ contains the formula

$$\neg(((\phi)_{\sigma HU_1})_{\sigma HU_2} \wedge \bigvee_{\substack{g \in (\omega)_{\sigma F} \\ f \sim_\sigma g}} \sigma) \rightarrow ((f)_{\sigma HU_2} \leftrightarrow f_{U_1}),$$

which is true by definition of f_{U_2} and f_{U_1}, if f unifies with an atom of F; and true by formula 6.4, otherwise.

If f in $U_2(U_1(T))$ unifies with an atom of F, then $U_2(U_1(T))$ contains the formula

$$\neg(((\phi)_{\sigma HU_1})_{\sigma HU_2} \wedge \bigvee_{\substack{f \sim_\sigma g \\ g \in F}} \sigma) \rightarrow (f \leftrightarrow f_{U_2}).$$

Since $(\phi)_{\sigma HU}$ is true iff $((\phi)_{\sigma HU_1})_{\sigma HU_2}$ is true, by the definition of M_{U_2} and formula 6.4 this formula is also satisfied by M_{U_2}. This establishes that M_{U_2} satisfies the formulas added during Step 4 of U_1 and U_2, and that M_{U_2} is a model of an alternative world of $U_2(U_1(T))$.

To show that models produced by U_1 and U_2 represent alternative worlds produced by U, suppose M_{U_2} is a model of $U_2(U_1(T))$. Let M_U be a model differing from M_{U_2} only in the following: f_U has the truth valuation in M_U of f_{U_1} in M_{U_2} if the data atom f unifies with an atom of σHU_1, and of f_{U_2} otherwise. Then M_{U_2} and M_U represent the same alternative world, and again we must show that M_U satisfies all the formulas of $U(T)$.

Let α be a formula of T. Then $(\alpha)_{\sigma_{HU}}$ occurs in $U(T)$. M_U satisfies $((\alpha)_{\sigma_{HU_1}})_{\sigma_{HU_2}}$, and therefore M_U satisfies $(\alpha)_{\sigma_{HU}}$.

Now consider formulas added to T in Step 1 of U: for each data atom f that occurs in ω but not T, $U(T)$ contains the formula

$$(f)_{\sigma_{HU}} \rightarrow \bigvee_{\substack{g \in T \\ f \sim_\sigma g}} \sigma. \tag{6.5}$$

For f in $(\omega)_{\sigma_F}$, M_U satisfies the formula of $U_2(U_1(T))$

$$(f)_{\sigma_{HU_1}} \rightarrow \bigvee_{\substack{g \in T \\ g \sim_\sigma f}} \sigma,$$

which implies that M_U satisfies formula 6.5 as well.

For data atoms f in σ_F, M_U satisfies the formula of $U_2(U_1(T))$

$$(f)_{\sigma_{HU_2}} \rightarrow (\bigvee_{\substack{g \in T \\ g \sim_\sigma f}} \sigma \vee \bigvee_{\substack{g \notin T \\ g \in (\omega)_{\sigma_F} \\ g \sim_\sigma f}} \sigma). \tag{6.6}$$

In formula 6.6, suppose $(f)_{\sigma_{HU_2}}$ is true in M_U. If the left-hand disjunct of 6.6 is true, then formula 6.5 is satisfied. Otherwise, for some g from the right-hand disjunct, g is true in M_U; therefore M_U must satisfy an instantiation of formula 6.5 for g. It follows that a left-hand disjunct of 6.6 must be true in M_U, and therefore 6.5 is satisfied by M_U.

The formulas added to $U(T)$ during Step 4 of U take the form, for f unifying with a data atom of ω,

$$\neg((\phi)_{\sigma_{HU}} \wedge \bigvee_{\substack{g \in \omega \\ g \sim_\sigma f}} \sigma) \rightarrow (f \leftrightarrow f_U) \tag{6.7}$$

If f unifies with a data atom of $(\omega)_{\sigma_F}$, and f occurs in T, ϕ, or $(\omega)_{\sigma_F}$, then M_U

satisfies the formula of $U_2(U_1(T))$

$$\neg(((\phi)_{\sigma_{HU_1}})_{\sigma_{HU_2}} \wedge \bigvee_{\substack{g \in (\omega)_{\sigma_F} \\ g \sim_\sigma f}} \sigma) \rightarrow ((f)_{\sigma_{HU_2}} \leftrightarrow f_{U_1}).$$

For f any data atom of $U(T)$ unifying with an atom of σ_F, M_U also satisfies

$$\neg(((\phi)_{\sigma_{HU_1}})_{\sigma_{HU_2}} \wedge \bigvee_{\substack{g \in F \\ g \sim_\sigma f}} \sigma) \rightarrow (f \leftrightarrow f_{U_2}). \tag{6.8}$$

If f does not unify with data atoms of both $(\omega)_{\sigma_F}$ and σ_F, then formula 6.7 is satisfied. Otherwise, if the left-hand disjunct of formula 6.8 is true in M_{U_2}, then by definition of M_U, formula 6.7 is satisfied in M_U. If the left-hand disjunct is false, then the right-hand one must be true; since the occurrence of a data atom g in F implies that g also occurs in ω, it follows that 6.7 is again satisfied for M_U.

Now consider the formula added to $U(T)$ during Step 3 of U: $(\phi)_{\sigma_{HU}} \rightarrow \omega$. By the same argument used in the forward direction of this proof, $((\phi)_{\sigma_{HU_1}})_{\sigma_{HU_2}}$ is true in M_{U_2} iff $(\phi)_{\sigma_{HU}}$ is true in M_{U_2}. It remains to show that ω is true when $((\phi)_{\sigma_{HU_1}})_{\sigma_{HU_2}}$ is true in M_{U_2}.

When $((\phi)_{\sigma_{HU_1}})_{\sigma_{HU_2}}$ is true in M_{U_2}, M_{U_2} must satisfy $((\omega)_{\sigma_F})_{\sigma_{HU_2}}$,

$$\bigwedge_{f \in F} (f \leftrightarrow f_F),$$

$$\bigvee_{\substack{g \in (\omega)_{\sigma_F} \\ f \sim_\sigma g \\ or \ \sigma = F}} \sigma \rightarrow (f_F \leftrightarrow (f)_{\sigma_{HU_2}}),$$

and formula 6.8. But these together imply that M_{U_2} satisfies $(\omega)_{\sigma_F}$. By definition of M_{U_2}, if $(\omega)_{\sigma_F}$ is true in M_{U_2}, then ω must be true in M_{U_2}. Therefore M_{U_2} satisfies the formulas added during Step 3 of U.

As M_U satisfies all the formulas added to T during the Update Algorithm for U, we conclude that $\text{Worlds}(U_2(U_1(T))) = \text{Worlds}(U(T))$.

Proof of Splitting Rule 4.   Let M be a model of T, and let M_{U_1} be a model such that $\text{World}(M_{U_1}) \in \text{Worlds}(U_1(M))$. First, by the arguments of Theorem 5.1, $(\phi_2)_{\sigma_{U_1}}$ is true in M_{U_1} iff ϕ_2 is true in M. It follows that Splitting Rule 4 is true for all models M of T where $\neg\phi_1 \wedge \neg\phi_2$, $\phi_1 \wedge \neg\phi_2$, or $\neg\phi_1 \wedge \phi_2$ is true. If $\phi_1 \wedge \phi_2$ is true in M, then ω will be inserted into M twice. But insertion of a formula is idempotent; for any update U, Worlds$(U(U(M)))$ = Worlds$(U(M))$. It follows that U is equivalent to the sequence of updates U_1 and U_2.

Proof of Splitting Rule 5.   Let M be a model of T, and let M_{U_1} be a model such that World$(M_{U_1}) \in$ Worlds$(U_1(M))$. By the proof of Theorem 5.1, $H(U)$ will be true in M_{U_1} iff ϕ is true in M. Therefore ϕ and ϕ' are true in M iff $(\phi)_{\sigma_{HU_1}}$ and $(\phi')_{\sigma_{HU_1}}$, respectively, are true in M_{U_1}. Reusing the proof of Splitting Rule 4, it follows that Worlds$(U_2(U_1(T)))$ = Worlds$(U(T))$.

Proof of Splitting Rule 6.   We will show that U_1 and U_4 are equivalent, and the proofs for the rest follow. Let M be a model of T, and let σ_1 be the null substitution for M. Let M_{U_1} be a model produced from M by the Update Algorithm for update U_1. Then $\phi \wedge \sigma$ is true in M iff $(\phi)_\sigma \wedge \sigma$ is true in M. If $\phi \wedge \sigma$ is false in M, the theorem follows. If $\phi \wedge \sigma$ is true in M, then σ_1 logically entails σ, so if ω is true in M_{U_1} then $(\omega)_\sigma$ is also. This implies that World$(M_{U_1}) \in$ Worlds$(U_4(T))$.

For the other direction, let M be as before, and let M_{U_4} be a model produced from M by U_4. Suppose that $(\phi)_\sigma \wedge \sigma$ is true in M, as otherwise the theorem follows. Then $(\omega)_\sigma$ is true in M_{U_4}. Since σ_1 logically entails σ, $((\omega)_\sigma)_{\sigma_1}$ is identical to $(\omega)_{\sigma_1}$, so $(\omega)_{\sigma_1}$ is true in M_{U_4}. It follows that World$(M_{U_4}) \in$ Worlds$(U_4(T))$.

6.7.3. The Splitting Algorithm

The Splitting Algorithm shows how to split update hyperedges in the lazy graph. Suppose an update U is to be split into the sequence of updates U_1 $\cdots U_n$. Intuitively, the job of the Splitting Algorithm is to move back in time to the moment when U was added to the lazy graph, and instead of adding U, successively add U_1 through U_n. Then all the updates that arrived after U can be added back into the lazy graph. As the proof of correctness for the Splitting Algorithm will illustrate, this can be done quite efficiently as long as in all vertical splits (Splitting Rule 5), ϕ' contains only equality atoms.

The Splitting Algorithm

Input: A lazy graph G containing update U, and the sequence of updates U_1 and U_2, produced by splitting U in accordance with Splitting Rules 1–4; or produced by Splitting Rule 5, if ϕ' contains only equality atoms; or a single update U_1, produced in accordance with Splitting Rule 6.

Output. An equivalent lazy graph G' in which U has been replaced by the new updates U_1 and/or U_2, as appropriate.

Procedure. A sequence of three steps:

Step 1. Add new nodes. Set G' to be G. Remove the nodes of U, the update hyperedge of U, and all arcs incident to nodes of U from G'. Apply the NAP algorithm to add update hyperedge U_1 to the family hyperedge of U in G'; but only consider as possible ancestors of U_1 those nodes that were ancestors of U in G. Repeat for U_2, if U_2 exists; but allow nodes of U_1 also to become ancestors of nodes in U_2.

Step 2. Check arcs to children of U. If there is an arc in G from a node of U to a node g not in U, apply Step 2 of the NAP algorithm and create, if Step 2 so requires, an arc from a node of U_1 or U_2 to g in G'.

Step 3. Reestimate costs for children of U. If there was an arc in G from a node of U to a node g not in U, then the cost information for g may change in G'. In particular, the number of unifications for g may decrease if some atom f of U that unified with g no longer occurs in T or in any pending ancestor of g. Adjust the unification counts to reflect these changes.

Example 6.12.   Given the lazy graph of Figure 6.4, if update U_1 is split horizontally according to Splitting Rule 2, the Splitting Algorithm produces

U_3: *insert* Emp(Pratt, ϵ_1) $\vee$ H(1) and
U_4: *insert* Mgr(Nilsson, ϵ_2) $\leftrightarrow H(1)$,

shown in the lazy graph produced by the Splitting Algorithm in Figure 6.6.

The part of the Splitting Algorithm in serious need of formal justification is its assumption that U_1 and U_2 have no descendants or ancestors other than those nodes that were ancestors or descendants of U. Theorem 6.3 shows that this assumption is in fact warranted. According to Theorem 6.3, close examination of any seemingly missing arcs of G' will show that the unifications under which those conflicts would occur will never materialize.

Theorem 6.3.   *Let S be a sequence of updates and queries containing update or query U. Let G be a lazy graph, created with the NAP and Splitting Algorithms, with topological sort S. Let G' be the lazy graph produced from G by the Splitting Algorithm when U is split into U_1 and U_2 (just U_1 if splitting in accordance with Splitting Rule 6). Let S' be the sequence created by replacing U in S by $U_1 U_2$ (just U_1 if splitting in accordance with Splitting Rule 6). Let G'' be the lazy graph greated by using the NAP algorithm to insert sequentially the updates and queries of S' into an initially empty lazy graph. Then if S_1 and S_2 are reverse topological sorts of G' and G'', respectively, then S_1 and S_2 are equivalent.*

The proof of this theorem will show that there may be arcs that the NAP

Figure 6.6. Splitting Algorithm example.

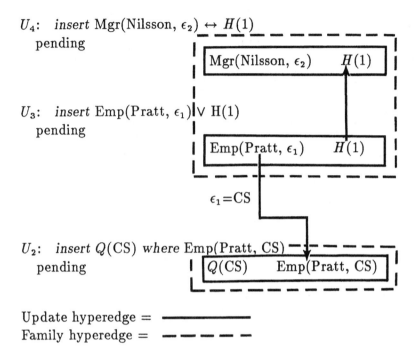

U_4: *insert* Mgr(Nilsson, ϵ_2) $\leftrightarrow$ $H(1)$
   pending

U_3: *insert* Emp(Pratt, ϵ_1) $\lor$ H(1)
   pending

$\epsilon_1 = CS$

U_2: *insert* $Q(CS)$ *where* Emp(Pratt, CS)
   pending

Update hyperedge = ————————
Family hyperedge = — — — — —

algorithm would include but the Splitting Algorithm does not; but for any such arc, external factors will prevent the conflict predicted by the arc from materializing. First a bit of terminology: we will use ϕ_U and ω_U to refer not only to those parts of U, but also to the sets of nodes on the lazy graph hyperedge for U whose labels occur in ϕ_U and ω_U, respectively.

Proof of Theorem 6.3.   Assume inductively that all splits previously performed in G have this property. Then if an arc labeled σ appears in G'' and not in G' (a *new* arc), its presence cannot lead to a violation of Theorem 6.3 unless one endpoint of the arc is in U_1 or U_2 and the other is outside U_1 and U_2. Suppose first that the endpoint is in U_1.

Looking at the formula that defines U_1 for the splits of Splitting Rule 1, there are no data atoms in U_1 that do not also occur in U; and the selection clause ϕ is the same as for U. Therefore, by Step 2 of the NAP algorithm, no new arc could possibly have an endpoint in U_1.

Looking at the formula that defines U_1 for the splits of Splitting Rule 2, there is only one data or history atom, $H(U_1)$, that did not also occur in U; and the selection clause ϕ is the same as it was in U. Therefore, by Step 2 of the NAP algorithm, any new arc must have $H(U_1)$ as an endpoint. But by definition $H(U_1)$ does not occur in any other update except U_2, or unify with any atom in any update except U_2. Therefore there can be no new arc with an endpoint in U_1.

For Splitting Rule 3, the same argument holds as for Splitting Rule 2.

For Splitting Rule 4, again there are no new atoms in U_1; however, ϕ has changed, so perhaps some unification that failed test (2) or (3) of Step 2 of the NAP algorithm will now succeed. However, for test (2), if $\sigma \wedge (\phi_1 \vee \phi_2)$ is unsatisfiable, then $\sigma \wedge \phi_1$ must be unsatisfiable as well. For test (3), if $\phi_1 \vee \phi_2$ logically entailed α, then so does ϕ_1. Therefore there can be no new arcs with an endpoint in U_1.

For Splitting Rule 5, by assumption ϕ' contains no non-equality atoms. Therefore there are no new data or history atoms in U_1, and by the argument for Splitting Rule 4, there can be no new arcs with an endpoint in U_1.

For Splitting Rule 6, there may indeed be new atoms in ω or ϕ, created by applying σ to previously existing atoms. However, if σ_1 is the label of the new arc, by Step 2 of the NAP algorithm, it must be the case that $\sigma_1 \wedge \phi \wedge \sigma$ is satisfiable, and so that arc should have been in G all along. We conclude that there can be no new arcs with an endpoint in U_1, for any type of split.

Now consider new arcs with an endpoint in U_2 and, say, U' as the other endpoint. For Splitting Rule 1, the only new atom in U_2 is $H(U)$. But by the argument used above for U_1 of Splitting Rule 1, no new arc can have $H(U)$ as an endpoint. Therefore if there is a new arc between U_2 and U', it must be because that arc formerly failed test (2) or (3) of the NAP algorithm Step 2, and now passes the test.

If test (3) was failed, suppose first that U_2 lies at the head of the new arc, and update or query U' lies at the tail of the arc. Let T be a relational theory with model M. Then by the definition of test (3), if ϕ_{U_2} is true in M, it must be the case that α, defined in test (3), is also true in M. As α contains only equality atoms, this property still holds for the descendants of M after any sequence of updates is applied to M. But this means that when U' is executed, its selection clause must be false in all the descendants of M. This means that the conflict predicted by the new arc can never materialize, as the result of applying U and U' to M is independent of the order in which they are applied. The proof is symmetric if U' lies at the head of the new arc and U_2 at the tail.

If test (2) was failed, $\sigma \wedge \phi$ was unsatisfiable. By the arguments of Theorem 5.1, $(\sigma \wedge \phi)_{\sigma HU_1}$ will also be unsatisfiable; by the same arguments, after any sequence of history substitutions, this property still holds. Therefore if $H(U)$ is true in a model, it must be the case that σ is false in that model, and therefore the predicted conflict does not actually occur because the unification needed for the dependency does not take place.

Consider the split of Splitting Rule 2. The same argument applies to $H(U)$ as for Splitting Rule 1. As $H(U_1)$ does not unify with any atom outside of U_1 and U_2, the theorem follows for that type of split.

The case of Splitting Rule 3 is identical to that of Splitting Rule 2.

For Splitting Rule 4, the arguments used for Splitting Rule 1 eliminate the possibility that any new arc from outside could have a history atom of $(\phi_2)_{\sigma HU_1}$ as an endpoint. Therefore if there is a new arc with U_2 as an endpoint, it must be because that arc formerly failed test (2) or test (3) of the NAP algorithm Step 2, and now passes these tests. If test (2) was failed, $\sigma \wedge (\phi_1 \vee \phi_2)$ was unsatisfiable, which implies that $\sigma \wedge \phi_2$ was unsatisfiable. By the arguments of Theorem 5.1, $(\sigma \wedge \phi_2)_{\sigma_{HU_1}}$ will also be unsatisfiable. And if test (3) was failed with selection clause $\phi_1 \vee \phi_2$ for U, then test (3) must still be failed when the selection clause is changed to ϕ_2. It follows that there can be no new arcs with an endpoint in U_2.

For Splitting Rule 5, ϕ' contains no non-equality atoms, so there are no new non-equality atoms in U_2 other than $H(U)$. By the argument used for Splitting Rule 1, no new arc can have $H(U)$ as an endpoint. The only remaining possibility is that some substitution now passes tests (2) and (3) of Step 2 of the NAP algorithm, but the argument used for Splitting Rule 1 also rules that out. We conclude that Theorem 6.3 is true.

6.8. Assertions

To drive the Lazy Algorithm, we need a policy on when updates should be processed and executed. At the very least, queries should force the execution of as many updates as are necessary to give a correct answer to the query. But update processing and execution cannot be entirely query-driven: early execution or at least special handling is required for assertions that are entered in response to a query rejection. For example, if the user is told that a query about an employee cannot be executed because of the atom Emp(ϵ, CS), the user might assert a value for ϵ and then reenter the query. The cost estimation function must take note of this new assertion about ϵ and reduce the cost estimates of pending updates in which ϵ occurs. Furthermore, the new information about ϵ can be used to reduce the size of the relational theory, in effect retroactively reducing the cost of all earlier updates that contained ϵ. Since the earlier updates have become more affordable than they originally were, their estimated costs should be decreased in accordance with the savings realized in T. We omit the algorithm for this aspect of lazy evaluation.

By letting update execution be entirely query-driven, we would miss some other opportunities to reduce the size of the relational theory and to reduce the cost estimates of other updates. For example, it is a good idea to execute helpful assertions (ones that narrow down the range of possible values for a null) right away. If helpful updates are being blocked from execution by expensive ancestors or by the presence of expensive atoms in the same update, it may be worthwhile to use the Lazy Algorithm to force execution of the helpful part of the update, rather than hold it in abeyance until query processing begins.

Another argument for early execution of assertions is that the user interface routines will probably force processing and execution of as many pending assertions as possible before presenting the user with the answer to a query, even though not all assertions need be executed before the query is executed. This is necessary if the most exact answer to a query is to be given, because any assertion can eliminate an alternative world that was relevant to the query, and in the process eliminate some candidate answer to the query.

6.9. Costs and Benefits of the Lazy Algorithm

As mentioned earlier, we have no nice worst-case theorems telling when a query or update U will be processable. This is due to the difficulty of splitting the selection clause ϕ of an update; if ϕ were as easy to split as ω is, then an excellent characterization would be possible of the benefits of the Lazy Algorithm. For this reason, we characterize the behavior of the Lazy Algorithm for a certain class of selection clauses ϕ. This characterization depends on three assumptions:

Assumption 1. The non-interacting ϕ requirement: *Let Q be the incoming query to be processed by the Lazy Algorithm. Then no data atom that occurs in ϕ in any proper ancestor of Q in the lazy graph can also occur in ω of another ancestor of Q.*

Assumption 1 says that any data atom read by a parent or higher ancestor of Q cannot also be written by an ancestor of Q.

Assumption 2.   *The cost estimation function must satisfy the following equation for any hyperedge or set of nodes U in the lazy graph:*

$$EstCost(U) = \sum_{f \in U} \begin{cases} 0, & f \text{ an equality atom;} \\ 1, & f \text{ a history atom;} \\ EstCost(f), & f \text{ a data atom.} \end{cases}$$

For a particular data atom node f, $EstCost(f)$ must depend only on the cost information stored at that node in the lazy graph.

The purpose of Assumption 2 is to ensure that the cost estimation function does not depend on hard-to-handle factors such as the number of update hyperedges in the lazy graph or the distance of an update from a root in the lazy graph. This is needed in order to establish a simple relationship between the estimated cost of the nodes of an update before and after the update is split.

Assumption 3. Judicious use of history atoms: *Let Q be an incoming query. At the time Q is added to the lazy graph, every history atom arc (i.e., an arc having an endpoint labeled with a history atom) in the lazy graph must have one endpoint in an executed update.*

History arcs should rarely prevent execution of an otherwise affordable update. The purpose of a history arc is to make sure that a history atom is defined before it is used; a split of U into U_1 and U_2 should always be performed so that if U_1 defines the history atom and U_1 is an ancestor of the query or update that is to be executed, then U_1 is not an ancestor solely because of history atom arcs. For example, consider the update

U: *insert* Emp(Pratt, ϵ) $\wedge$ Mgr(Nilsson, CS) *where* Mgr(Kennedy, EE)

and the incoming query

Q: *insert* Q(Nilsson) *where* Mgr(Nilsson, CS).

Suppose that Emp(Pratt, ϵ) makes U too expensive, and so U is split according to Splitting Rule 1 into

U_1:   *insert* Emp(Pratt, ϵ) *where* Mgr(Kennedy, EE)

U_2:   *insert* Mgr(Nilsson, CS) *where* $H(U)$,

where U_1 defines $H(U)$. This was a most foolish choice of splits, because Q still depends on U_1 through a history atom definition arc for $H(U)$. Either Mgr(Kennedy, EE) should have been used as the selection clause of U_2, or else Emp(Pratt, ϵ) should have been split out of U into U_2 rather than into U_1. Any reasonable choice of splitting heuristics should satisfy assumption 3.

Theorem 6.4 below gives a simple sufficient condition for queries to be accepted by the Lazy Algorithm. First a bit of terminology: For any formula α, let $\|\alpha\|$ be the number of different data and history atoms in α. EstCost(ϕ_U) is the sum of the estimated costs of nodes of ϕ_U.

Theorem 6.4.   *Let Q be an incoming query. If assumptions 1, 2, and 3 are satisfied, then Q will be accepted by the Lazy Algorithm if Q is affordable*

*and for each update family F in the lazy graph that contains a parent of Q,
the difference between the cost bound for F and the amount spent so far on
executed updates of F is at least*

$$\sum_{\substack{U \in F \\ U \text{ parent of } Q}} \left(\text{EstCost}(\phi_U) + \|\omega_U\| - 2 + \sum_{\substack{f \in \omega_U \\ g \in Q \\ f \sim_\sigma g}} (\text{EstCost}(f) + 3) \right). \quad (6.9)$$

Theorem 6.4 implies that when assumptions 1, 2, and 3 are satisfied, there
is a quick test for acceptability that only requires looking at the parents of
the query, rather than all ancestors of the query. The proof of the theorem
will show what splits to use to achieve this bound.

Proof of Theorem 6.4.   Let us examine how to split a particular parent U of
Q to achieve the bound in formula 6.9. Suppose f_1 through f_n are the data atoms
of ω_U that have arcs going out to atoms in Q. Then first split U horizontally
according to Splitting Rule 3, removing all data atoms of ω_U from ω_{U_1} except f_1
through f_n. Then U_1 is still an ancestor of Q, with the same estimated costs for
its nodes as those nodes had in U before the split, by assumption 2; and with the
same arcs going to Q as went from U to Q. U_2, however, is not an ancestor of Q,
by assumption 1.

The next step is to separate out the data atoms of ω_{U_1} into individual updates.
To accomplish this, split U_1 $n-1$ times according to Splitting Rule 3, removing data
atom f_i from U_1 on the ith split. By assumption 2, these splits will not alter the
cost information for any node of a split update that originally appeared in U. Note
that there is no need to define a new history atom $H(U)$ at each split of Splitting
Rule 3; every update that is split off can use the same selection clause $H(U)$, defined
by U_1 with the formula $H(U) \leftrightarrow \phi_U$. (This optimization was mentioned earlier.)
The small savings realized through reuse of $H(U)$ has been included in formula 6.9.

In the lazy graph resulting from this second round of splits, there are n updates
split off from U that are now ancestors of Q; for simplicity, rename the updates in
the graph as necessary so that these n updates are called U_1' through U_n'. We now
review the form and estimate the costs of U_1' through U_n', beginning with U_1'.

Only one data atom occurs in $\omega_{U_1'}$: f_n. All other data atoms of ω_U have been
replaced by history atoms in $(\omega)_{U_1'}$: there will be $\|\omega_U\| - 1$ different history atoms
in $\omega_{U_1'}$. By assumption 2, each history atom has an estimated cost of 1. The
selection clause of U_1' is the same as that for U. By assumption 2, it follows that
$\text{EstCost}(\phi_{U_1'}) = \text{EstCost}(\phi_U)$. U_1' defines a new history atom $H(U)$, using the

formula $H(U) \leftrightarrow \phi$. Therefore the estimated cost of U_1' is no more than

$$\text{EstCost}(f_n) + (\|\omega_U\| - 1) + \text{EstCost}(\phi_U) + 1.$$

U_2' through U_n' all take the form

$$insert\ (f \leftrightarrow (f)_{c_i}) \wedge ((\bigvee_{\substack{g \in S \\ f_i \sim_\sigma g}} \sigma) \quad \rightarrow (f_F \leftrightarrow (f)_{d_i})))_{\sigma'}, \text{ where } H(U),$$

for some constants c_i and d_i, where S is the set of atoms remaining in ω at the time f is being split out of ω. This formula has an upper bound on estimated costs of $\text{EstCost}(f) + 3$.

Summing the estimated costs of U_1 through U_n produces an upper bound estimate of

$$\text{EstCost}(f_n) + (\|\omega_U\| - 1) + \text{EstCost}(\phi_U) + 1 + \sum_{1 \le i < n} (\text{EstCost}(f_i) + 3),$$

which simplifies to

$$\|\omega_U\| - 2 + \text{EstCost}(\phi_U) + \sum_{1 \le i \le n} (\text{EstCost}(f_i) + 3). \qquad (6.10)$$

If these two stages of splitting are applied to all the parents of Q, then summing formula 6.10 over the new parents of Q gives formula 6.9. However, the theorem is not quite proven: Q may still have ancestors in the lazy graph other than its parents. It will require two more rounds of splitting to remove these undesirable ancestors. These rounds of splits, however, will not change the estimated costs of the parents of Q.

Let V be a parent of Q in the lazy graph after the first two rounds of splitting. To eliminate unwanted ancestors of V, let ϕ' be the disjunction of all the substitutions labeling arcs that go from V to Q. Split V vertically on ϕ' according to Splitting Rule 5, producing updates V_1 and V_2. Splitting V with Splitting Rule 5 does not change the cost estimates for the nodes of V, because vertical splitting does not change the atoms or history atoms of the split update.

After this third stage of splitting, suppose there is still a parent A of V_1 such that A is not a parent of Q. Then by assumptions 1 and 3, there must be a data atom f of ω_A that unifies with an atom f' of ω_{U_1} under a most general substitution σ'. Since f' is the only data atom in ω_{U_1}, f' must unify with some atom g of Q under a most general substitution σ. Further, by definition of U_1, σ must be one

Figure 6.7. Portion of simplified lazy graph.

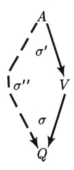

of the substitutions in the selection clause ϕ' of ϕ_{U_1}: ϕ' is

$$\phi_U \wedge \bigvee_{\substack{g \in Q \\ f' \sim_\sigma g}} \sigma.$$

Since A is a parent of V_1, by Step 2 of the NAP algorithm it must be the case that $\sigma' \wedge \phi_U \wedge (\bigvee_{\substack{g \in Q \\ f \sim_\sigma g}} \sigma)$ is satisfiable; therefore for some choice of σ, $\sigma' \wedge \sigma$ must be satisfiable. This implies that f unifies with g under substitution $\sigma' \wedge \sigma$. Yet A is not a parent of Q; therefore it must be the case that there is no arc from f to g because that arc fails test (2) or (3) of the NAP algorithm Step 2.

First consider the case where the arc fails test (3). In this case there is an equality formula α such that, say, ϕ_A logically entails α and ϕ_Q logically entails $\neg \alpha$. Let ϕ' be the formula $\neg \alpha$, and split V_1 vertically with Splitting Rule 5 on ϕ', creating updates V_3 and V_4. Then by test (3) of the NAP algorithm Step 2, V_4 is not a parent of Q, and A is not a parent of V_3. Therefore A is no longer an ancestor of Q by any path that goes through V_3 or V_4.

Now consider the case where the arc from f in A to g in Q passed test (3) but failed test (2) of Step 2 of the NAP algorithm. In this case either $\sigma'' \wedge \phi_Q$ or $\sigma'' \wedge \phi_A$ must be unsatisfiable, where σ'' is the most general substitution under which f and g unify. A simplified diagram of the relevant portion of the lazy graph, including the illegal arc σ'' from A to Q, appears in Figure 6.7.

Let Σ be the set of all choices for σ'', that is, the set of all substitutions σ'' such that $f \in \omega_A$, $g \in Q$, and $f \sim_{\sigma''} g$. Let ϕ' be $\bigvee_{\sigma'' \in \Sigma} \tau(\sigma'')$, where $\tau(\sigma'')$ is σ'' if $\sigma'' \wedge \phi_A$ is unsatisfiable, and is $\neg \sigma''$ otherwise. Split V_1 vertically with Splitting Rule 5 on ϕ', creating updates V_3 and V_4. We will now show that there is no path from A to Q through V_3 or V_4.

Suppose that $\sigma'' \wedge \phi_Q$ is unsatisfiable. Then ϕ_Q logically entails $\neg \sigma''$. Since σ'' is at least as general as σ, $\neg \sigma''$ logically entails $\neg \sigma$. It follows that $\sigma \wedge \phi_Q$ is also unsatisfiable. Therefore no arc labeled σ can go from V_3 or V_4 to Q, by test (2) of the NAP algorithm Step 2. Further, ϕ_{U_3} logically entails $\bigvee_{\sigma'' \in \Sigma} \tau(\sigma'')$.

Figure 6.8. Portion of simplified lazy graph.

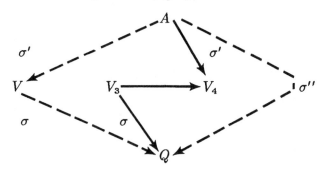

Therefore ϕ_{U_3} logically entails $\neg\sigma''$, and ϕ_{U_3} logically entails $\neg\sigma$ and $\neg\sigma'$ as well. We conclude that there can be no arc labeled σ from V_3 to Q and no arc labeled σ' from A to V_3, when $\sigma'' \wedge \phi_Q$ is unsatisfiable.

Following the same line of reasoning when $\sigma'' \wedge \phi_A$ is unsatisfiable leads to the conclusion that no arc labeled σ' can go from A to V_3 or V_4, no arc labeled σ can go from V_4 to Q, and no arc labeled σ' can go from A to V_4, when $\sigma'' \wedge \phi_Q$ is unsatisfiable.

It follows that the only arcs between A, V_3, V_4, and Q fall into the following three classes:

1. Arcs from V_3 to V_4.
2. Arcs labeled σ from V_3 to Q, when $\sigma'' \wedge \phi_A$ is unsatisfiable.
3. Arcs labeled σ' from A to V_4, when $\sigma'' \wedge \phi_Q$ is unsatisfiable.

Figure 6.8 depicts a simplified lazy graph containing A, V_3, V_4, Q, the phantom arc σ'' from A to Q, and for clarity V and its arcs as well, though of course the Splitting Algorithm would have removed V from the lazy graph before V_3 and V_4 were inserted.

Note that there is no path from A to Q via V_3 or V_4. Therefore after applying this final round of splitting to all ancestors of Q that are not parents of Q, all such ancestors will no longer be ancestors of Q, and the theorem follows.

As an improvement to this theorem, arcs coming into an update that represent read/write dependencies need not prevent execution of that update, because history predicates can be used as a versioning mechanism to eliminate the read/write conflicts. Therefore one can execute updates in the lazy graph without following a pure topological sort, as read/write arcs need not determine execution order. For example, given

U_1: *insert* Emp(Pratt, CS) *where* Emp(Pratt, English),

U_2: *insert* $\neg$Emp(Pratt, English),

there is a read/write conflict between U_1 and U_2. However, U_2 can be executed ahead of U_1 as long as U_1 reads Emp(Pratt, English, U_2) rather than Emp(Pratt, English).

The situation is a bit more complex if the read/write dependency arc has a substitution label other than T. For example, if U_1 were

insert Emp(Pratt, CS) *where* Emp(Pratt, ϵ),

then U_1 could not get by with reading Emp(Pratt, ϵ, U_2), for Emp(Pratt, ϵ, U_2) may be true in models where Emp(Pratt, ϵ) never was true. This anomaly can occur whenever Emp(Pratt, ϵ) does not already occur in T at the time U_2 is executed. If U_2 is executed before U_1, the solution is for U_1 to be replaced by

insert Emp(Pratt, CS)
where (Emp(Pratt, ϵ) $\wedge$ ($\epsilon \neq$ English)) $\vee$
$\qquad$ (Emp(Pratt, ϵ, U_2) $\wedge$ ($\epsilon =$ English)).

CHAPTER SEVEN

INTEGRITY CONSTRAINTS

Would martyrs have sung in the flames for a mere inference, however inevitable it might be?
—William James, *The Varieties of Religious Experience*

Database management systems usually offer a means of expressing simple pieces of information that are best thought of as *knowledge* rather than *data*. For example, the information that an employee can belong to only one department is modeled in the database world by an integrity constraint called a functional dependency. These integrity constraints can be examined at update time to ensure that a requested update will not produce a nonsensical database state in which, for example, an employee is listed as a member of two different departments.

How might relational theories be extended to handle integrity constraints? Suppose we are given a set of integrity constraints and a relational theory containing incomplete information, such that the integrity constraints are not logically entailed by the database. Then naturally the relational theory's query processor must consider these integrity constraints when forming answers to queries, as otherwise queries may be answered imprecisely or, under some semantics for queries, incorrectly. For example, suppose that the theory contains the formula Emp(Nilsson, EE) ∨ Emp(Nilsson, CS). If asked whether Nilsson might possibly be in both CS and EE, the answer is "yes," if no integrity constraints are present, and "no," if we have the constraint that each employee can be in only one department.

What is less obvious is that queries may not be answered correctly unless the relational theory's *update* processor also explicitly considers the integrity constraints while performing updates. In this chapter we describe the types of query-answering errors that may occur if the update processor does not properly process universally quantified integrity constraints, and we provide algorithms for the resolution of these problems. Our suggested enforcement technique is to make the intensional information in D that is *relevant* to T and the current update U into extensional information, by transforming that information into a small set of ground formulas called a cover, and adding the cover to T before performing U. The transformation process is made efficient by considering the semantics of U and by using the theory's query processor to find the violations of D that require attention.

7.1. Introduction

Suppose that a user of an ordinary relational database requests an update that would lead to a database state that violates an integrity constraint. There are several possible ways of resolving this conflict, and the correct choice of action is a policy decision that must be based on the intended semantics of the particular integrity constraint being violated. For example, the database management system's possible enforcement policies include

- Reject the update.
- Perform the update and make additional changes in the database to make it obey the integrity constraint.
- Perform the update and ignore the temporary inconsistency.

In addition to these roles, integrity constraints play another important part in databases with incomplete information, that of identifying and eliminating "impossible" completions of the incomplete database. For example, if an integrity constraint states that managers can only manage one department at a time and we know that Mgr(Nilsson, CS) ∨ Mgr(Nilsson, EE) is true, then the model where Nilsson manages both CS and EE is inconsistent with the integrity constraint and can be eliminated immediately. As yet another possible enforcement policy, if a requested update would create models that violate the integrity constraint and the update is known to be correct, then the integrity constraint can be changed. As an example of the use of the latter policy, if the database includes a completion axiom encoding a type of closed-world assumption, and the requested update inserts the fact that an additional atom such as Mgr(Nilsson, CSL) is true, then the completion axiom should be modified to permit the new atom to be true. These five integrity constraint enforcement policies are summarized in Table 7.1.

All five of these integrity constraint enforcement policies are reasonable; the correct choice of a policy for a particular integrity constraint depends

Table 7.1. *Integrity constraint enforcement policies.*

> *If an update U applied to model M would create a model M' that violates integrity constraint α, then ...*

1.	Reject U.
2.	Make additional changes in M' so that it does not violate α.
3.	Ignore the temporary inconsistency and permit a later update U' to remove the violation of α in M'.
4.	Eliminate M' permanently.
5.	Change α.

---

on the semantics of the integrity constraint and of the database, and we delegate this decision to the database administrator. The remainder of this chapter presents a mechanism (called *strict enforcement*, or simply *enforcement*), to enforce integrity constraints by permanently weeding out models that violate integrity constraints, to be employed as the database administrator sees fit, in conjunction with any of the model-based semantics introduced in Chapters 2 and 3. En route we will point out how to perform *passive enforcement*, that is, to ignore temporary inconsistencies between the database body and its axioms—perhaps not a logically sound procedure, but one used daily by humans with spectacular success.

Chapter 8 shows how to provide the type of integrity constraint enforcement in which additional changes will be made in the body of the relational theory whenever an update causes an integrity constraint to be violated. The mechanisms of Chapter 8 are needed in applications where it is unreasonable to expect the user to be able to list explicitly all of the facts that have changed in the world, and the update processor needs to shoulder that burden. For example, consider the update *insert* Emp(Chien, EE). If we have a functional dependency stating that each employee is in at most one department, and Emp(Chien, CS) is a sentence of T, then this update will produce an inconsistent theory if the integrity constraint is enforced via the mechanisms introduced in this chapter; on the other hand, the effect intended by the user was probably that of *insert* Emp(Chien, EE) $\wedge$ ¬Emp(Chien, CS). Under the approach presented in Chapter 8, the requested update would make Emp(Chien, CS) false as a side effect, and the result theory would remain consistent.

Associated with T is a set of universally quantified integrity constraints that are to be strictly enforced. For simplicity we will assume that this set consists of a single integrity constraint D; to enforce a set of integrity constraints, one simply enforces each integrity constraint in turn. $T+D$ is the theory containing the formulas of T plus D. We will write D without quantifier symbols; its variables will be implicitly universally quantified. The class of update semantics under consideration is the model-based semantics, for updates not containing variables.

A *banned model* is a model of T that is not a model of D. A model M is *rescued* by an update U if M is banned and $U(M)$ includes a model M' that satisfies D and is not a member of $U(T+D)$. A particular update algorithm *enforces* D for an update U if for every relational theory T, there are no rescued models in $U(T)$. Under the Update Algorithms of Chapters 4 and 5, if an update U removes all violations of D from a banned model M, then M will be rescued by U, i.e., an updated version of M will satisfy both D and the updated version of T.

Let us illustrate this by a simple example of a banned model rescue. Let the body of T be

Mgr(Nilsson, CS) $\lor$ Mgr(Nilsson, EE),

and let D be

$(\mathrm{Mgr}(x,\,y) \land \mathrm{Mgr}(x,\,z)) \rightarrow y = z,$

stating that a manager can only manage one department. This theory has three classes of models, in which Nilsson manages just CS, just EE, or both CS and EE. The latter of these models is banned, as it does not satisfy D. Let U be an update stating that if Nilsson manages both EE and CS, then he should now only manage English:

insert Mgr(Nilsson, English) $\land \neg$Mgr(Nilsson, CS) $\land \neg$Mgr(Nilsson, EE)
    where Mgr(Nilsson, CS) $\land$ Mgr(Nilsson, EE).

U should not change the models of $T+D$, because the selection clause of U is false in all models of $T+D$. But using the Update Algorithm Versions I or II, the result models are the two original models in which Nilsson manages CS and EE, plus a third model in which Nilsson manages the English department. All three of these models satisfy $T+D$. The banned model in which Nilsson manages both CS and EE was rescued by U.

7.2. Preventing Model Rescues

What sort of axiom enforcement is provided by an update algorithm that does not explicitly take integrity constraint axioms into account? Rescued models arise because update algorithms that do not consider D provide passive axiom enforcement, using D only to shape answers to queries. As mentioned in the introduction to this chapter, passive enforcement will be the best choice for some applications. If D is to be strictly enforced, however, then the models produced by these update algorithms will be incorrect. How can one avoid rescuing models? Proposition 7.1 hints at a method: add a set of formulas to the body of T that are implied by $T+D$ and that prevent rescues when T is updated.

Definition. *A set C of formulas is a* cover *for U, D, and T if Models$(T+D) = $ Models$(T + D + C)$ and there are no rescued models in $U(T + C)$.*

The remainder of this chapter is devoted to a discussion of means of generating covers. Our first candidate cover is very simple:

Proposition 7.1. $\{D\}$ *is a cover for U, D, and T.*

The proof of Proposition 7.1 is trivial: there are no banned models in $T+D$, so there can be no rescues. Proposition 7.1 suggests that a cover can be used to prevent rescues by adding it to the body of T before performing U. However, the cover $\{D\}$ cannot be added directly to the body of T because D may contain variables, and the body of T cannot. In the spirit of Proposition 7.1, rescues can be avoided by converting the universally-quantified intensional information in D into ground extensional information. In principle the set *HugeCover* containing all ground instantiations of D can be used to prevent rescues. Unfortunately, in general *HugeCover* is much too large for this to be practical. For example, as L contains an infinite set of constants, then *HugeCover* will also be infinite even for the simplest functional dependency. The remainder of this section discusses how to generate a smaller cover than *HugeCover*, in polynomial time.

7.2.1. Generating a Small Cover
Proposition 7.2 suggests a method of obtaining a smaller cover than *Huge-Cover*.

Proposition 7.2. *Under all the model-based semantics discussed in Chapters 2 and 3, if C is a cover for U, D, and T, then so is the subset of C consisting of all formulas containing an atom that unifies with a data atom of ω.*

Proof of Proposition 7.2.   Let α be a formula of C, and let M be a banned model in which α is false. Under all these model-based semantics, in the first-order case M can only be rescued by U if ω contains an atom that unifies with a data atom of α under M's null substitution. In the propositional case, M can only be rescued if a propositional symbol of ω appears in D.

Proposition 7.2 plus a few simple techniques can be used to construct a very generous cover just by syntactic examination of the body of T; but in general this cover is still rather large. There is a better way of finding a small cover: *use the query processor itself* to build a *SmallCover*. Before describing the construction of *SmallCover*, let us describe our model of query processing.

Definitions.   *A binding b is a substitution of data constants and nulls for variables. Binding b is* complete *for a formula α if b assigns constants to exactly the variables of α.*

For our purposes, a query Q is a quantifier-free formula. (The empty query is identical to the query T.) A natural-seeming definition of the answer to a query is that the answer to Q is the set of all complete bindings b for Q such that the query processor proved that $(Q)_b$ was true in all models of T. Under this definition, the answer to a query contains just those bindings which surely satisfy the query. In our work in this chapter, we will also be interested in bindings that satisfy the query in some, rather than all, of the models of T. This leads to a second candidate definition: the answer is the set of all complete bindings b for Q such that the query processor determined that $(Q)_b$ was true in some model of T.

Unfortunately, due to the presence of an infinite set of nulls, under the second definition queries will almost always have infinite answers. In addition, under both the first and second definitions, it will not always be possible for the query processor to determine whether a particular binding should be in the answer, in a reasonable amount of time. The answer should therefore permit the inclusion of bindings b such that the query processor was unable, in the time it allotted itself, to determine whether or not $(Q)_b$ was true in any models of T. To eliminate the problem of infinite answers for most queries, we rework the definition slightly, so that the answer need only include a representative set of bindings:

Definition.   *The* answer *to query Q against relational theory T is a set X of complete bindings with the following property: if in a model M of T,*

$(Q)_b$ *holds for some complete binding b, there must exist a binding $b' \in X$ such that $(Q)_b$ unifies with $(Q)_{b'}$ under M's null substitution.*

The result of a query Q includes both "definite" and "maybe" answers—bindings that surely satisfy Q as well as bindings that *may* satisfy Q. The query processor may of course offer additional facilities for users beyond those described here (e.g., the division of bindings into "definite" and "maybe" query answers); but our results do not make use of such facilities.

If the query processor returns the empty binding, then Q is a ground formula that may follow from T. If the query processor returns no bindings, then $(Q)_b$ is false in all models of T, for all bindings b. Finally, Answer(Q) is the set of all formulas $(Q)_b$, where b is a binding returned by the query processor for query Q.

Example 7.1. If Q is T, then the query processor should return the set of bindings $\{\{\ \}\}$, and Answer$(Q) = \{T\}$. If Q is F, then the query processor should return the set of bindings $\{\ \}$, and Answer$(Q) = \{\ \}$. For the query Emp$(x,$ Complaint$)$, the query processor might return the set of bindings $\{\{x = \text{Smith}\}, \{x = \text{Chu}\}\}$, in which case Answer$(Q)$ would be $\{\text{Emp(Smith, Complaint)}, \text{Emp(Chu, Complaint)}\}$. For the query Mgr$(x,\ y)$, the query processor might return the set of bindings $\{\{x = \text{Liu}, y = \text{Complaint}\}, \{x = \text{Liu}, y = \text{Toy}\}\}$, in which case Answer$(Q)$ would be $\{\text{Mgr(Liu, Complaint)}, \text{Mgr(Liu, Toy)}\}$.

Now let us turn to the problem of using the query processor to create a small cover. The following definition formalizes the idea, suggested by Proposition 7.2, of a "seed" binding.

Definition. *Let p be a binding such that for some data atom $R(c_1, \ldots, c_n)$ of ω and some atom $R(d_1, \ldots, d_n)$ of D, $R(c_1, \ldots, c_n)$ unifies with $R(d_1, \ldots, d_n)$ under most general substitution p. Let SeedBindings be the set of all such choices of p.*

Seed bindings are used as a starting point in the following algorithm for construction of a small cover. Recall that the query processor ordinarily will refer to D when trying to determine the answer to a query; Step 3 of the algorithm turns off this integrity constraint checking, effectively temporarily deleting D. Essentially the algorithm asks the query processor which atoms of ω might be involved in a violation of D in some model of T.

Algorithm for Computing *SmallCover*

1.   Let *SmallCover* be the empty set.
2.   Compute *SeedBindings*.
3.   Turn off integrity constraint checking in the query processor.
4.   For each p in *SeedBindings*, add to *SmallCover* the negation of every formula in Answer$(\neg(D)_p)$.

Example 7.2.   Let D be the functional dependency

$(\mathrm{Emp}(x, y) \wedge \mathrm{Emp}(x, z)) \rightarrow (y = z)$,

and let the body of T be

$\mathrm{Emp}(\mathrm{Liu}, \mathrm{Complaint}) \vee \mathrm{Emp}(\mathrm{Liu}, \mathrm{Shipping}) \vee \mathrm{Emp}(\mathrm{Liu}, \mathrm{Toy})$.

If U is

insert $\mathrm{Emp}(\mathrm{Liu}, \mathrm{Toy})$,

then *SeedBindings* contains the two bindings

$\{x = \mathrm{Liu}, y = \mathrm{Toy}\}$,
$\{x = \mathrm{Liu}, z = \mathrm{Toy}\}$.

We will consider only the first of the pair, as the other case is symmetric. The query posed in Step 4, $\neg(D)_p$, is logically equivalent to

$\mathrm{Emp}(\mathrm{Liu}, \mathrm{Toy}) \wedge \mathrm{Emp}(\mathrm{Liu}, z) \wedge (\mathrm{Toy} \neq z)$.

The bindings given in reply by the query processor will presumably be

$\{\{z = \mathrm{Complaint}\}, \{z = \mathrm{Shipping}\}\}$.

This means that Answer$(\neg(D)_p)$ is

$\{\mathrm{Emp}(\mathrm{Liu}, \mathrm{Toy}) \wedge \mathrm{Emp}(\mathrm{Liu}, \mathrm{Complaint}) \wedge (\mathrm{Toy} \neq \mathrm{Complaint})$,
$\mathrm{Emp}(\mathrm{Liu}, \mathrm{Toy}) \wedge \mathrm{Emp}(\mathrm{Liu}, \mathrm{Shipping}) \wedge (\mathrm{Toy} \neq \mathrm{Shipping})\}$.

Therefore *SmallCover* is the set

$\{\neg(\mathrm{Emp}(\mathrm{Liu}, \mathrm{Toy}) \wedge \mathrm{Emp}(\mathrm{Liu}, \mathrm{Complaint}) \wedge (\mathrm{Toy} \neq \mathrm{Complaint}))$,
$\neg(\mathrm{Emp}(\mathrm{Liu}, \mathrm{Toy}) \wedge \mathrm{Emp}(\mathrm{Liu}, \mathrm{Shipping}) \wedge (\mathrm{Toy} \neq \mathrm{Shipping}))\}$,

which can be written more concisely as

$\{\neg\mathrm{Emp}(\mathrm{Liu}, \mathrm{Toy}) \vee \neg\mathrm{Emp}(\mathrm{Liu}, \mathrm{Complaint})$,
$\neg\mathrm{Emp}(\mathrm{Liu}, \mathrm{Toy}) \vee \neg\mathrm{Emp}(\mathrm{Liu}, \mathrm{Shipping})\}$.

There are three major problems with the *SmallCover* algorithm. First, there is no guarantee that the query $\neg(D)_p$ has a finite answer; second, even if its answer is finite, there is no guarantee that its answer can be found in acceptable time (say, polynomial in the size of T); and third, even if its answer can be found in polynomial time, there is no guarantee that the query processor will know how to do so. Let us examine each of these problems in turn.

First, in the case where the answer to $\neg(D)_p$ is inherently infinite, one can use a very simple transformation on D, described in Section 4, to produce an equivalent (for our purposes) query with guaranteed finite answer.

Second, it is quite true that determining whether a formula Q is true in any models of T cannot be done in polynomial time in general. However, the query processor will have been built with this problem in mind, and will have some means of curtailing too-expensive computations by giving less precise answers than would be possible given unlimited computing resources. In other words, the query processor will only search for the answer to Q for time polynomial in the size of T. The query processor is in the best possible position to give a small cover for rescuable models in a small amount of time; it is the ideal tool for this purpose.

Finally, it may be that the query processor does not know how to compute answers to queries that, for example, contain certain types of negation; these queries are discussed in Section 4. There is, however, a class of integrity constraints that any query processor should be able to handle, and this is the topic of the next section.

7.2.2. Safe Integrity Constraints

We begin by defining safe variables, formulas, and integrity constraints.

Definition. *A variable x in a quantifier-free conjunctive formula α is a safe variable iff*

1. $\alpha \models (x = y)$, *for some variable y that appears in a positive non-equality conjunct of α; or*
2. $\alpha \models (x = c)$, *for some constant c.*

A bit of terminology: $\mathrm{DNF}(\alpha)$ and $\mathrm{CNF}(\alpha)$ are the disjunctive and conjunctive normal forms of α, respectively.

Definitions. *A quantifier-free conjunctive formula α is safe if all its variables are safe. A quantifier-free formula β is safe if all disjuncts of DNF(β) are safe and all contain the same variables. An integrity constraint D is safe if the formula $\neg D$ is safe. The unsafe variables of integrity constraint D are the unsafe variables of the formula $\neg D$.*

Example 7.3.   In the formula $R(x) \wedge \neg R(y) \wedge \neg S(x) \wedge (z = c) \wedge (w \neq z)$, x and

z are safe, and y and w are unsafe. $R(x) \wedge \neg S(x)$ is a safe *formula* but an unsafe *integrity constraint*, because $\neg R(x) \vee S(x)$ is unsafe. $R(x) \vee \neg P(x, y)$ is an unsafe formula but a safe integrity constraint.

Proposition 7.3.   *All functional, multivalued, and join dependencies are safe.*

Theorem 7.1.   *If query Q is safe, then there is a choice of Answer(Q) such that Answer(Q) is finite.*

Proof of Theorem 7.1.   Assume that query Q is in DNF. A reasonable answer to Q is the union of the answers to the disjuncts of Q. Ground disjuncts clearly have finite answers, so consider a disjunct d of Q containing a variable x. Recall that the completion axioms of T guarantee that any data atom true in a model M of T will unify with a data atom represented in the (finite) completion axioms of T, under M's null substitution. By rule 1 in the definition of safe variables, then, one need only consider a finite number of bindings for x that could possibly make d true in any model of T. It follows that Q has a finite answer.

Any query processor should be able to construct a finite answer to a safe DNF query Q in the following manner. First, a conservative approach is to consider each disjunct d of Q separately, searching for appropriate bindings for the variables of d, and to return all bindings found for all disjuncts. Second, given a conjunctive formula d, process d by first propagating any variable bindings specified directly in d, such as $x = c$ in $R(x, y) \wedge (x = c) \wedge \neg S(y) \wedge (x = z)$. Then find possible bindings for the variables appearing in the positive non-equality literals of d, such as x and y in $R(x, y)$; ordinary relational database techniques can be used for this. By the definition of a safe formula, once all these variables have been bound and their bindings propagated through conjuncts such as $x = z$, no unbound variables remain in d. The final step in processing is to test whether the bound version of d is satisfiable in T.

An integrity constraint D need never be considered unsafe due to the presence of different sets of variables in different disjuncts of $\text{DNF}(\neg D)$. To see this, replace D by a set of integrity constraints, consisting of the conjuncts of $\text{CNF}(D)$. Because D is universally quantified, D is logically equivalent to the new set of integrity constraints. As each new integrity constraint is a disjunctive formula, its negation will contain only one disjunct.

In the remainder of this paper, we assume that D has been preprocessed in this manner if necessary, so that all disjuncts of DNF($\neg D$) contain the same variables.

7.2.3. Covers for Safe Integrity Constraints

We have shown that when D is safe, the queries posed by the *SmallCover* algorithm have finite answers that any query processor should be able to find. It remains to show that *SmallCover* will actually prevent rescues when D is safe.

Theorem 7.2.   *If D is safe, then SmallCover is a cover for U, D, and T.*

Theorem 7.2 does not depend on the restrictions placed on model universes in Chapter 3. In particular, the theorem still holds if there are elements in the universes of models that are not named by any term of L. This holds because when a model violates a safe integrity constraint D, then D must be violated in M by elements that are named in L.

Proof of Theorem 7.2.   Let p be a binding in *SeedBindings*. Since the negation of every formula in Answer($\neg(D)_p$) is logically entailed by D, it must be the case that Models($T+D$) = Models($T+D+SmallCover$), and the first point of the definition of a cover is satisfied. It remains to verify that there are no rescued models in $U(T+SmallCover)$.

Let M be a banned model of T. By the definition of a standard model, there exists a complete binding b such that $(D)_b$ is false in M. For M to be rescued, a data atom α of ω must unify with an atom of $(D)_b$ under M's null substitution. Let β be an atom of D such that α unifies with $(\beta)_b$ under M's null substitution. Then there is a binding p in *SeedBindings* such that α unifies with β under most general substitution p; as p was chosen to be as general as possible, α, $(\beta)_p$, and $(\beta)_b$ must all unify under M's null substitution. As $(D)_b$ is false in M, there must be a binding b' such that $\neg(D)_{b'}$ is in Answer($\neg(D)_p$), and $\neg(D)_{b'}$ and $\neg(D)_b$ unify under M's null substitution. Therefore M is not a model of $U(T+SmallCover)$, and *SmallCover* is a cover for U, D, and T.

7.3. Unsafe Integrity Constraints

This section shows how to enforce unsafe integrity constraints, such as $R(a) \rightarrow R(x)$. The enforcement techniques are based on an implicit closed-world assumption active in the database world—the assumption encoded in the completion axioms. Intuitively, unsafe integrity constraints should be hard to enforce because a banned model may violate them in an infinite number of ways. In practice, however, this does not pose a problem, as we can replace $R(a) \to R(x)$ by a safe integrity constraint that is easily enforced.

The need for an infinite supply of update identifiers in L assures that all standard models have infinite universes. Using this assumption, we will replace D by a set SafeVersion(D) of safe integrity constraints that is equivalent to D in the sense that Models($T+D$) = Models($T+$SafeVersion(D)), for any relational theory T. Instead of enforcing D, we simply enforce SafeVersion(D). The algorithm to perform this transformation is given below.

Algorithm for Computing SafeVersion(D)

1.   Let SafeVersion(D) be the empty set.
2.   For each satisfiable disjunct d of DNF($\neg D$), perform the following:
       a.   Remove all conjuncts of d that contain an unsafe variable.
       b.   Add $\neg d$ to SafeVersion(D).

Example 7.4.   Consider the unsafe integrity constraint $R(a) \to R(x)$. DNF($\neg D$) is $R(a) \wedge \neg R(x)$. In Step 2a, the conjunct $\neg R(x)$ containing the unsafe variable x is removed. By Step 2b, then, SafeVersion(D) contains just $\neg R(a)$.

The SafeVersion algorithm may seem peculiarly circuitous in the way that it first negates D and then effectively renegates it in Step 2. Why not just remove the unsafe subformulas of D directly? The following example shows why a clean solution to the problem requires the use of negations: the more straightforward approach would reduce D to a tautology rather than to a contradiction.

Example 7.5.   Consider the unsafe integrity constraint $R(x)$. DNF($\neg D$) is $\neg R(x)$. In Step 2a, d is reduced to the empty formula, which is equivalent to T. In Step 2b, F is added to SafeVersion(D).

Example 7.6.   Consider the integrity constraint $(x = y) \vee (x \neq y)$, which is a tautology but does not satisfy the definition of a safe integrity constraint. If unsatisfiable disjuncts of $\neg D$ were not ignored in Step 2, then SafeVersion(D) would contain the truth value F.

Clearly SafeVersion(D) contains only safe integrity constraints. Theorem

7.3 shows that these integrity constraints are equivalent to D, and therefore D can be enforced by running the *SmallCover* algorithm on SafeVersion(D).

Theorem 7.3.   *If L contains an infinite set of constants, then for any theory T, Models($T + D$) = Models(T+SafeVersion(D)).*

The proof of Theorem 7.3 uses UnsafePart(D), which intuitively is the non-tautological disjuncts of D not present in SafeVersion(D).

Definition.   *If D is a disjunctive integrity constraint, then* UnsafePart(D) *is the disjunction of the negations of the formulas discarded during Step 2a of computing SafeVersion(D).*

Example 7.7.   If D is $R(a) \rightarrow R(x)$, then D can be rewritten as the disjunctive integrity constraint $\neg R(a) \lor R(x)$, and UnsafePart(D) is $R(x)$.

Proof of Theorem 7.3.   Let D be an unsafe integrity constraint; without loss of generality, we assume that D is a disjunctive formula, that D is not a tautology, and that D', the single formula in SafeVersion(D), is in DNF. If D' is true in a model, then D must also be true there, as the disjuncts of D' are a subset of those of D. It remains to prove that D' must be true in any model M of T where D is true.

Assume that D is true in M. If UnsafePart(D) is the empty formula, then D' is true in M, so let us consider the case where UnsafePart(D) contains at least one disjunct. If D' is false in M, then by the definition of a standard model, for some complete binding b, $(D')_b$ is false in M. Since $(D)_b$ is true in M, it follows that (UnsafePart(D))$_b$ is true in M. In the remainder of the proof, we derive a contradiction by showing that (UnsafePart(D))$_b$ is in fact false in M, through construction of a binding that falsifies (UnsafePart(D))$_b$.

By an *outside constant*, we mean a constant whose interpretation in M is different from that of any constants in D, b, or T.

Let d be a disjunct of (UnsafePart(D))$_b$. We first show that unless d is of the form $x = y$ or $x \neq y$, for variables x and y, d is easily falsified by bindings containing outside constants. By the definition of D', d must contain an unsafe variable. If d is a data atom, then by the completion axioms d will be false in M if any of its variables are bound to an outside constant. Further, d cannot be the negation of a data atom, as then the variables in d would be safe. If d is of the form $x = c$, for c a constant, then d will be false in M when c is bound to an outside constant. Finally, d cannot have the form $x \neq c$, as then x would be a safe variable.

To complete the proof we need only demonstrate the existence of a complete binding, using outside constants, that falsifies the disjuncts of (UnsafePart(D))$_b$ of the form $x = y$ and $x \neq y$. This can be done by first dividing the variables of

$(\text{UnsafePart}(D))_b$ into equivalence classes so that x and y are in the same class iff $(\text{UnsafePart}(D))_b$ contains a disjunct of the form $x \neq y$. If the resulting classes are C_1 through C_n, then assign outside constant c_i to equivalence class C_i. Clearly this binding falsifies all inequality literals. As by assumption D is not a tautology, all equality literals must be falsified as well. Finally, by assumption L contains an infinite set of outside constants (e.g., update identifiers), so it is possible to construct this outside binding.

7.4. Extensions

There are a number of heuristics that can be used to improve these enforcement techniques. The most important is to consider what U actually *does*, i.e., take into account the exact semantics of U. As an example, if D is a functional dependency, then rescues will never be caused by updates that insert positive literals. For example, if managers can only manage one department, then inserting Mgr(Nilsson, English) cannot cause rescues, as this insertion cannot remove violations of the manager rule; it can only cause new violations. In an implementation of strict enforcement, simple heuristics such as this should be used to yield more efficient enforcement of all common types of integrity constraints.

Another improvement can be gained by considering the meaning of selection clauses in updates and queries. The selection clause ϕ of an update *insert ω where ϕ* selects a subset of the models of T in which U is to take place; in other models, no change occurs. This means that rescues can only occur in banned models where ϕ is true, and integrity constraint enforcement need only consider such models. To adapt to this new situation in the SafeVersion algorithm, rather than asking the query $\neg(D)_p$ we can ask $\neg(D)_p$ *where ϕ*, as we are only interested in violations of $(D)_p$ in models of ϕ. The benefit of allowing selection clauses lies in potentially smaller query answers and therefore smaller covers.

Another area of extension is to allow variables in updates. As in ordinary relational systems, updates with variables are eventually reduced to a set of ground updates to be performed simultaneously. Enforcement then consists of enforcing D for this set of ground updates.

One might wish to extend this technique to theories operating under the open-world assumption. In general, however, strict enforcement is not possible for an open-world version of T (created by removing its completion axioms), because there is no finite ground cover. For example, consider the functional dependency

---

D: $(\mathrm{Emp}(x, y) \land \mathrm{Emp}(x, z)) \rightarrow (y = z)$

and the relational theory T with body

Emp(Smith, Complaint).

Under the open-world assumption, this integrity constraint is violated in the models of T where

$\exists x \; (\mathrm{Emp}(\mathrm{Smith}, x) \land x \neq \mathrm{Complaint})$

is true. If U is

insert ¬Emp(Smith, Complaint),

then *SeedBindings* contains the binding $\{x = \mathrm{Smith}, y = \mathrm{Complaint}\}$. The banned models of T that will be rescued by this update are those in which Smith is an employee of the complaint department plus one other department; since the other department could be anything at all, there is no way to create a finite ground cover for U, D, and T under the open-world assumption.

This lack of algorithmic techniques is no great drawback, however, as strict enforcement is philosophically at odds with the open-world assumption anyway. The open-world assumption implies a lack of omniscience. An open-world theory and its updates do not necessarily capture all possible relevant information about the world; quite possibly world changes are occurring that are outside the current scope of the database. In the current example, it would be rash to replace T's body,

Emp(Smith, Complaint),

by

Emp(Smith, Complaint)
¬Emp(Smith, Toy)
¬Emp(Smith, Shipping)
. . . ,

even though both have the same models when D is added; T' implies that all future changes in Emp(Smith, Complaint), Emp(Smith, Shipping), etc., will be known to us and presented in updates. Chapter 8 presents a method of constraint enforcement that is more suitable for open-world theories.

7.5. Computational Complexity

The increase in size of T incurred in enforcing D—i.e., the size of the answer to the queries in *SmallCover*—depends on the cleverness of the query processor, on D, and on the body of T. Since D is known ahead of time and will change only rarely if at all, it can be preanalyzed and templates for *SmallCover* prepared. Let k be the number of different atoms in ω, and let R be the maximum number of data atoms in T over the same predicate. For generality, we assume that nulls are permitted in T and U.

Theorem 7.5.   *If D is a functional, multi-valued, join, or predicate-inclusion dependency, then SmallCover contains $O(kR)$ atoms in the worst case and zero atoms in the best case.*

Theorem 7.5 follows straightforwardly from the definition of *SmallCover*, so we will not give its proof here.

The worst-case costs given in Theorem 7.5 may seem high, particularly when extended to updates containing variables. However, in an actual database application, a number of mitigating factors lead one to expect that *SmallCover* will be quite small on average. First, the variables in an update play a different role than in queries. The typical update in a real database does *not* modify multiple tuples. It selects and changes just one tuple. Variables in such an update play the role of placeholders for "don't-care" values while a selection is being done on a key, and do not lead to large numbers of database modifications per update request.

Second, in practice, for example in the case of a functional dependency, not very many data atoms in T will agree on their "ruling" attributes, as the atoms will be sparse within the cross product of their domains. The worst-case estimates assume that *every* data atom of U "conflicts" with *every* data atom in T; in practice, a constant number of conflicts is to be expected. Our heuristic of focussing on the current update should work well, especially when coupled with heuristics related to the semantics of the update.

Finally, one very reasonable restriction for a practical database management system is to forbid null values to occur in keys. This action would drastically reduce the size of *SmallCover* for functional dependencies.

7.6. Related Work

In the previous sections of this chapter, we have investigated a means of enforcing integrity constraints across updates. A number of researchers have examined the related question of integrity constraint enforcement when computing answers to queries (e.g., [Grahne 84, Imielinski 83, 85, Lerat 86]).

In their work, the goal is to make it unnecessary for the query processor to consider integrity constraints during query evaluation, for certain subclasses of relational theories. As mentioned earlier, this is not a practical goal for relational theories in general, as doing so even in the case of a functional dependency might enlarge the body of the theory by a polynomial factor. For that reason, we have suggested heuristics to focus the integrity constraint instantiation process, so that the body of T would not be excessively enlarged.

For example, Imielinski and Lipski considered the problem of ensuring that the answer to a query Q is the same whether it is applied to T or to $T+D$, given that the user's query language is restricted to various sets of operators, and the integrity constraints are universally quantified [Imielinski 83]. The query language restriction is used as leverage for more efficient integrity constraint enforcement: instead of ensuring that Models(T) = Models$(T+D)$, one need only ensure that for all permitted queries Q, the answer to Q is the same whether Q is applied to T or $T+D$. Imielinski and Lipski consider the case where the body of the theory is simply a set of data atoms possibly containing nulls. D may contain equality-generating and total-tuple-generating dependencies; these are both safe integrity constraint classes. Their approach is to apply a modified "chase" procedure to the theory body, and thereby eliminate the need to consider D during processing of the permitted queries. In order to enforce integrity constraints across updates, however, one must use more than a chase procedure:

Example 7.8.   Let D be a functional dependency stating that an employee can only work in one department:

$(\text{Emp}(x, y) \land \text{Emp}(x, z)) \rightarrow (y = z)$,

and let T have the body

Emp(ϵ_1, Toy)
Emp$(\epsilon_2, \text{Complaint})$.

Models where $\epsilon_1 = \epsilon_2$ are banned, as ϵ_1 and ϵ_2 must be different employees. Emp satisfies the chase procedure of [Imielinski 83]. If update U is

insert $\neg\text{Emp}(\epsilon_1, \text{Toy}) \land \text{Mgr}(\epsilon_1, \text{Complaint})$ *where* $\epsilon_1 = \epsilon_2$,

then U should not change the models of T, as the selection clause is false in all models of T. Under the Update Algorithm, however, U rescues models where $\epsilon_1 = \epsilon_2$, making ϵ_1 the manager of the Complaint department in those models.

For the case of functional dependencies, one can use an extended chase procedure to ensure that Models(T) = Models$(T+D)$ [Grahne 84, Lerat 86]. For the extended chase, one must allow the body of T to contain both data atoms and inequalities. Once the extended chase is applied to T, the update processor need not consider D while performing updates, as long as the body of T is of this special form. If the body of T contains other types of formulas, such as disjunctions, the extended chase can no longer be used. For example, in Example 7.8, suppose that the body of T were

$\text{Emp}(\epsilon_1, \text{Toy}) \vee \text{Emp}(\epsilon_2, \text{Complaint})$.

One cannot use a chase procedure on these two data atoms, as the chase would lead one to conclude that $\epsilon_1 \neq \epsilon_2$, which is not justified.

CHAPTER EIGHT

ADDING KNOWLEDGE TO RELATIONAL THEORIES

"... You believers make so many and such large and such unwarrantable assumptions."

"My dear, we must make assumptions, or how get through life at all?"

"Very true. How indeed? One must make a million unwarrantable assumptions, such as that the sun will rise tomorrow, and that the attraction of the earth for our feet will for a time persist, and that if we do certain things to our bodies they will cease to function, and that if we get into a train it will probably carry us along, and so forth. One must assume these things just enough to take action on them, or, as you say, we couldn't get through life at all. But those are hypothetical, pragmatical assumptions, for the purposes of action; there is no call actually to believe them, intellectually. And still less call to increase their number, and carry assumption into spheres where it doesn't help us to action at all. For my part, I assume practically a great deal, intellectually nothing."
—Rose Macaulay, *Told by an Idiot*

Relational theories contain little *knowledge*, that is, *data about data*. The exact line between knowledge and data is hard to pinpoint; for our purposes, the distinguishing characteristic of knowledge will be our reluctance to change it in response to new information in the form of an update. Under this categorization, the integrity constraints discussed in Chapter 7 are a form of knowledge. The closed-world assumption per se constitutes knowledge, since we are unwilling to retract it in the face of contradicting information; however, its syntactic embodiment in the completion axioms undergoes regular revision, and so is closer to data. The body of a relational theory is data.

If one attempts to apply the techniques of previous chapters to applications in artificial intelligence (AI), the first major obstacle is the need for means of handling knowledge during updates, means other than that of strict enforcement. For example, if we have a piece of knowledge that $p \rightarrow q$, and the pieces of data $\neg p$ and $\neg q$, then the desired result of the update *insert p* in AI applications is not the inconsistent theory, but rather a model in which both p and q are true. One may think of *insert p* as a stone tossed into a pond: making p true causes ripples felt by other propositions throughout the theory. The problem of determining what additional changes must result from inserting a formula ω, other than simply making ω true in all models, is known in AI circles as the *ramification* problem [Finger 87]. The dual question of what in a model will be unaffected by an update is known as the *frame* problem. Closely related is the *qualification* problem: what facts about the world might prevent a formula ω from becoming true as the result of an action?

The frame, ramification, and qualification problems have provided the theme for many literary works. One example is the nursery rhyme

> *For want of a nail, the shoe was lost.*
> *For want of a shoe, the horse was lost.*
> *For want of a horse, the rider was lost.*
> *For want of the rider, the battle was lost.*
> *For want of the battle, the kingdom was lost,*
> *And all for the want of a horseshoe nail!*

The potential ramifications can be enormous for even the loss of a horseshoe nail. The qualification problem looms similarly large for the king: just to keep his kingdom, the king may have to inform himself about the status of every nail in every hoof in the land. Any formal means of reasoning about action must also come to grips with these two problems.

In this chapter we will explore the use of model-based and formula-based semantics as tools in the AI application of reasoning about the effects of actions in the physical world. Through consideration of a series of examples, the potential advantages of a minimal-change model-based semantics in this application will become apparent. In addition, we will show that general-purpose update techniques alone do not solve the problems of the application; rather, they are a useful tool that can carry much though not all of the burden of computing the effects of actions. The examples we use will be based on those of Chapter 2, plus an additional type of example (closely related to Examples 2.6 and 2.7) to show the dependence of formula-based semantics on the syntax of T. The problem of syntax dependence carries over to the case where knowledge is present in T, with the additional wrinkle that formula-based semantics differentiate strongly between information that is directly stated in T and that is unstated but still derivable from T. We will restrict our attention to the frame and ramification problems; the qualification problem is very similar.

Formula-based approaches have difficulties with the frame, ramification, and qualification problems, due to the formula-based equation of the *state of the world* with the *description of the state of the world*. In particular, the frame principle says that as little as possible changes in the world when an action is performed. Formula-based semantics translate this into "as little as possible in the description of the world changes when an action is performed." Of course, a minimal change in the world does not necessarily correspond to a minimal change in the description of the world, and vice versa. This makes formula-based approaches excessively sensitive to the syntax of the description of the world, and leads to incorrect handling of incomplete information. For formula-based semantics to be a useful tool in reasoning about action, the syntax of the formulas in T must be tightly controlled.

Model-based semantics suffer from a similar problem, but at a higher level of abstraction: they are sensitive to the choice of language used to describe the world. As the unit of change in model-based approaches is the atom truth valuation, there must be a close correspondence between the units of change in the world and the atoms of the language L. The language can be augmented with new predicates to create this correspondence if it is lacking initially.

Neither formula-based nor model-based approaches provide a complete solution to the problems encountered in reasoning about action; one must bring additional domain-dependent knowledge and techniques to bear on the problem in order to provide a full solution. We do believe, however, that one necessary component of a full solution is a general-purpose theory revision mechanism.

Ginsberg and Smith have suggested the use of a formula-based "when in doubt, throw it out" (WIDTIO) semantics in reasoning about action, which they call the Possible Worlds Approach (PWA) [Ginsberg 88ab]. In Section 8.1 of this chapter, we sketch a simple action scenario, a simplified version of that used in [Ginsberg 88a], to serve as an example throughout the remainder of the chapter. Section 8.2 presents an extension of the minimal-change model-based semantics, called the Possible Models Approach (PMA), that deals with knowledge as well as data. Sections 8.3 and 8.4 show how formula-based semantics encounter difficulties with the frame and ramification problems, respectively, and show that a model-based semantics will not suffer from these particular anomalies. Section 8.5 discusses problems with the formula-based treatment of multiple candidate result theories, and Section 8.6 describes problems with the PMA in reasoning about action.

8.1. An Example Action Scenario

In reasoning about action, it becomes clear that those formulas of T that represent knowledge—for example, those stating inviolable properties of the physical world—should be not be altered by updates: these "nonupdatable" formulas should always be present in T'. For example, in trying to move a block to a position already occupied by another block, it is not reasonable to remove the axiom stating that only one object can occupy any given position. Throughout this chapter, we will assume that any formulas we try to add to T are consistent with the nonupdatable formulas of T, as otherwise the action is undefined.

The types of theories under consideration, then, consist of a set of nonupdatable sentences and a finite set of updatable sentences (the body). Although there are no syntactic restrictions on updatable sentences, all the examples in this chapter will have ground theory bodies. In this application, the closed-world assumption is not needed, so we will omit the completion axioms. For simplicity, when writing nonupdatable formulas we will omit universal quantifiers, so that all free variables will be implicitly universally quantified over the scope of the entire formula.

For the purposes of this chapter, we can also simplify L and the definition of standard models. Let us omit from L all nulls and update identifiers, so that the only constants in L are data constants. We will also eliminate the history predicates. Then a standard model is simply a set of data atoms over L, as each constant c designates a separate universe element c.

Imagine Aunt Agatha's living room: two ventilation ducts on the floor, a bird cage, a newspaper, a television, and a magazine (Figure 8.1). The bird cage, newspaper, TV, and magazine must be either on the floor or on the ducts. Only one object fits on a duct at a time, and if an object is on a duct, then the duct is blocked. If both ducts are blocked, then the room becomes stuffy. This living room is described by the following nonupdatable formulas, adapted from [Ginsberg 88a], which will be part of T throughout this chapter:

$$\text{duct}(x) \leftrightarrow [x{=}\text{duct1} \vee x{=}\text{duct2}]$$
$$\text{location}(x) \leftrightarrow [\text{duct}(x) \vee x{=}\text{floor}]$$
$$[\text{on}(x, y) \wedge \text{on}(x, z)] \rightarrow y{=}z \tag{8.1}$$
$$[\text{on}(x, y) \wedge \text{on}(z, y)] \rightarrow [z{=}x \vee y{=}\text{floor}] \tag{8.2}$$
$$[\text{duct}(d) \wedge \exists x\, \text{on}(x, d)] \leftrightarrow \text{blocked}(d) \tag{8.3}$$
$$[\text{blocked}(\text{duct1}) \wedge \text{blocked}(\text{duct2})] \leftrightarrow \text{stuffy} \tag{8.4}$$
$$\text{on}(x, y) \rightarrow [\text{location}(y) \wedge \neg\text{location}(x)] \tag{8.5}$$

Figure 8.1. A living room.

$$\exists y \; \text{on}(x, y) \vee \text{location}(x) \qquad\qquad (8.6)$$

The first formula says that there are exactly two ducts, and the second states that the only locations are the ducts and the floor. Formula 8.1 says that an object can only be in one place at a time, and formula 8.2 says that only one object can occupy a given position at a particular time. Formula 8.3 says that only ducts can be blocked, and that a duct is blocked iff it has something sitting on top of it. According to formula 8.4, the room will be stuffy iff both ducts are blocked. Formula 8.5 does a bit of type checking, by ensuring that if $\text{on}(x, y)$ is true then y is a location and x is not a location. Note that formula 8.5 implies that no stacking of objects is permitted in the living room. Finally, formula 8.6 says that every object must be somewhere.

These formulas are the mental model that Agatha has of her living room. Agatha herself is off washing dishes in the kitchen; her faithful robot servant, Tyro, will carry out any actions that she requests. In particular, Tyro is capable of moving living room objects from one spot to another.

Associated with each action is a formula ω, describing what must be true in the world after that action takes place, known as the *postcondition* of the action. Each action also has a precondition, a formula which must be true of the world in order for the action to be executable. To reason about the effect of an action on the world, one checks to make sure that the associated precondition is true, and then inserts ω into the theory describing the world.

8.2. Definition of the Possible Models Approach

The PMA is an extension of the minimal-change semantics to the case where knowledge is present. To reason about the effect of performing an action with postcondition ω, the PMA considers the effect of the action on each possible state of the world, that is, on each model of T. The PMA changes the truth valuations of the atoms in each model as little as necessary in order to make both ω and the nonupdatable formulas of T true in that model. The possible states of the world after the action is performed are all those models thus produced.

Let us say that models M_1 and M_2 *differ on an atom* α if α appears in exactly one of M_1 and M_2.

Definition.   *Let M be a model of T and U the update* insert ω. *Under the PMA, $U(T)$ is given by MB3:*

$$\text{Models}(U(T)) \;=\; \bigcup_{M \in \text{Models}(T)} U(M),$$

and $U(M)$ is the set of all models M' such that

(1) ω *and the nonupdatable formulas of T are true in M'.*
(2)   *No other model satisfying (1) differs from M on fewer atoms, where "fewer" is defined by set inclusion.*

The PMA is a model-based semantics, although it violates principle MB2 (requiring that only atoms of ω can change truth valuation); that principle is only appropriate for categorization of update semantics where knowledge is not present in T. The semantics of the PMA depends only on the models of the knowledge and updatable formulas of T, and not on the formulas used to describe those models. Except for the division of formulas into knowledge and data statements, the PMA is entirely syntax-independent.

One can easily extend other model-based semantics that are as restrictive as the minimal-change semantics, to handle the case where knowledge formulas occur in T. The disadvantage of these semantics in this application is that they are likely to prune away the model of T that is most intuitively desirable. For example, Dalal's semantics uses a cardinality test to pick out minimally-changed models. That means that one can alter the effect of an update under Dalal's semantics just by introducing new predicates whose meaning is synonymous with that of preexisting predicates. We believe that cardinality counting introduces too great a degree of language dependence when reasoning about the effects of actions.

8.3. The Frame Problem

This section contains two examples that illustrate the difficulties that a formula-based approach encounters with the frame problem. To sum up the conclusions of this section, difficulties arise because the frame problem cannot be solved by simply requiring that the changes made in T as the result of an action be minimal.

8.3.1. Example 8.1

As an initial description of the state of the world, consider the body for T

$$on(TV, duct1)$$
$$on(birdcage, duct2)$$
$$on(magazine, floor).$$

Note that the whereabouts of the newspaper are not explicitly known. By the definition of standard models, and by the nonupdatable formulas 8.2 8.5, and 8.6 given for "on," it follows that the newspaper must be on the floor. In other words, the state of the world is completely determined by the information in T.

Suppose Agatha now asks Tyro to move the TV to the floor. Suitable preconditions for move(x, y) are that y be the floor, y be clear, or that x already be on y: on$(x, y) \lor \neg$on$(z, y) \lor y$=floor. The postcondition is on(x, y). We will assume that the "move" action is unqualified, in the sense that it is guaranteed to succeed if the preconditions for "move" logically follow from T.

In order, then, to reason about the effect of moving the TV to the floor, it suffices to insert on(TV, floor) into T. Under any formula-based approach, the result is the set of updatable formulas

$$\text{on(TV, floor)}$$
$$\text{on(birdcage, duct2)}$$
$$\text{on(magazine, floor).}$$

The frame principle seems to tell us that the newspaper should still be where it was, i.e., on the floor, but this does not logically follow from the new theory; the newspaper may have flitted to duct1 when the TV was removed, according to the new theory. To see that this is not objectionable, imagine that duct1 and duct2 ventilate the room by powerfully sucking new air in through the windows. In this case, the vacuum caused by moving the TV to the floor might well result in the newspaper flying to duct1. Rather, the problem is that *only* the newspaper can have changed position; why not, say, the magazine? Both the magazine and the paper were lying on the floor; why should only the newspaper be affected by moving the TV?

What has gone wrong? The problem is that the formula-based semantics assume that the frame problem will be solved by making a *minimal change* in the formulas of T. Minimality is therefore measured only by the effect of a change on the formulas present in T, rather than by considering the effect of a change on the world itself. This confers second-class status upon those formulas that can be derived from T, such as the location of the newspaper, and also makes the semantics too reluctant to retract the formulas present in T.

One might think that the use of reason maintenance techniques would help to avoid the problems of Example 8.1. Reason maintenance is the process of keeping track of *why* particular facts are believed [de Kleer 86]. For example, for each atom we could keep a list of all the combinations of circumstances that would cause us to believe that that atom was true (or false). For example, we might believe that the TV is on the floor because that is entailed by a nonupdatable formula, because that was stated in an update request, or because there is no place else that it could be, due to the known locations of the other objects in the room. Believing any member of these three categories of reasons would cause us also to believe that the TV was on the floor. Reason maintenance allows one to stop believing in a fact once the underlying support for that fact is no longer itself believed.

For example, one might believe that the room was stuffy because the air ducts were blocked; if the air ducts were then unblocked, one might wish to retract automatically the belief that the room is stuffy.

Reason maintenance is a bookkeeping technique that can be used in conjunction with any update semantics; it is a tool, rather than a philosophy. In Example 8.1, the addition of reason maintenance will not eliminate the formula-based anomaly, because the update eliminates the reasons for believing that the newspaper was on the floor. On the other hand, reason maintenance would be helpful for determining whether the room was stuffy.

What does the PMA do with Example 8.1? The model of T is[14]

$$on(TV, duct1)$$
$$on(birdcage, duct2)$$
$$on(magazine, floor)$$
$$on(newspaper, floor)$$
$$blocked(duct1)$$
$$blocked(duct2)$$
$$stuffy.$$

The PMA agrees with the formula-based approaches that when the TV is moved to the floor, all the other objects can stay where they are, or the newspaper or the magazine can fly to duct1. In addition, under the PMA *the bird cage can move from duct2 to duct1*, and the resulting void at duct2 can be left open or filled by the newspaper or the magazine. (To see this, recall that the nonupdatable formulas of T must be true in every result model. The nonupdatable formulas 8.3 and 8.4, governing "stuffy" and "blocked", are key players in computing the result models.) The six result models are:

on(TV, floor)	on(TV, floor)	on(TV, floor)
on(birdcage, duct2)	on(birdcage, duct2)	on(birdcage, duct2)
on(magazine, floor)	on(magazine, floor)	on(magazine, duct1)
on(newspaper, floor)	on(newspaper, duct1)	on(newspaper, floor)
blocked(duct2)	blocked(duct1)	blocked(duct1)
	blocked(duct2)	blocked(duct2)
	stuffy	stuffy

---

[14] For brevity, the "location" and "duct" atoms will not be listed in the example models.

on(TV, floor)   on(TV, floor)   on(TV, floor)
on(birdcage, duct1)   on(birdcage, duct1)   on(birdcage, duct1)
on(magazine, floor)   on(magazine, duct2)   on(magazine, floor)
on(newspaper, floor)   on(newspaper, floor)   on(newspaper, duct2)
blocked(duct1)   blocked(duct1)   blocked(duct1)
                           blocked(duct2)   blocked(duct2)
                           stuffy   stuffy.

Are these extra models intuitively acceptable? As Ginsberg and Smith point out, the physics of the ducts are unspecified by the nonupdatable formulas of T. One duct might blow air, and the other suck air; the ducts might preferentially attract certain objects. None of these common sense physics constraints are specified in the nonupdatable formulas of T; there is nothing in T to indicate that changes of location should be minimized in preference to changes in the stuffiness of rooms; hence there is no way to eliminate the unwanted models using vanilla PMA. Formula-based approaches do not have any semantic means of eliminating these models, either; they were only eliminated under the formula-based semantics because the location of the bird cage was explicitly stated in T, as opposed to being merely derivable. In other words, the physics knowledge needed to keep the bird cage from moving was encoded syntactically into the formula-based theory, rather than being stated declaratively.

Clearly the PMA would benefit from the introduction of additional pruning heuristics. The maximum benefit would come from the addition of a module that could reason about causal effects. Lacking such a module, we can duplicate many of its effects simply by specifying preferences for minimizing changes in PMA predicates in a manner analogous to prioritization in circumscription. For example, suppose the physics of Agatha's living room are such that changes of location are to be minimized in preference to changes in duct blockage and room stuffiness. If this is done, then the sole minimally-changed model in which on(TV, floor) and all nonupdatable formulas are true is

on(TV, floor)
on(birdcage, duct2)
on(magazine, floor)
on(newspaper, floor)
blocked(duct2),

the intuitively desired model.

Prioritization of predicates is an easily encoded heuristic that helps us cope with the problem of proliferation of models. Prioritization is by no means a philosophically satisfactory treatment of causality, which must await the development of a general theory of causality. In the current application, one could also supply the necessary physics knowledge either directly in T or through special analysis tools used in conjunction with general-purpose update techniques [Forbus 89].

For a formal definition of prioritization under the PMA, partition the predicates of T into sets $S_1, \ldots, S_n$ such that the priority of minimization of changes in predicates in S_i is higher than for those in S_j iff $i < j$. (If desired, individual atoms rather than entire predicates can be prioritized.) Say that two models agree on an atom α if they do not differ on α.

Definition.   *Let M be a model of T and U: insert ω an update under the prioritized PMA. Then $U(T)$ is given by MB3, and $U(M)$ is the set of all models M' such that*

(1)   *ω and the nonupdatable formulas of T are true in M'.*
(2)   *There is no other model M'' such that for some $1 \leq i \leq n$,*
    o   *M'' satisfies (1);*
    o   *M'' and M' agree on all atoms over predicates in $S_1, \ldots$*
              S_{i-1}; and
    o   *M'' differs from M on fewer atoms over predicates in S_i*
              than does M', where "fewer" is defined by set inclusion.

The remaining examples do not make use of the magazine; for that reason, let us assume that Tyro has removed the magazine from the living room, and it ceases to exist from the viewpoint of T.

8.3.2. Example 8.2

The frame problems of formula-based approaches are exacerbated when incomplete information is present. Even if the locations of all objects are known initially, incomplete information will be introduced if Agatha requests actions that are abstract. For example, consider the updatable formulas

$$\text{on(TV, duct1)}$$
$$\text{on(birdcage, floor)}$$
$$\text{on(newspaper, floor)}$$

and Agatha's request that Tyro please remove the TV from duct1. The "remove" action is abstract in the sense that the new location of the TV is unspecified; it is a realistic request in the sense that a useful robot *should* be able to deal with requests like "Take the top off the toothpaste." Reasonable preconditions for remove(x, y) are that y not be the floor and that x be on y, both of which are true for remove(TV, duct1) in Agatha's theory. A suitable postcondition for remove(x, y) is ¬on(x, y). Therefore the formula-based result of performing Agatha's request is

$$¬on(TV, duct1)$$
$$on(birdcage, floor)$$
$$on(newspaper, floor),$$

in which the location of the TV is uncertain. As Example 8.1 illustrated, this type of incomplete information can lead to anomalies when reasoning about subsequent actions, because derivable information is not explicitly represented.

Under the PMA, the initial model is

$$on(TV, duct1)$$
$$on(birdcage, floor)$$
$$on(newspaper, floor)$$
$$blocked(duct1).$$

Without prioritization of predicates, the PMA says that the bird cage or newspaper may fly over to duct1 when the TV is removed, and that an object may move onto duct2. The six result models are

on(TV, floor)	on(TV, floor)	on(TV, floor)
on(birdcage, floor)	on(birdcage, duct1)	on(birdcage, floor)
on(newspaper, floor)	on(newspaper, floor)	on(newspaper, duct1)
	blocked(duct1)	blocked(duct1)
on(TV, duct2)	on(TV, duct2)	on(TV, duct2)
on(birdcage, floor)	on(birdcage, duct1)	on(birdcage, floor)
on(newspaper, floor)	on(newspaper, floor)	on(newspaper, duct1)
blocked(duct2)	blocked(duct1)	blocked(duct1)
	blocked(duct2)	blocked(duct2)
	stuffy	stuffy.

If changes in "on" are minimized preferentially, then the first and fourth of the six models above will be the result models.

8.4. The Ramification Problem

Formula-based semantics employ backward pruning; that is, they will eliminate models of T that differ sufficiently from the information conveyed in ω. As explained in Chapter 2, this makes formula-based semantics unsuitable for applications in which one needs to guarantee that the actual state of the world is at all times reflected in some model of T. Example 8.3 shows the effect of backward pruning in reasoning about action; it is a domain-specific version of Examples 2.1 and 2.5.

8.4.1. Example 8.3

Agatha, still working in the kitchen, thinks of her favorite TV program soon to begin, and remembers that the TV overheats and turns off unless it gets extra ventilation. She calls out to Tyro and asks him to put the TV on one of the ducts. If her initial set of updatable formulas is

$$\text{on(TV, floor)}$$
$$\text{on(birdcage, floor)}$$
$$\text{on(newspaper, floor)},$$

and her request is formulated as the action postcondition on(TV, duct1) $\lor$ on(TV, duct2)[15], then the result theory is

$$\text{on(TV, duct1)} \lor \text{on(TV, duct2)}$$
$$\text{on(birdcage, floor)}$$
$$\text{on(newspaper, floor).}$$

Next Agatha remembers that she can't see the TV from the couch if the TV is on duct2, and she asks Tyro to put the TV on duct1. Inserting on(TV, duct1) into T produces the new set of updatable formulas

$$\text{on(TV, duct1)} \lor \text{on(TV, duct2)}$$
$$\text{on(TV, duct1)}$$
$$\text{on(birdcage, floor)}$$
$$\text{on(newspaper, floor).}$$

(Note that the formula on(TV, duct1) $\lor$ on(TV, duct2) is still part of the theory; its presence will cause backward pruning in the next update.) After the show, Agatha asks Tyro to take the TV off duct1. The result theory is

$$\text{on(TV, duct1)} \lor \text{on(TV, duct2)}$$
$$\neg\text{on(TV, duct1)}$$
$$\text{on(birdcage, floor)}$$
$$\text{on(newspaper, floor)},$$

---

[15] The same anomaly occurs if the postcondition is expressed as $\exists x(\text{on(TV, }x) \land (x{=}\text{duct1} \lor x{=}\text{duct2}))$ (assuming quantifiers are permitted in the body), or by an equivalent formula.

which logically implies that the TV is on duct2, when intuitively the TV could be anywhere but on duct1.

What does the PMA do with Example 8.3? Recall that no principles of physics are encoded in T; further, whatever the physical principles are, they are not known to manifest themselves in the same manner from moment to moment (which is quite reasonable, if, for example, the ventilation system cycles on and off). After Agatha's series of requests in Example 8.3, under the plain PMA the objects in her living room could be nearly anywhere. If instead changes in the location of objects are minimized in preference to changes in other predicates, then the final resulting PMA models are

$$
\begin{array}{ll}
\text{on(TV, duct2)} & \text{on(TV, floor)} \\
\text{on(birdcage, floor)} & \text{on(birdcage, floor)} \\
\text{on(newspaper, floor)} & \text{on(newspaper, floor).} \\
\text{blocked(duct2)} &
\end{array}
$$

Recall that one form of backward pruning is given by formula 2.1,

$$\text{Models}(U(T)) = \text{Models}(T \cup \{\omega\}), \qquad (2.1)$$

when $T \cup \{\omega\}$ is consistent. It follows from FB1 that formula-based semantics use backward pruning. Any model-based semantics that uses backward pruning will also experience the anomaly of Example 8.3; i.e., disjunctive information can lead to unintuitive results, because the incorporation process treats the case where $T \cup \{\omega\}$ is consistent as a special case.

Chapter 2 pointed out that for particularly simple theories and updates, different semantics often agree on the results of the updates. For example, one can apply a prioritized model-based semantics satisfying the Gärdenfors Postulates to the problem of reasoning about movement of blocks, using many of the same examples as [Ginsberg 88ab], and obtain satisfactory results, in spite of the backward pruning required by the Gärdenfors Postulates, if suitable simplifying assumptions are employed, e.g., that the locations of all blocks are known at all times, and, further, have been computed and are available directly in T. In this simplified scenario, the anomalies discussed in this chapter should not arise; reasoning with complete information is much easier than reasoning with incomplete information, and under simplifying assumptions as strong as these, most model-based and formula-based semantics will give satisfactory results.

8.5. Multiple Extensions

Example 8.4 illustrates a formula-based anomaly that arises when more than one possible world can result from an action.

8.5.1. Example 8.4

Suppose that the body of T is

on(TV, floor)
on(newspaper, duct2)
on(birdcage, floor)
¬stuffy.

Ginsberg and Smith show that moving the TV to duct1 leads to two candidate formula-based result theories: one in which the newspaper flies off duct2 and the room remains unstuffy; and one in which the newspaper does not move and the room becomes stuffy. As Ginsberg and Smith remark, this is quite reasonable, for without more information one cannot know whether the force of air from the blocked heating system will blast the newspaper off the duct.

Suppose, however, that ¬stuffy is *not* present in T initially. It is of course, still derivable from T. Yet moving the TV to duct1 now gives only one candidate result theory:

on(TV, duct1)
on(newspaper, duct2)
on(birdcage, floor).

What does the PMA do with Example 8.4? Whether ¬stuffy is included in T or not, the intuitively desired result models are produced:

on(TV, duct1)	on(TV, duct1)
blocked(duct1)	blocked(duct1)
on(newspaper, duct2)	on(newspaper, floor)
on(birdcage, floor)	on(birdcage, floor).
blocked(duct2)	
stuffy	

8.5.2. Resolution of Ambiguous Actions

Recall that a WIDTIO semantics is one in which the theory body resulting from an update with multiple candidate result theories is the set of formulas that appear in all the candidate result theories. In other words, one takes the intersection of all candidate result theories, giving in the case of Example 8.4 the set of updatable formulas on(TV, duct1)

on(birdcage, floor).

Chapter 2 pointed out that WIDTIO enjoys a number of advantages:

- One retains only formulas that are true "no matter what."
- WIDTIO has a better time complexity (NP^{NP}) than the contending formula-based approaches (all exponential in the size of T).
- WIDTIO does not lengthen T excessively ($O(1)$ atoms added if size of postconditions is bounded). All the contending formula-based approaches will on occasion add a number of atoms that is exponential in the size of T.

WIDTIO emphasizes deletion of formulas from T, with the result that after a series of actions, one may know less and less about the state of the world, so that intuitively true propositions become unprovable. As formula-based semantics behave very poorly in the presence of incomplete information, the method chosen for dealing with multiple candidate result theories should not delete any more than absolutely necessary.

Recall that the cross-product approach is to roll the candidate result theories into a single theory by, roughly speaking, taking a disjunction of all the formulas in the cross product of the candidate theories. In light of the difficulty that formula-based semantics have with disjunctive information, this approach would also be ill-advised. The set-of-theories approach seems the most promising of the three formula-based choices.

The formula-based anomalies associated with multiple candidate result theories do not arise under model-based approaches adhering to formula 2.2. The result of an action is exactly the union of all candidate models under these semantics; no extra models are introduced, and no candidate models are pruned.

8.6. Problems with the Possible Models Approach

This section describes the problems with the PMA and other model-based approaches in the application of reasoning about action: language dependence and measures of minimality, algorithms, and building a complete system.

8.6.1. Language Dependence and Measures of Minimality

Formula-based approaches depend on the syntax of T; model-based approaches do not, except for the distinction between knowledge and data formulas. Syntax dependence would not be a flaw in the formula-based approaches if there were some means of "normalizing" the syntactic form of T so that the intuitively desirable effects of an action would be obtained. No such set of normalization guidelines exists at this time, however.

Like formula-based semantics, model-based semantics are language-dependent, in the sense that these semantics are affected by the choice of language used to describe the world. This reflects the model-based assumption that the possible states of the world are the models of a theory, and therefore a minimal change in the world is a minimal change in a model.

For example, suppose that out in the world there are two facts that may possibly hold, p and q, and an action, A, whose effect is to make p or q false. Suppose that the language used to describe this world uses just the propositions a, b, and c, and that p and q are encoded in a, b, and c as follows:

p is true iff a and b both hold;
q is true iff a and c both hold.

The postcondition of A can be expressed as $\neg a \lor \neg b \lor \neg c$. But look at the models that result if A is applied when p and q are both true:

| a | b | a |
| b | c | c |

In the second of these three models, both p and q have become false, which is not a minimal change in the world. (The choice of language in this example may not be as capricious as it first seems; perhaps for some actions, a, b, and c are the right way to describe matters.) To remove the anomaly, one would need to add two additional propositions to represent p and q, and add nonupdatable formulas stating that p was true iff a and b were true, and q was true iff a and c were true. If the postcondition of A is changed to $\neg p \lor \neg q$, then the desired models will result.

General-purpose update semantics cannot avoid the problem of language dependence. Philosophically, the language dependence problem suggests that minimization of changes in atom truth valuations may not always be the right way to reflect changes in the world. This problem has already been noted and addressed by the philosophical community, in work on, for example, mathematical measures of the closeness of different worlds. Another step in this direction has been taken in the AI community, with the idea of minimizing changes in new semantic units called *situations* [Baker 89].

Philosophical holes in our definition of minimality need not prevent the PMA from being a useful tool in an actual application, of course. There is reason to believe that system builders choose the language that most closely models the world, if only to make matters simpler for themselves. The more closely the language mirrors the world, the better behaved the PMA will be; and the more useful the PMA as a tool, the less special-purpose domain-dependent machinery will be needed for the application to augment the capabilities of the PMA.

8.6.2. Algorithms

The PWA may not be as useful a tool in reasoning about action as the PMA, but at least there is a simple and elegant procedure, described in Chapter 2, for reasoning about PWA actions. PMA implementations are a topic of current research. For small problems, one can work with partial descriptions of the models themselves [Forbus 89], rather than operating directly on T, and this seems to be the most promising implementation approach.

8.6.3. Building a Complete System

The PMA does not "solve" the frame, ramification, and qualification problems; as Section 8.6.1 showed, one can quickly concoct scenarios where the PMA, or any other update semantics, cannot express a desired change, or cannot pick out the intuitively desired world in a philosophically satisfactory manner. Rather, the interesting question is that of determining the range of effectiveness of the PMA as a tool in this application, and the design of additional domain-dependent tools and mechanisms that can work in conjunction with the PMA in computing the effect of an action. Such additional mechanisms might deal with causality, quantitative or qualitative reasoning, temporal reasoning, reason maintenance, and reasoning about prior states of the world, as the PMA does not itself address any of these issues.

For example, the PMA does not incorporate any notion of reason maintenance. (Interestingly, Harmon argues that the same holds to some degree in human belief revision, in situations where an entirely rational agent might find reason maintenance imperative [Harmon 86].) If an atom f is true in a PMA model, then f will continue to be believed for as long as possible, even if the original reasons for believing f evaporate. For example, suppose a PMA theory T contains a nonupdatable formula stating that heavy smoking implies a high risk of cancer, and an updatable formula stating that John is a heavy smoker. If John quits smoking and T is updated accordingly, then

T would still imply that John has a high risk of getting cancer, because that is consistent with the new information that John is a non-smoker.

A syntactic solution to this problem, which may suffice in some situations, is to separate the set of predicates on which reason maintenance is to be performed from the remainder of the theory. To achieve this, one would confine the predicates appearing in T to those where reason maintenance was unneeded. A second theory T_1 (or theories, if appropriate) would contain the definitions of the predicates requiring reason maintenance. The truth valuations of those secondary predicates would depend entirely on the current sets of predicate truth valuations for T, and would not depend on information about the past state of the world. For example, we might place in T_1 the nonupdatable formula stating that smoking produces a high cancer risk, and keep formulas about the habits of patients, such as John's smoking, in T. Then when John stopped smoking, whether he was a high cancer risk would become unknown. For this scheme to work properly, every model of T must be extensible to one or more models of $T \cup T_1$. In other words, T_1 cannot constrain the models of T; T_1 can only add truth valuations of new predicates to those models.

Semantic approaches to the reason maintenance problem are much more difficult to devise. One might try to add an understanding of causality to the system; this is an area of current research [Gärdenfors 88b, Lifschitz 87, Shoham 88]. Alternatively, one could manually identify those pairs of pieces of information whose truth valuations can change independently of one another, and use that information to alert an update algorithm to cases where reason maintenance is required [Myers 88].

The task of building a complete system for reasoning about the effects of an action is complicated by our inability to devise a precise standard of correctness. In other words, we have no precise statement of what the effect of an action should, in general, be. This makes it difficult to locate the boundary of the effectiveness of proposed approaches, and to establish limited subdomains within which a particular approach can be guaranteed to provide correct answers.

CHAPTER NINE

IMPLEMENTATION

'... But I say to hell with common sense! By itself each segment of your experience is plausible enough, but the trajectory resulting from the aggregate of these segments borders on being a miracle.'
—Stanislaw Lem, *The Chain of Chance*

This chapter describes simulation experiments conducted with the Update Algorithm, and presents the results from these experiments. The goal of the simulation was to gauge the expected performance of the update and query processing algorithms in a traditional database management system application. The implementation was tailored to this environment, and for that reason the techniques used and results obtained will apply only partially, if at all, to other application environments, such as knowledge-based artificial intelligence applications. In particular, the following assumptions and restrictions were made.

- Update syntax was modified and restricted, to encourage use of simple constructs.
- A fixed data access mechanism (query language) was assumed.
- A large, disk-resident database supplying storage for the relational theory was assumed.
- Performance was equated with the number of disk accesses required to perform queries and updates after a long series of updates, and the storage space required after a long series of updates.

These assumptions and restrictions are all appropriate to traditional database management scenarios; they will be discussed in more detail in later sections. We begin with a brief high-level description of the implemented system, and then examine its components in more detail. The chapter concludes with a description of the experimental results.

9.1. Overview

The Update Algorithm Version II was chosen for simulation. This version of the Update Algorithm permits both nulls and variables to occur in update requests. We assume that a statistical profile of the "average" update is known in advance, so that it is possible to gear the implementation of the Update Algorithm toward this expected case, rather than orienting the implementation toward the worst case as was done in the presentation of the Update Algorithm in Chapters 4 and 5. Orienting the implementation toward the average case allows us to optimize the algorithm to improve performance during update processing. A query processor simulator was also constructed; because the expected case is also known during traditional query processing, the query processing algorithms were also thoroughly optimized. Both the query and the update processing routines made use of a heuristic satisfiability tester to help optimize performance. The implementation is coded entirely in C and is approximately 121 Kbytes long in executable form. The program is main-memory based, i.e., disk storage and accessing are simulated.

Lazy evaluation was not implemented; for that reason, to keep the size of the relational theory within reasonable limits, nulls were not permitted to occur in attributes on which joins were performed in the selection clauses of updates[16].

The exact pattern of the data, and the individual queries and updates, are determined using random numbers and probability distributions, as described in Section 9.4. Updates and queries are modeled chiefly in terms of their *selectivity* rather than their syntax. In other words, because the goal of the implementation is a count of the disk accesses required for processing, the exact syntax of a selection clause is unimportant; what matters is how many disk accesses are required to process that selection clause. Profiles for updates and queries were chosen on the basis of selectivity classes rather than on the basis of syntactic features such as numbers of disjuncts and conjuncts. For example, all selection clauses that require accessing 10 data atoms of T are identical for the purposes of performance measurement, whether those selection clauses contain just single data atoms or conjuncts and disjuncts galore.

The implemented version of update syntax differs from that presented

---

[16] A more thorough investigation is needed into efficient heuristic techniques for minimizing the size of the formulas added to the theory during updates. Simplification heuristics are vital for efficient execution.

in Chapter 3. The goal of the modifications was to tailor syntax to the operations expected to be most common in ordinary database management systems. This decision is expected to have the side effect of mildly discouraging the use of less common (and presumably harder to perform) forms of update requests. The restricted syntax does, however, have the same expressive power as the original syntax; some changes to the relational theory that could be accomplished in one update may, however, now require multiple updates. The exact restrictions on syntax are described in Section 9.5.

9.2. Data Structures and Access Techniques for Relational Theories

The relational theory is mapped into a set of data structures for storage on disk. The data structures required fall into five general categories:

- Data atom space.
- History atom space.
- Equality atom space.
- Logical relationship space.
- Data structures for satisfiability testing.

The unique name axioms and completion axioms are implicitly present and are not stored. Figure 9.1 shows a simplified version of these data structures for the relational theory with body $R(a) \vee R(\epsilon)$.

In the following four subsections we give a high-level overview of each type of data structure. The final subsection gives the full details of the data structures.

9.2.1. Data Atom Space
Data atom space is organized much as ordinary database tuple storage, with data atoms packed into disk blocks and accessed using B-tree indices on their attributes. In fact, to obtain the running time estimates given in Chapters 4 and 5, all data atoms in a relational theory T must have a lookup and insertion time of $O(\log R)$, where R is the maximum number of data atoms in T over the same predicate.

9.2.2. History Atom Space
As presented in Chapters 4 and 5, the Update Algorithm makes heavy use

Figure 9.1. Data atom and logical relationship space.

Body of T: $R(a) \lor R(b)$, $R(a) \lor R(\epsilon)$.

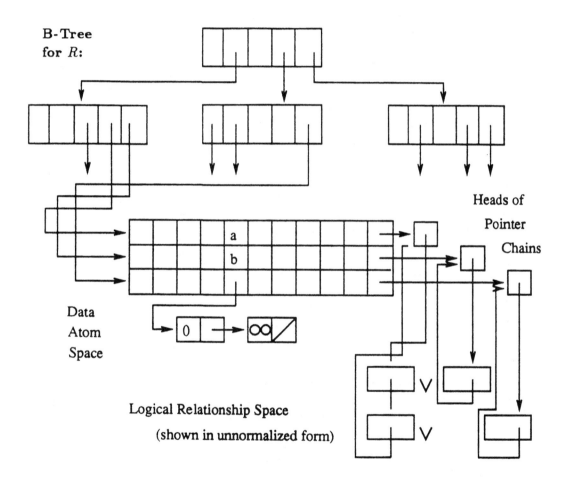

of history atoms. But history atoms are not strictly necessary; there is no reason to introduce them when there is an equivalent method of performing a particular update that uses less space than would be required using history atoms [Hegner 87, Weber 86]. For this reason, the implementation of the Update Algorithm only uses history atoms when it is difficult or impossible to get along without them. For example, the "typical" update in practice is expected to have a very simple selection clause, one that is true in all alternative worlds. If ω is also simple, one can almost always "update in place," and no data atoms need be replaced by history atoms—Steps 2 and 4 of the Update Algorithm become superfluous.

History atoms are stored separately from data atoms. Much less information must be stored for a history atom than for a data atom, because little is important about a history atom except its unique ID. In particular, its attribute values are only important insomuch as they determine which other history atoms that atom unifies with; and if there are no unifications with other atoms, then nothing need be stored for that atom other than its unique ID. Further, the set of atoms with which a history atom unifies is fixed at the time an update is performed. Since we expect few unifications in practice, the implementation reduces all history atoms f_U to unique IDs $h_1, h_2, \ldots$ (predicate constants, in the language of mathematical logic). If some history atom h_1 unifies with another atom h_2 under most general substitution σ, then the additional formula $\sigma \rightarrow (h_1 \leftrightarrow h_2)$ must also be stored in T. This simplification of history atoms is expected to reduce the size of T greatly, as history atom unifications will be rare.

9.2.3. Equality Atom Space
Equality atoms that are true in all alternative worlds have special data structures dedicated to them. Restrictions on the possible values of a null are stored in the same disk block as one of the data atoms in which that null occurs (its *home* data atom). In addition, if the null is known to be equal to any other nulls (e.g., $\epsilon_1 = \epsilon_2$), the data structure for each data atom in which the null occurs includes a pointer to a list of those other nulls.

9.2.4. Logical Relationship Space
An *outside logical relationship* of a data atom f is a formula in T that contains f and other atoms. For example, if f only occurs as a separate formula in T, then f does not take part in any outside logical relationships. If the formula $f \vee \alpha$ occurs in T, however, then f participates in an outside logical relationship.

The history substitution step (Step 2) is the bottleneck for the Update Algorithm. To make renaming fast and achieve the time bounds presented in Chapters 4 and 5, all occurrences of a data atom f in T must be represented on disk by pointers to a block of storage where f is actually kept, so that the substitution of f_U for f, if required, can be done in constant time. In other words, rather than storing the formulas of T directly, the formulas are mapped into a data structure that contains pointers into a separate name space where names of data atoms are kept—data atom space.

All occurrences of the same atom or history atom in logical relationship space are linked together in a chain whose head is either an index entry for a data atom or a history atom unique ID.

To facilitate satisfiability testing, logical relationships are not stored as they would appear in T, but rather are converted into a normal form that is convenient for satisfiability testing. This normal form uses only one logical operation, a variant on exclusive-or called *exact-or* that takes one or more arguments. If a set of atoms is related by exact-or, then exactly one of those atoms must be true in any model of the relational theory. Exact-or differs from exclusive-or in that exact-or is not associative—not a proper operator at all. When normalized, the body of the relational theory is just a list of *alternative sets*, or sets of pointers to atoms, related by exact-or. It is extremely easy to write a heuristic satisfiability tester in C (described in Section 9.2.5) that works on alternative sets. The potential pitfall of using alternative sets is that like any other normal form, conversion to alternative sets may exponentially increase the length of a formula in the worst case.

9.2.5. Data Structures for Satisfiability Testing

A heuristic satisfiability tester is an important part of an efficient implementation of the Update Algorithm. "Heuristic" means that when testing satisfiability of a formula α, in addition to the obvious responses of "satisfiable" and "unsatisfiable," the satisfiability tester may decide that it is too hard to tell whether α is satisfiable, and respond accordingly. This satisfiability tester is guaranteed to stop in a number of steps that is polynomial in the number of stored atoms.

To test satisfiability efficiently, once a decision has been made by the tester on the truth valuation of an atom f, all other occurrences of f in T must be located quickly. To achieve this, in the implementation all occurrences of the same data atom in the body of T are linked together in a list whose head is an index entry.

The other data structure needed for heuristic satisfiability testing is an array of bits to keep track of the decisions made so far on atom truth valuations.

9.2.6. Details of Data Structures

In agreement with traditional relational database terminology, in this discussion the arguments to a predicate are called *attributes* and the values for those attributes in a particular data atom are called *attribute values*.

For an efficient implementation, more must be stored on disk for each data atom than just its attribute values. The following data structure description shows what data structure fields our implementation stores for a three-attribute data atom; there are 13 fields, the last three of which contain the attribute value information for the data atom.

1.   Data atom ID(s).
2.   Does this data atom contain nulls or participate in outside logical relationships? (Yes/No)
3.   Does this data atom participate in outside logical relationships? (Yes/No)
4–6.   Are the attribute values of attributes 1–3 null? (Yes/No for each attribute)
7–9.   Pointers to MarkLists for attributes 1–3.
10.   Pointer to AltSetList.
11–13. Attribute value or pointer to null for attributes 1–3.

The data structure for data atoms contains pointers to MarkLists, AltSetLists, and nulls. Let us first describe the data structures used for nulls.

If an *insert* request is received for a data atom that includes a null as an attribute value, then a flag is set for that attribute in a header for the data atom, and in place of the attribute value a pointer is stored to a null data structure in the same block of disk storage. The null data structure consists of an ordered list of begin/end range values, with a provision for open ranges. This gives a reasonable simulation of nulls in a variety of domains (e.g., strings, integers, reals). The implementation uses a linked list, but there might be a better choice; the actual data structure is not important for performance measurement, as long as one can get the null information during the same disk access as the rest of the data atom.

MarkLists are lists of the equality atoms in which a null occurs. "Marked nulls" is the traditional name in the database literature for the case when two nulls are known to be equal to one another. The actual data structure used is a header followed by a linked list of data atom IDs and attribute numbers. The performance measurements assume that each MarkList can be fully contained on a block of disk storage.

One of the drawbacks of using exact-or normal form is that pure disjunctions are difficult to express. To make pure disjunction easier to implement, we allow the use of multiple data atom IDs for the same data atom.

The data structure for an AltSetList looks like that used for a MarkList. The main difference between them is that some atom IDs in an AltSetList refer to history atoms. (Exact-or normal form tends to introduce many history atoms.) A history atom unique ID is just an index into the History-AtomArray; in that array a list is stored for each history atom, containing pointers to the alternative sets where that history atom appears.

Associated with the AltSetLists are a few extra bits to help the satisfiability testing routine remember which truth valuations have been decided so far. The bits are arranged so that the satisfiability tester would not have to hop all over disk to turn those bits off after the testing is done; they are kept together in one array, hashed on data atom and history atom ID. This array is to be loaded into main memory when the database is first opened.

The HistoryAtomArray fits on as many contiguous blocks of disk as its length requires. Its storage is managed by a manager that keeps track of free slots. Each slot represents a different history atom, and contains a pointer to a list of the alternative sets that that history atom occurs in.

9.3. Implementation of the Update Algorithm

The Update Algorithm as implemented does not resemble its presentation in Chapter 5. This is because the presentation in Chapter 5 was geared toward streamlined handling of the general case, that is, the worst case. In contrast, the implemented version is geared toward streamlined handling of the expected case. We expect the "typical" data atom in the relational theory to be true in all alternative worlds, and hence the implementations of the query and update algorithms are oriented heavily toward dealing with data atoms that are true (or false) in all alternative worlds.

This orientation leads to the use of a hierarchical architecture for the update processor. At the top of the hierarchy are procedures that work correctly when data atoms do not contain nulls and are not involved in any outside logical relationships. At the lowest level are routines that know how to handle arbitrary outside logical relationships. The implemented version of the Update Algorithm operates at all times in the highest possible level of this uncertainty hierarchy. A simplified version of the hierarchy for ground queries and updates follows.

1.   All atoms involved in this query/update are true in all alternative worlds, so process this request as though in an ordinary database.

2.   There are nulls in one of the atoms involved in this request, but the nulls are not relevant to this particular request, so they can be ignored. Further, the atoms are not involved in any outside logical relationships.

3.   There are nulls in one of the atoms involved in this request, but the atom and its nulls are not involved in any outside logical relationships, so the uncertainty can be dealt with locally.

4.   Some atoms or nulls of the request are involved in outside logical relationships, and a heuristic satisfiability tester needs to be called before any updates are performed or the query answer is returned.

The determination of the correct level of the hierarchy is done as rapidly as possible; dedicated fields in the stored data atom are maintained to give that information. The determination of the correct level of the hierarchy is done separately for each set of bindings to variables in the update or query.

The hierarchy is organized in accordance with the expected frequency of different types of uncertainty in the relational theory. For example, nulls are expected to be the most common type of uncertainty, and nulls are expected to be less frequent in the "important" attributes (i.e., those appearing in joins or equality atoms in ϕ and ω). For that reason, the implementation is optimized to work most efficiently at higher levels of the hierarchy. In particular, if no uncertainty is present at all, then queries and updates will be processed with as few disk accesses as though the database management system had never heard of uncertainty (barring effects due to the higher space required for tuple storage). This ensures that one needn't pay for the expressive power of the relational theory unless one uses it.

Conceptually, a practical implementation of the Update Algorithm will begin by instantiating the variables of the update or query request U, attempting to satisfy the selection clause ϕ of U. The process of instantiation will be guided by the use of safe selection clauses, construed in this implementation to mean roughly that each instantiation of a variable should be a most general choice that will lead a data atom of ϕ to unify with a data atom already in the relational theory. The instantiation process stops as soon as ϕ is satisfied and all variables in ω are bound. As an example optimization used in the implementation, at this point the bound version ϕ' of ϕ is minimized in length. For example, all atoms in ϕ' that are known to be true (resp. false) in all alternative worlds are replaced by the truth value T (resp. F). In the average case, ϕ' will be reduced to T if the request is an insertion. In the worst case, ϕ' should be reduced to a conjunction of a very small number of literals, say no more than three. This important minimization reduces the number of atoms that must be added to T to perform U.

9.4. Simulation Data

This section describes the data used as input to the performance measurement runs.

For performance measurement, a relational theory containing "real" data (e.g., employees, managers, and departments) could not give sufficiently empirical results. For example, what would constitute a "representative" set of queries and updates? Therefore for performance measurement, we have chosen the important parameters of individual queries and updates randomly according to pre-specified probability distributions (described below). The individual queries and updates are reduced to a set of statistical profiles, so that data atoms are selected to satisfy selection clauses according to the dictates of probability distributions.

A simple approach to queries is to divide query answers into three categories: sets of data atoms known to satisfy the query, sets of data atoms known to satisfy the query in some alternative worlds but not in others, and sets of data atoms that may possibly satisfy the query. The latter class consists of those sets of data atoms for which the heuristic satisfiability tester was unable to reach a conclusion.

The relational theory T used for performance measurement contains three database predicates, each with three attributes. Indexes are stored for all three attributes. At the beginning of a run, all three database predicates have the same number of data atoms occurring in T; the exact number is a parameter set at the beginning of the run, typically 1000 or 200. Nonnull data atom attribute values are distributed uniformly over an infinite range. The chance of nulls occurring as attribute values in data atoms, both initially and when data atoms are added using *insert* and *modify*, is controlled by probabilities selected at the beginning of a performance run. These probabilities control the number of introduced data atoms having zero, one, and two nulls as attribute values. In addition, the type of range restrictions, if any, on nulls at the time of their home data atom insertion is controlled by probabilities set at the beginning of a performance run. Nulls can be unrestricted, meaning they can take on any value in the underlying attribute domain; or they can be restricted to a range, the size of which is chosen uniformly on an interval also selected at run time; or they can be restricted to a set of three values. Of course these restrictions can be altered by subsequent updates.

Disk block size is also a parameter set at run time. Data atom size is set to 100 bytes. A block packing factor of 69% (derived from empirical and theoretical studies; see [Wiederhold 87]) is assumed.

9.5. Updates and Queries

We first cover the syntax for updates and queries, then look at the method used to generate particular profiles of updates and queries for performance measurement.

Rather than using one single update operation, four operators are made available: *insert*, *delete*, and *modify* (all discussed in Chapter 3), and also an operation called *assert*, with syntax and semantics as follows:

assert ϕ: Eliminate every alternative world of T where ϕ is false.

The mix of the different types of updates and queries is controlled by parameters selected at the start of each performance measurement run.

In the implemented version of update requests, no more than one data atom f can occur in ω. The formula ω can contain just f, or $f \vee \top$ (written $maybe(f)$ for ease of programming), or either of these in conjunction with range restrictions on nulls. Further, any nulls in f cannot already occur in T. (Assertions can be used later to equate pairs of nulls.) More complicated ωs containing additional atoms can be simulated using multiple updates within one transaction.

9.5.1. Selection Clause Profiles

As implemented, processing of every selection clause other than $\top$ begins with a selection phase. The relation and attribute for the initial selection is chosen randomly from a uniform distribution. These selections fall into five different types, based on the number of data atoms they select.

1.   One data atom is selected via index lookup on attribute value. Any additional data atoms with nulls that could be equal to that attribute value are included in the result.

2.   A small set of data atoms is selected via index lookup. A uniform distribution is used to determine the size of the set, which can range between zero and a parameterized upper limit (typically 50 data atoms). Any additional data atoms with nulls that could be equal to that attribute value are included in the result.

3.   A percentage of the data atoms over a predicate are selected via index lookup. The percentage is selected using an Erlang distribution ($m = 2$, $l = 2$, total = 2.5) that typically selects 10% of the data atoms over a predicate. The Erlang distribution (see e.g. [Wiederhold 87]) is often used to model natural phenomena; the graph of its probability distribution starts off at $m = 2$ at a high probability, quickly rises to its maximum, then falls into a long tail. Any additional data atoms with nulls that could be equal to that attribute value are included in the result.

4.   Range selection: All data atoms within two delimiting points in an attribute index are selected. Size of range is chosen uniformly from an interval selected at the beginning of the performance run. (A Zipfian distribution [Knuth 73] would have been more appropriate, as discussed below, but was bypassed due to the difficulty of implementing it.) Any additional data atoms with nulls that could fall within that range are included in the result.

5.   A sequential scan is conducted of the data atoms in the relational theory over some predicate, resulting in the eventual selection of a small set of data atoms over that predicate. Again, the size of the set is chosen uniformly from an interval selected at the beginning of the performance run, and any additional data atoms with nulls that could be equal to that attribute value are included in the result.

The type of the selection clause of the current request is selected at run time using random numbers and expected distributions of selection clause types for queries and for updates. Updates are strongly biased towards selection of individual data atoms (type 1) or the truth value T, in accordance with traditional database updates. (Of course, if every data atom in the relational theory has a null for some attribute, then even a type 1 selection clause could return all the data atoms in the theory.) Further, no selection clauses of type 3 are allowed in updates, as it is our belief that the number of tuples changed by an update is not generally a function of the size of the database.

Once the size of the result of a selection has been decided, the actual data atoms satisfying the selection must be chosen. The implementation uses a uniform probability distribution to select data atoms from the predicates. Choice of predicate for the selection is also made uniformly.

9.5.2. Join Profiles

After the initial selection phase, between zero and two joins are executed. Expected percentages of updates and queries with zero, one, and two joins are chosen at the beginning of the performance measurement run; generally updates are expected to have a high likelihood of having no more than one join. After the initial selection phase, the order of joining of relations is chosen, using a uniform distribution.

9.5.3. Projection

Projection is not modeled, because it is not expected to have a large effect on the comparative disk access costs for relational theories and complete-information relational databases.

9.6. Update Implementation Technique

It was our belief that the most economical route in the long run was to minimize the amount of information in logical relationship space, at the expense of data atom space. In other words, if there are two ways to represent the result of an update in the relational theory, and one way adds more to data atom space but less to logical relationship space than does the other, then the former method is preferred. The idea is to have as much information as possible stored in a simple, flat format that will not require use of expensive procedures for analysis. With this goal in mind, the implementation avoids having to store equality atoms by making heavy use of a procedure called *tuple splitting* [Keller 85b], described briefly below.

Consider a relational theory with body $Emp(\epsilon, CS)$. Suppose an update arrives with selection clause $Emp(Chien, CS)$. Then, loosely speaking, the data atom $Emp(\epsilon, CS)$ satisfies that selection clause in some alternative worlds and not in others. If the update is *insert* $Mgr(Nilsson, CS)$ *where* $Emp(Chien, CS)$, then the truth valuation of the new data atom $Mgr(Nilsson, CS)$ is going to depend on the value of ϵ. We chose to avoid proliferation of atoms such as $\epsilon = Chien$ by *splitting* $Emp(\epsilon, CS)$ into two stored data atoms $Emp(Chien, CS)$ and $Emp(\epsilon, CS)$, where (1) the new data atom $Emp(\epsilon, CS)$ has a range restriction $\epsilon \neq Chien$, and (2) the two data atoms appear together in an alternative set. Then the selection clause is satisfied by the data atom Emp(Chien, CS) in all of the alternative worlds where Emp(Chien, CS) is true, and is not satisfied by the other stored data atom in any world where that data atom is true. In the implementation, whenever a data atom only satisfies the selection clause of an update in some of the worlds where that data atom is true, then that data atom is split until this is no longer the case. When a data atom is split, its alternative sets must be changed, and also all tuples on its mark list may require splitting to preserve the alternative worlds of the relational theory. We prefer not to present the details of this process, as it is quite intricate.

9.7. Experimental Results and Discussion

In this section we describe the behavior of the implementation with respect to two parameters: disk accesses required to execute a set of queries after a certain number of updates has been completed, and size of relations (i.e., number of stored data atoms over the same predicate) after a series of updates. We first examine relation size, then disk access count, and then give some general comments.

9.7.1. Relation Size

As described earlier, the input to a simulation run consists of three relations/predicates, each with three attributes, and each with the same number of stored data atoms. Each stored data atom is known to be true in all alternative worlds at the beginning of the run. Then a long series of hundreds or thousands of updates is applied while the size of the three relations is monitored. Most of our runs used an initial relation size of 200 data atoms, for reasons discussed below; experiments were also performed with initial sizes of 1000 and 20. These runs were all very interesting to watch; a number of phenomena deserve mention. First we describe the parameter settings used for this set of runs, summarized in Table 9.1.

These parameters are intended to model a scenario where 80% of the incoming *insert* requests are for data atoms that are to be true in all alternative worlds. Of the remaining 20%, one null appears in 18% of the data atom insertion requests, and two nulls appear in the remaining 2%. Every inserted data atom has some non-null as an argument, because one attribute is required to be null-free, to permit joins at a reasonable cost for large relations. In keeping with this 80/20 approach, a *modify* request has an 80% chance of modifying an attribute value to be a constant, and a 20%

Table 9.1. *Major input parameters for a series of runs.*

200	Number of data atoms in each relation at start of run
20	Upper bound on "small set" size for type 2 selection clauses
.20	Percentage of updates that are insertions
.40	Percentage of updates that are modifications
.20	Percentage of updates that are deletions
.20	Percentage of updates that are assertions
.20	Percentage of modifications that introduce set nulls
.80	Percentage of type 1 selection clauses for insertions
.20	Percentage of type 2 selection clauses for insertions
.58	Percentage of type 1 selection clauses for modifications
.34	Percentage of type 2 selection clauses for modifications
.00	Percentage of type 3 selection clauses for modifications
.06	Percentage of type 4 selection clauses for modifications
.02	Percentage of type 5 selection clauses for modifications
.75	Percentage of type 1 selection clauses for deletions
.15	Percentage of type 2 selection clauses for deletions
.00	Percentage of type 3 selection clauses for deletions
.05	Percentage of type 4 selection clauses for deletions
.05	Percentage of type 5 selection clauses for deletions
.20	Percentage of type 1 selection clauses for queries
.20	Percentage of type 2 selection clauses for queries
.20	Percentage of type 3 selection clauses for queries
.20	Percentage of type 4 selection clauses for queries
.20	Percentage of type 5 selection clauses for queries
.40	Percentage of queries with no joins in the selection clause
.35	Percentage of queries with one join in the selection clause
.25	Percentage of queries with two joins in the selection clause
.50	Chance of an inserted set null having an unrestricted domain
.80	Chance of an inserted tuple having no nulls
.18	Chance of an inserted tuple having one null
.02	Chance of an inserted tuple having two nulls

Figure 9.2. Relation size after a series of updates.

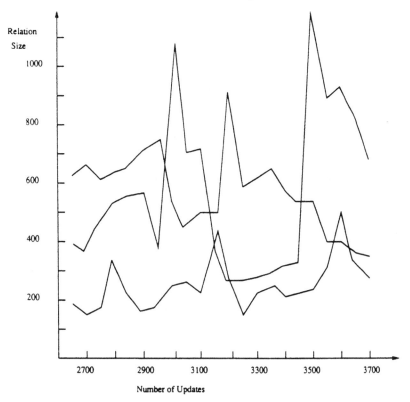

chance of modifying it to be a null. Half of the unknown values in inserted data atoms are restricted to small sets, containing three possible values initially. These represent inserted data atoms like Emp(ϵ, CS) $\wedge$ (ϵ=Chien $\vee$ ϵ=Nilsson). The other half of the inserted nulls have unrestricted ranges, meaning that they can assume any value from an infinite domain. Emp(ϵ, CS) is an example of this type of unrestricted insertion.

The breakdown of update types in the sample run of Figure 9.1 is 40% *modify* requests and 20% each *insert*, *delete*, and *assert* requests. The sensitivity of our results to the value of the *assert* parameter will be discussed below.

Figures 9.2 and 9.3 show the number of stored data atoms for each of the three relations over a long series of updates, taken from a run with an initial relation size of 200 data atoms. Figure 9.2 gives a close-up view of the behavior of the relations between updates 2700 and 3700. The starting and stopping points were taken at random from a run of over 6000 updates.

Figure 9.3. Relation size after a series of updates.

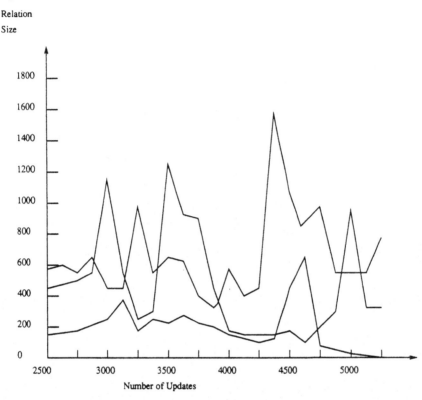

Figure 9.3 takes a longer-term view, covering updates 2500 through 5250. These figures bring out two important points about this typical run:

- Relation size does not increase with time.
- Relation size has a high variance.

Figures 9.2 and 9.3 show sudden, dramatic rises in relation size, followed immediately by major collapses. What causes those dramatic peaks? Over such a long series of updates, events with low probability of occurring at any one moment have a high probability of occurring at some point. The peaks in relation size are caused by repeated splits of data atoms like Emp(ϵ, CS): a long series of updates all have selection clauses containing an atom that unifies with Emp(ϵ, CS), and that data atom is split again and again, causing a sudden explosion in the size of the alternative sets of the data atom. Then the law of averages has its effect: an *assert* request establishes that a data atom in one of those large alternative sets is true in all alternative worlds, and the entire huge alternative set vanishes with that *assert* request. Graphs on a larger scale than those of Figures 9.2 and 9.3 would show that such explosions typically take place within a short series of perhaps 30 updates, and vanish even more quickly.

Of course any practical implementation of the Update Algorithm would need to prevent sudden bursts in relation size: the growth and collapse use a lot of resources. The obvious means of controlling growth is a limit on the number of times any one tuple can be split before more complete information on its nulls is required.

Sudden collapses in relation size, other than those following a sudden burst in size, are very rare. This is because the base size of the relation—its size when not in a dramatic peak—is determined not by data atoms that have been split many times, but by data atoms that are either true in all alternative worlds or at most have been split just a few times. There is no way to delete many of these data atoms within a few updates, because the number of data atoms selected by the *delete* operator is not a function of relation size.

Figures 9.2 and 9.3 do not show the initial growth of the relations from 200 to their eventual base size of approximately 400 data atoms. Recall that at the beginning of a simulation run, all data atoms are known to be true in all alternative worlds. The initial phase of growth lasts for several hundred updates, as the initial data atoms in the relations are replaced by data atoms that are not so likely to be true in all alternative worlds. As such data atoms are likely to be split several times before they are *deleted* or *asserted*, the long-term expected size of the relation is greater than its initial size.

We had planned to do the simulation runs with much larger initial relation sizes, say 10,000 or more tuples. However, our hardware platform did not take kindly to keeping all the data structures for statistics for such large relations. In addition, the random numbers we used so heavily gave terrible locality to the data atom access patterns. We tested the behavior of relations with initial sizes of between 20 and 5000 tuples to see what relationship held between starting size and eventual size, with the hope that a smaller starting size would suffice. We found that in all cases, the relation size after a long series of updates is a function of the initial relation size, and that for initial sizes over 100 tuples, the relations grew to between 1.5 and 2 times their initial size before stabilizing. For example, an initial relation size of 1000 tuples grew to an average base size of 2000 tuples after a series of 1500 or more updates. Smaller starting sizes had to grow proportionately more before reaching stability; relations of fewer than 80 tuples stood in danger of being wiped out by an unlucky sequence of *assert* and *delete* requests. For example, the smallest relation in Figure 9.2 drops down below 100 tuples after update 4500, and to size zero soon thereafter. Even 1500 updates later, that relation still had fewer than 20 data atoms. This opened up the possibility that 100 data atoms was a size threshold for stability; however, this hypothesis was discredited by a separate simulation run using initial sizes of 20 data atoms. In this latter run, the relation size stabilized at a base of 100 tuples. From the group of test runs we conducted, we concluded that simulation runs with an initial relation size of 200 data atoms were adequate for our purpose of understanding long term statistical trends in relation size.

The exact pattern of relation size peaks and valleys is highly variable. For example, changing the random number seed, or changing the initial relation size from 200 to 199 or 201 data atoms, was found to lead to a very different pattern of growth and shrinkage, though an unchanged relation base size.

What effect did assertions have in keeping down the size of the relations? A sample run with the assertion routines disabled showed slow, steady growth in the size of the relations, so that an initial relation size of 200 data atoms had grown to over 20,000 data atoms in the three relations after approximately 850 updates.

When the percentage of *assert* requests was lowered to 10% by disabling the *assert* routine half the time, then after 1000 updates, the three relations of initial size 200 had grown to a combined base size of over 3500 tuples. After 1500 updates, the combined base size was over 6000 tuples. Relations of initial size 100 headed towards size infinity at the same steady pace.

The second phase of experimentation involved measuring disk accesses required for a series of queries after a long series of updates. From examination of the pattern of growth and shrinkage, we determined that 1000 updates were sufficient to "randomize" the initial relations fully and to stabilize the relation sizes. The base relation size remained the same from the 1000th update on through the 10,000th, which was the largest number of iterations we tried.

Because relation size was subject to dramatic temporary fluctuations, we did not want to measure the disk access cost of queries at a moment when the relations were at an unrealistic size peak that would not have been permitted in a more practical setting. However, this turned out not to be a problem, as for the test runs we used in measuring disk accesses, the relation sizes were all quite reasonable after exactly 1000 updates.

9.7.2. Disk Access Measurements

We wished to compare the performance during query processing of a relational theory and a complete-information relational database. The first task of such a comparison is to decide what constitutes a fair comparison: what should be the characteristics of the complete-information database? To determine this, we examined the internal state of a relational theory after a long series of updates, in order to determine the approximate size of each of its relations in its alternative worlds by examining the cardinality of its alternative sets. In the process we garnered information about the number and makeup of the alternative sets in a relational theory after a long series of updates.

The relational theory used in this discussion was generated by applying a series of 1000 updates to relations of initial size 200. This theory was described in the previous section, and the major input parameters for the theory are listed in Table 9.1. At the end of the generation process, the three relations had sizes 485, 600, and 358, respectively. Examination of the alternative sets of the theory showed that an alternative world of this theory would have approximately 225, 199, and 139 tuples, respectively, in its three relations. The largest alternative set found contained 130 data atoms, most of them from relation three. This correlated with the findings of test runs on complete-information relations of initial size 200, which showed that the average relation size was still approximately 200 tuples after 1000 updates. We concluded that a fair comparison could be obtained by running the queries on a complete-information relational database with 200 tuples in each relation.

We then ran a series of random queries on the complete-information database, using simulation to count the number of disk accesses needed to answer the queries. Experimental runs of 100 to 500 queries on this complete-information database showed wide variation—as much as a factor of three—in the seeks, latencies, and block transfers needed, depending on the choice of a random number seed. We traced this problem to the presence of joins whose result was the cartesian product of the two relations. To achieve greater stability, such joins were prohibited. Once this step was taken, disk access requirements were fairly uniform over different choices of random number seeds. We averaged the results from eight typical runs of 100 queries to get complete-information seek, latency, and block transfer totals. These figures are shown in Table 9.2.

Another factor threatened to prevent a realistic comparison. If joins are done on attributes containing unrestricted nulls, then data atoms containing

Table 9.2. *Disk accesses during processing of 100 queries.*

	Seeks	Disk Block Transfers
Complete Information	7, 750	9, 440
Incomplete Information	25, 821	28, 502

nulls on those attributes will match with every data atom in the joining relation. The volatility of this type of n^2 join had already been demonstrated in the complete-information case. To avoid spurious comparisons, we chose to restrict joins to the null-free attribute of each of the relations. This is a very strong assuption with a marked effect on our results.

As mentioned earlier, we assume that each alternative set and mark list fits on one block of disk storage. When the satisfiability tester is called, it recursively visits all alternative sets that each selected data atom appears in, all alternative sets that the atoms in those sets appear in, and so on. Once an alternative set has been visited during a query, it is completely read into memory at that time and remains in memory until the end of that query. Similarly, once a MarkList is referenced it is assumed to remain in memory until the end of the query. At the end of each query, the alternative sets and mark lists are flushed from memory.

The disk access requirements shown in Table 9.2 for the incomplete-information theory are the averages of a set of six runs taken with different random number seeds at query time and otherwise identical input data; the same input data for queries were used as for the complete-information database.

Table 9.2 shows that the presence of incomplete information causes a threefold increase in disk access costs for a series of queries. Examination of the raw data showed that most of the extra cost does not come from accesses to alternative sets and mark lists; rather, the more mundane accessing of data atom space records alone more than doubles the average disk access requirements. Since there are twice as many stored data atoms in the incomplete-information theory as in the complete-information database, this is not surprising.

9.7.3. Discussion
When the simulation project began, it was unclear what level of *assert* re-

quests would be required to keep the relational theory from growing without bound. We found that 20% assertions provided size stability, and 10% produced slow growth, when 40% of the updates were modifications and the rest were evenly split between insertions and deletions. As for disk access costs, the presence of incomplete information in the database caused an approximate doubling in the number of stored data atoms and an approximate threefold increase in disk accesses required during query processing, for the case where joins were not permitted on attributes containing unrestricted nulls. This increase seems reasonable, since intuitively the presence of nulls will cause many more data atoms to appear to satisfy the selection clause of an incoming query.

One unusual feature of the implementation is its use of tuple splitting in an attempt to avoid complicated logical inferences over data atoms. It is not clear whether tuple splitting has any advantages as an implementation strategy. On the one hand, tuple splitting made the relation size a clear indicator of the proliferation of uncertainty within the relational theory. On the other hand, tuple splitting was responsible for the sudden spurts and drops in relation size. In a practical implementation of this approach, those irregularities in relation size would have to be ironed out by establishing limits on the permissible number of splits. This points out another potential advantage of tuple splitting, in that it is easy to detect the most common situations where uncertain data will have a big impact on processing costs. On the other hand, such record-keeping could probably be incorporated into a more direct implementation of logical relationships as well. Finally, it is not clear to what extent the high disk access requirements for the database were due to the use of tuple splitting.

The simulation uses a uniform probability distribution to select data atoms from a relation during the selection phase of query and update processing. A more realistic model (and one which would lead to more optimistic results) would be to use Zipf's law [Knuth 73] with a distribution that directed 90% of the updates to 10% of the relational theory data atoms, 90% of that 90% to 10% of that 10%, and so on; and that directed 80% of the queries to 20% of the relational theory data atoms, 80% of that 80% to 20% of that 20%, and so on. Zipf's law would improve the in-memory performance of the implementation, because it would tend to localize uncertainties into little clusters. The most expensive processing occurs when a chain of interrelated uncertainties sprawls across the relational theory; a Zipfian distribution would tend to keep uncertainty local. Because processing cost may be exponential in the length of the chain of interrelated uncertainty,

short localized chains—in particular, chains of guaranteed bounded length—
would put a tight cap on the CPU cost of query answering. In particular,
if chain lengths are bounded by a constant, then query answering will no
longer be $\mathcal{NP}$-complete[17]; the worst-case running time of a query will be
polynomial in the size of the relational theory. This $O(1)$ *hypothesis*—the
belief that chains will be of bounded length—is a very important point, so
let us elaborate on it a bit.

It is not uncertainty per se that makes query processing expensive; in-
memory processing only gets expensive when attribute values are uncertain
and they depend on other uncertain values, which in turn depend on other
uncertain values, and so on. For example, if we do not know Smith's salary,
and we do not know the number of orders outstanding in the warehouse,
and we do not know who Smith's boss is, query processing does not thereby
become expensive and problematic; it only really becomes a problem if in
addition Smith's salary *depends on* who Smith's boss is, and that in turn
depends on the number of orders outstanding in the warehouse, and so on.
The length of that chain of uncertainty is what determines the cost of query
processing. We hypothesize that in practice, that chain of uncertainty is
short: $O(1)$, i.e., of length bounded by a constant. In other words, Smith's
salary is not going to depend on data atoms far off in another corner of
the relational theory. Zipf's law, which has been observed to hold for many
natural phenomena, supports the $O(1)$ hypothesis. Of course there is no
formal method to prove or disprove this hypothesis; consider it an argument
against entropy in the relational theory, where entropy is defined as the
Murphy's-Law state of affairs wherein the length of chains of interrelated
uncertainties grows as the size of the relational theory.

Entropy does have an ally, however. Since people are naturally messy,
their relational theories will tend to get messy and cluttered with old, irrelevant uncertainties. A certain amount of energy will have to be expended into
keeping the relational theory clean with *assert*. Feedback on performance
bottlenecks should suffice to motivate periodic clean-ups.

---

[17] Or co-$\mathcal{NP}$-complete, depending on the exact query language allowed [Vardi 86].

BIBLIOGRAPHY

[Abiteboul 85]   S. Abiteboul, G. Grahne, "Update Semantics for Incomplete Databases," *Proceedings of the Eleventh International Conference on Very Large Data Bases*, Stockholm, pp. 1–12, August 1985.

[Alchourrón 85]   C. E. Alchourrón, P. Gärdenfors, and D. Makinson, "On the Logic of Theory Change: Partial Meet Contraction and Revision Functions," *The Journal of Symbolic Logic*, **50**:2, pp. 510–530, June 1985.

[Appelt 88]   D. Appelt and K. Konolige, "A Practical Nonmonotonic Theory for Reasoning about Speech Acts," *Proceedings of the 26th Annual Meeting of the Association for Computational Linguistics*, Buffalo NY, pp. 170–178, June 1988.

[Atzeni 87]   P. Atzeni and M. C. De Bernardis, "A New Basis for the Weak Instance Model," *Proceedings of the Sixth Symposium on Principles of Database Systems*, San Diego, pp. 79–86, March 1987.

[Baker 89]   A. Baker and M. Ginsberg, "Temporal Projection and Explanation," *Proceedings of the Eleventh International Joint Conference on Artificial Intelligence*, Detroit, pp. 906–911, August 1989.

[Bancilhon 81]   F. Bancilhon and N. Spyratos, "Update Semantics of Relational Views," *ACM Transactions on Database Systems* **6**:4, pp. 557–575, December 1981.

[Biskup 81]   J. Biskup, "Null Values in Database Relations," in *Advances in Data Base Theory* 1, H. Gallaire, J. Minker, and J. M. Nicolas, eds., Plenum Press, 1981.

[Borgida 85]   A. Borgida, "Language Features for Flexible Handling of Exceptions in Information Systems," *ACM Transactions on Database Systems*, **10**:4, pp. 563–603, December 1985.

[Chamberlin 76]   D. D. Chamberlin, M. M. Astrahan, K. P. Eswaran, P. P. Griffiths, R. A. Lorie, J. W. Mehl, P. Reisner, and B. W. Wade, "SEQUEL 2: A Unified Approach to Data Definition, Manipulation, and Control," *IBM Journal of Research and Development* **20**:6, November 1976.

[Clark 78]   K. L. Clark, "Negation as Failure," *Logic and Databases*, H. Gallaire and J. Minker, eds., Plenum Press, New York, 1978.

[Codd 79]   E. F. Codd, "Extending the Relational Data Base Model to Capture More Meaning," *ACM Transactions on Database Systems* 4:4, pp. 397–434, December 1979.

[Dalal 88]   M. Dalal, "Investigations into a Theory of Knowledge Base Revision: Preliminary Report," *Proceedings of the Seventh National Conference on Artificial Intelligence*, Minneapolis, pp. 475–479, August 1988.

[Davidson 84a]   J. E. Davidson, *Interpreting Natural Language Database Updates*, PhD Thesis, Department of Computer Science, Stanford University, 1984.

[Davidson 84b]   J. E. Davidson, "A Natural Language Interface for Performing Database Updates," *Proceedings of the First International Conference on Data Engineering*, Los Angeles, pp. 69–76, April 1984.

[Dayal 82]   U. Dayal and P. A. Bernstein, "On the Correct Translation of Update Operations on Relational Views," *ACM Transactions on Database Systems* 7:3, pp. 381–416, September 1982.

[de Kleer 86]   J. de Kleer, "An Assumption-Based TMS," *Artificial Intelligence* 28:2, pp. 127–162, 1986.

[de Kleer 87]   J. de Kleer and B. C. Williams, "Diagnosing Multiple Faults," *Artificial Intelligence* 32:1, pp. 97–130, April 1987.

[Doyle 79]   J. Doyle, "A Truth Maintenance System," *Artificial Intelligence* 12:3, pp. 231–272, July 1979.

[Drummond 86]   M. Drummond, "Plan Nets: A Representation of Action and Belief for Automatic Planning Systems," PhD dissertation, Department of Artificial Intelligence, University of Edinburgh, 1986.

[Fagin 83]   R. Fagin, J. D. Ullman, and M. Y. Vardi, "On the Semantics of Updates in Databases," *Proceedings of the Second Symposium on Principles of Database Systems*, pp. 352–365, April 1983.

[Fagin 86]   R. Fagin, G. M. Kuper, J. D. Ullman, and M. Y. Vardi, "Updating Logical Databases," in *Advances in Computing Research* **3**, P. Kanellakis and F. Preparata, eds., JAI Press, 1986.

[Finger 87]   J. J. Finger, *Exploiting Constraints in Design Synthesis*, PhD thesis, Department of Computer Science, Stanford University, 1987.

[Foo 89]   N. Y. Foo and A. S. Rao, "Minimal Change and Maximal Coherence: A Basis for Belief Revision and Reasoning About Actions," *Proceedings of the International Joint Conference on Artificial Intelligence*, Detroit, pp. 966–971, August 1989.

[Forbus 89]   K. D. Forbus, "Introducing Actions into Qualitative Simulation," *Proceedings of the Eleventh International Joint Conference on Artificial Intelligence*, Detroit, pp. 1273–1278, August 1989.

[Gärdenfors 88a]   P. Gärdenfors and D. Makinson, "Revisions of Knowledge Systems Using Epistemic Entrenchment," *Proceedings of the Second Conference on Theoretical Aspects of Reasoning About Knowledge*, Asilomar, pp. 83–95, March 1988.

[Gärdenfors 88b]   P. Gärdenfors, *Knowledge in Flux: Modeling the Dynamics of Epistemic States*, Bradford Books, MIT Press, 1988.

[Ginsberg 86]   M. L. Ginsberg, "Counterfactuals," *Artificial Intelligence*, **30**:1, pp. 35–79, 1986.

[Ginsberg 88a]   M. L. Ginsberg and D. E. Smith, "Reasoning About Action I: A Possible Worlds Approach," *Artificial Intelligence* **35**:2, pp. 165–195, 1988.

[Ginsberg 88b]   M. L. Ginsberg and D. E. Smith, "Reasoning About Action II: The Qualification Problem," *Artificial Intelligence*, **35**:3, pp. 311–342, 1988.

[Goodman 83]   N. Goodman, *Fact, Fiction, and Forecast*, 4th ed., Harvard University Press, 1983.

[Grahne 84]   G. Grahne, "Dependency Satisfaction in Databases with Incomplete Information," *Proceedings of the Tenth International Conference on Very Large Data Bases*, Singapore, pp. 37–45, August 1984.

[Grahne 89]   G. Grahne, "Horn Tables: An Efficient Tool for Handling Incomplete Information in Databases," *Proceedings of the Eighth Symposium on Principles of Database Systems*, Philadelphia, pp. 75–82, March 1989.

[Harman 86]   G. Harman, *Change in View: Principles of Reasoning*, MIT Press, 1986.

[Hegner 87]   S. Hegner, "Specification and Implementation of Programs for Updating Incomplete Information Databases," *Proceedings of the Sixth Symposium on Principles of Database Systems*, San Diego, pp. 146–158, March 1987.

[Hintikka 62]   J. Hintikka, *Knowledge and Belief*, Cornell University Press, 1962.

[Imielinski 85]   T. Imielinski, "Abstraction in Query Processing," Technical Report, Department of Computer Science, Rutgers University, December 1985.

[Imielinski 83]   T. Imielinski and W. Lipski, "Incomplete Information and Dependencies in Relational Databases," *Proceedings of the International Conference on Management of Data*, San Jose, pp. 178–184, May 1983.

[Imielinski 84]   T. Imielinski and W. Lipski, "Incomplete Information in Relational Databases," *Journal of the ACM* **31**:4, pp. 761–791, October 1984.

[Jackson 89]   P. Jackson, "On the Semantics of Counterfactuals," *Proceedings of the Eleventh International Joint Conference on Artificial Intelligence*, Detroit, pp. 1382–1387, August 1989.

[Katsuno 89]   H. Katsuno and A. O. Mendelzon, "A Unified View of Propositional Knowledge Base Updates," *Proceedings of the Eleventh International Joint Conference on Artificial Intelligence*, Detroit, pp. 1413–1419, August 1989.

[Keller 82]   A. M. Keller, "Updates to Relational Databases Through Views Involving Joins," in *Improving Database Usability and Responsiveness*, P. Scheuermann, ed., Academic Press, New York, 1982.

[Keller 85a]   A. M. Keller, Algorithms for Translating View Updates to Database Updates for Views Involving Selections, Projections, and Joins," *Proceedings of the Fourth Symposium on Principles of Database Systems*, Portland, pp. 154–163, March 1985.

[Keller 85b]   A. M. Keller and M. Winslett-Wilkins, "On the Use of an
    Extended Relational Model to Handle Changing Incomplete Information,"
    IEEE Transactions on Software Engineering **SE-11**:7, pp. 620–633, July
    1985.

[Knuth 73]   D. E. Knuth, *The Art of Computer Programming*, Volume 3,
    Addison-Wesley, 1973.

[Laurent 88]   D. Laurent and N. Spyratos, "Partition Semantics for Incomplete
    Information in Relational Databases," *Proceedings of the International
    Conference on Management of Data*, Chicago, pp. 66–73, June 1988.

[Lerat 86]   N. Lerat, "Query Processing in Incomplete Logical Databases,"
    Proceedings of the First International Conference on Database Theory,
    Rome, September 1986; reprinted in *Lecture Notes in Computer Science:
    ICDT '86*, G. Ausiello and P. Atzeni, eds., Springer-Verlag, Berlin,
    pp. 260–277.

[Levesque 84]   H. Levesque, "Foundations of a Functional Approach to
    Knowledge Representation," *Artificial Intelligence* **23**, pp. 155–212, July
    1984.

[Lewis 73]   D. Lewis, *Counterfactuals*, Harvard University Press, Cambridge
    MA, 1973.

[Lifschitz 85]   V. Lifschitz, "Closed-World Databases and Circumscription,"
    Artificial Intelligence **27**:2, pp. 229–235, November 1985.

[Lifschitz 87]   V. Lifschitz, "Formal Theories of Action," *Proceedings of the 1987
    Workshop on the Frame Problem in Artificial Intelligence*, Lawrence KS, pp.
    35–37, 1987.

[Lipski 81]   W. Lipski, "On Databases with Incomplete Information," *Journal of
    the ACM* **28**, pp. 41–70, 1981.

[Liu 88]   K.-C. Liu and R. Sunderraman, "Indefinite and Maybe Information in
    Relational Databases," *Proceedings of the 4th International Conference on
    Data Engineering*, Los Angeles, pp. 250–257, February, 1988.

[McCarthy 86]   J. McCarthy, "Applications of Circumscription to Formalizing
    Common-Sense Knowledge," *Artificial Intelligence* **26**:3, pp. 89–118, 1986.

[Myers 88]   K. Myers and D. E. Smith, "On the Persistence of Derived
    Information," *Proceedings of the Seventh National Conference on Artificial
    Intelligence*, Minneapolis, pp. 496–500, August 1988.

[Nilsson 86]   N. J. Nilsson, "Probabilistic Logic," *Artificial Intelligence* **28**:1, pp.
    71–87, February 1986.

[Oddie 78]   G. Oddie, "Verisimilitude," from *The Logic and Philosophy of
    Scientific Change*, in *Acta Philosophica Fennica*, **30**:2–4, 1978.

[Papadimitriou 86]   C. H. Papadimitriou, *A Theory of Database Concurrency
    Control*, Computer Science Press, 1986.

[Pearl 88]   J. Pearl, *Probabilistic Reasoning in Intelligent Systems*, Morgan
    Kaufmann, 1988.

[Pollack 76]   J. L. Pollack, *Subjunctive Reasoning*, Reidel, Dordrecht, 1976.

[Reiter 80]   R. Reiter, "Equality and Domain Closure in First Order
    Databases," *Journal of the ACM* **27**:2, pp. 235–249, 1980.

[Reiter 84]   R. Reiter, "A Logical Reconstruction of Relational Database Theory," in M. L. Brodie, J. Mylopoulos, and J. W. Schmidt (eds.), *On Conceptual Modelling*, Springer-Verlag, 1984.

[Reiter 86]   R. Reiter, "A Sound and Sometimes Complete Query Evaluation Algorithm for Relational Databases with Null Values," *Journal of the ACM* **33**:2, pp. 349–370, 1986.

[Reiter 87]   R. Reiter, "A Theory of Diagnosis from First Principles," *Artificial Intelligence* **32**:1, pp. 57–96, April 1987.

[Rescher 64]   N. Rescher, *Hypothetical Reasoning*, North-Holland, 1964.

[Satoh 88]   K. Satoh, "Nonmonotonic Reasoning by Minimal Belief Revision," *Proceedings of the International Conference on Fifth Generation Computer Systems 1988*, ICOT, pp. 455–462, December 1988.

[Shoham 88]   Y. Shoham, *Reasoning About Change: Time and Causation from the Standpoint of Artificial Intelligence*, MIT Press, 1988.

[Stonebraker 85]   M. Stonebraker, ed., *The INGRES Papers*, Addison Wesley, Reading MA, 1985.

[Ullman 88]   J. D. Ullman, *Principles of Database and Knowledge Base Systems*, Volume I, Computer Science Press, 1988.

[Vardi 86]   M. Y. Vardi, "Querying Logical Databases," *Journal of Computer and System Sciences* **33**:2, pp. 142–160, October 1986.

[Vassiliou 79]   Y. Vassiliou, "Null Values in Data Base Management: A Denotational Semantics Approach," *Proceedings of the International Conference on Management of Data*, Boston, pp. 162–169, May 1979.

[Weber 86]   A. Weber, "Updating Propositional Formulas," *Proceedings of the First International Expert Database Systems Conference*, Charleston SC, pp. 487–500, April 1986.

[Wiederhold 87]   Gio Wiederhold, *File Organization for Database Design*, McGraw-Hill, 1987.

[Wiederhold 90]   Gio Wiederhold, *Semantic Database Design*, McGraw-Hill, 1990.

[Winslett 86a]   M. Winslett, "Is Belief Revision Harder Than You Thought?," *Proceedings of the Fifth National Conference on Artificial Intelligence*, Philadelphia, pp. 421–427, August 1986.

[Winslett 86b]   M. Winslett, "Updating Logical Databases With Null Values," *Proceedings of the First International Conference on Database Theory*, Rome, September 1986; reprinted in *Lecture Notes in Computer Science: ICDT '86*, G. Ausiello and P. Atzeni, eds., Springer-Verlag, Berlin, pp. 421–435.

[Winslett 86c]   M. Winslett, *Updating Databases with Incomplete Information*, PhD thesis, Department of Computer Science, Stanford University, December 1986.

[Winslett 88a]   M. Winslett, "A Framework for Comparison of Update Semantics," *Proceedings of the Seventh Symposium on Principles of Database Systems*, Austin, pp. 315–324, March 1988.

[Winslett 88b]   M. Winslett, "A Model-Theoretic Approach to Updating

Databases With Incomplete Information," *ACM Transactions on Database Systems*, **13**:2, pp. 167–196, June 1988.

[Winslett 88c]   M. Winslett, "Reasoning About Action Using a Possible Models Approach," *Proceedings of the Seventh National Conference on Artificial Intelligence*, Minneapolis, pp. 89–93, August 1988.

[Winslett 90]   M. Winslett and T. Chou, "Updates that Change the Universe," manuscript submitted for publication.

[Yuan 88]   L. Y. Yuan and D.-A. Chiang, "A Sound and Complete Query Evaluation Algorithm for Databases with Null Values," *Proceedings of the International Conference on Management of Data*, Chicago, pp. 74–81, June 1988.

[Yuan 89]   L. Y. Yuan and D.-A. Chiang, "A Sound and Complete Query Evaluation Algorithm for Databases with Disjunctive Information," *Proceedings of the Eighth Symposium on Principles of Database Systems*, Philadelphia, pp. 66–74, March 1989.

[Zadeh 79]   L. A. Zadeh, "Approximate Reasoning Based on Fuzzy Logic," *Proceedings of the Sixth International Joint Conference on Artificial Intelligence*, August 1979.

[Zaniolo 84]   C. Zaniolo, "Database Relations with Null Values," *Journal of Computer and System Sciences* **28**, pp. 142–166, 1984.

INDEX OF DEFINITIONS

Printed in the United States
By Bookmasters